Banking in Crisis

The University of Law, Braboeuf Manor, St. Catherines, Portsmouth Road, Guildford GU3 1HA Telephone: 01483 216788 E-mail: library-guildford@law.ac.uk

Cambridge Studies in Economic History

Editorial Board

PAUL JOHNSON   *University of Western Australia*
SHEILAGH OGILVIE   *University of Cambridge*
AVNER OFFER   *All Souls College, Oxford*
GIANNI TONIOLO   *Universita di Roma 'Tor Vergata'*
GAVIN WRIGHT   *Stanford University*

Cambridge Studies in Economic History comprises stimulating and accessible economic history which actively builds bridges to other disciplines. Books in the series will illuminate why the issues they address are important and interesting, place their findings in a comparative context, and relate their research to wider debates and controversies. The series will combine innovative and exciting new research by younger researchers with new approaches to major issues by senior scholars. It will publish distinguished work regardless of chronological period or geographical location.

A complete list of titles in the series can be found at
http://www.cambridge.org/economichistory.

Banking in Crisis

*The Rise and Fall of British Banking Stability,
1800 to the Present*

John D. Turner

CAMBRIDGE
UNIVERSITY PRESS

CAMBRIDGE
UNIVERSITY PRESS

University Printing House, Cambridge CB2 8BS, United Kingdom

Cambridge University Press is part of the University of Cambridge.

It furthers the University's mission by disseminating knowledge in the pursuit of education, learning and research at the highest international levels of excellence.

www.cambridge.org
Information on this title: www.cambridge.org/9781107609860

© John Turner 2014

First published 2014

Printed in the United Kingdom by Clay, St Ives plc

A catalogue record for this publication is available from the British Library

Library of Congress Cataloguing in Publication data

ISBN 978-1-107-03094-7 Hardback
ISBN 978-1-107-60986-0 Paperback

Contents

Figures

Tables

Acknowledgements

According to Winston Churchill, writing a book begins as an adventure, turns into a toy, then an amusement, then a mistress, then a master, then a tyrant, and just before you are about to surrender, you decide instead to slay the monster. I understand where Churchill was coming from, but throughout the writing of this book and the decade or more of underlying research, I have received the help and encouragement of family, friends, colleagues, librarians, archivists and countless scholars.

Lawrence H. White of George Mason University introduced me to banking history in his graduate class on money and banking, and he inspired me to take up the study of banking and financial history. Charlie Hickson guided me as a graduate student and later became my mentor and co-author. He taught me to think (and write) logically and introduced me to the powerful 'last-period problem'. I am indebted to all of my teachers – most particularly my parents, who nurtured my young mind.

As well as having great teachers, I have had the privilege of having great students over the years that stimulated my grey matter. In particular, I am indebted to those students who eventually became my co-authors and peers: Graeme Acheson, Gareth Campbell, Christopher Coyle, Clive Walker, Qing Ye and Wenwen Zhan.

The research that underpins this book benefitted greatly from the hospitality of the Bank of England, where I was a Houblon-Norman Fellow. I thank the trustees of the Houblon-Norman Fund for their support. During my time at the Bank, I benefitted immensely from discussions with Charles Bean, Charles Goodhart, Glenn Hoggarth, Kevin James, Andrew Large, Céline Gondat-Larralde, Hyun Song Shin and Geoffrey Wood. Sarah Millard and Jenny Mountain helped me to negotiate the Bank's archives and Kath Begley, the Bank's librarian, was exceptionally helpful in tracking down obscure publications from past eras.

At the conception of this book, I enjoyed the hospitality of Harvard Business School as the Alfred D. Chandler Jr Fellow. I thank the trustees of the fellowship for their financial support. Thanks also go to Walter Friedman, Patrick Fridenson, Geoffrey Jones, Elisabeth Koll, Christina

Lubinski, Noel Maurer, Aldo Musacchio and Tom Nicholas for the stimulating and friendly intellectual environment they provided.

The research that underpins this book received generous research funding from both the British Academy and the Economic and Social Research Council. I also had great research assistants who assisted me with this book: Jonny McCollum, Peter Neilly and Jill Turner deserve a special mention.

Over the years, I have enjoyed the assistance and insights of many bank archivists. I am particularly indebted to Edwin Green, formerly of HSBC, for his advice and encouragement. The access to archive material at Barclays Bank, Lloyds-TSB, the Royal Bank of Scotland Group and HSBC was very much appreciated. Thanks go to all of the archivists who assisted me, especially Jessie Campbell, Karen Sampson, Lucy Wright and Philip Winterbottom. I thank also the librarians and archivists at Guildhall Library in London for their assistance over the years.

My academy, Queen's University Belfast, supported me during the writing of this book. In particular, Rob Gilles, my Head of School, gave me all of the help an academic could ever want when writing a book.

Several scholars and colleagues read and provided valuable feedback on the book: Graeme Acheson, Vicky Barnes, Graham Brownlow, Gareth Campbell, Chris Colvin, Christopher Coyle, Alan Hanna, Charlie Hickson, Liam Kennedy, Donal McKillop, Owen Sims and Clive Walker. Richard Grossman, Lucy Newton and Cormac Ó Gráda participated in a roundtable workshop on an early version of my manuscript, and I am indebted to them for the meaningful advice they provided. Eve Richards provided valuable proofreading and encouragement on an early draft.

I presented an early overview of my book as a keynote address at the Future Research in Economic and Social History conference at London School of Economics and Political Science in December 2012. My thanks go to Rowena Gray and Paul Sharp, the conference organisers, for the invitation and also to Vincent Bignon, Alan Taylor and Stefano Ugolini for their comments.

This book is the result of an invitation by Luke Samy – then at the Winton Institute for Monetary History at Oxford University – to give a talk on the history of British financial stability. In the audience was Avner Offer, who subsequently invited me to submit a book proposal to Cambridge University Press. I thank Luke and Avner for their kind invitations. Michael Watson at Cambridge University Press has been a very encouraging and helpful editor.

Above the doors of Cambridge University's Cavendish Physics Laboratory is an inscription from Miles Coverdale's 1535 translation of Psalm 111: 'The workes of the LORDE are great, sought out of all that haue pleasure therin'. These words serve as my motto as a social scientist and an economic historian.

Finally, my wife, Karen, and son, Jack, had to endure my near-monastic existence during the writing of this book. Without their unstinting love and support, this book would never have been written. I therefore dedicate this 'slain monster' to them.

1 Introduction: Holding shareholders to account

> But we know that generations do not always act upon the experience of their predecessors. There are periods of confidence in which all ordinary maxims of prudence are neglected . . . and all banking is in its very nature liable to abuse.[1]
>
> Thomas Tooke

Looking to the past

My first introduction to banking was playing *Monopoly*, the popular board game, with my siblings on rainy Sunday afternoons in the early 1980s. I learned two things from *Monopoly*. First, if one wished to mortgage property, the bank would advance no more than 50 per cent of the property's value. In other words, the loan-to-value ratio was 50 per cent. Second, the banker, usually my brother, had to be constrained from cheating via a combination of monitoring, punishment and appropriate incentives. Fast-forward several decades and real British banks were granting mortgages with loan-to-value ratios of up to 125 per cent and British bankers, instead of being constrained to behave prudently and cautiously, were incentivised to increase bank leverage and take imprudent risks with other people's money. The lessons of my youth suggested that such a system was doomed to implode, which it duly did in spectacular fashion in the autumn of 2008.

The portents of the collapse of the British banking system, as well as the breakdown of the banking system in the United States and in European economies, appeared in the summer of 2007, when banks ceased lending to one another. By September 2007, Northern Rock was receiving emergency loans from the Bank of England and facing depositor runs, with long queues of depositors outside many of its branches shown on BBC news broadcasts. It took an announcement by Alastair Darling, the Chancellor of the Exchequer at the time, of a taxpayer guarantee for

---

[1] *Committee of Secrecy on the Bank of England Charter*, P.P. 1831–32 VI, Evidence of Thomas Tooke, q. 3918.

all of Northern Rock's deposits and various wholesale liabilities to bring the run on the Rock to an end.[2] The financial condition of Northern Rock was so poor that it was eventually nationalised in February 2008. Then, following the failure of Lehman Brothers in the United States on 15 September 2008, banking and financial systems across much of the developed world experienced a collapse, which resulted in taxpayer-funded bailouts and emergency loans unprecedented in their scale and scope. The United Kingdom was at the epicentre of the crisis, with the Royal Bank of Scotland, HBOS (the result of the Halifax and Bank of Scotland merger), Lloyds-TSB and Bradford and Bingley, as well as Northern Rock, all requiring taxpayer support to prevent their collapse.

The 2007–8 crisis has resulted in economists, policy makers and ordinary citizens now looking to past financial crises to understand more about the anatomy of banking crises and the appropriate policy responses of governments, monetary authorities and financial regulators. As a result, there is renewed interest in economic history and, in particular, financial history and historical banking crises.[3] For example, in its final report, the Parliamentary Commission on Banking Standards suggests that the 2007–8 crisis might not have happened had the lessons of past failures been heeded.[4] This book ties into this appreciation of the importance of historical research by analysing the stability of the British banking system in the past two centuries, from immediately before the point at which modern joint-stock banking emerges until the Great Crash of 2007–8.

Economists have been lambasted for the inability of the profession to predict the Great Crash of 2007–8.[5] One possibility is that the economics profession came to be dominated by the wrong ideology – that is, a blind faith in competition and the free market. Over time, those who disagreed with the new ideology were excluded from the profession so that there were few dissenting voices and the free market became the 'new policy metaphysics'.[6] Another more worrying possibility is that the profession

---

[2] House of Commons Treasury Committee, *Banking Crisis*, p. 45.

[3] Notable examples include Reinhart and Rogoff, *This Time Is Different*; Schularick and Taylor, 'Credit booms gone bust'; and Gorton, *Misunderstanding Financial Crises*.

[4] Parliamentary Commission on Banking Standards, *Changing Banking for Good*, vol. 1, pp. 15–16. This Commission recommended that the Bank of England's Financial Policy Committee should have an external member, 'with particular responsibility for taking a historical view of financial stability and systemic risk' (vol. 1, p. 62).

[5] See, for example, Buiter, 'The unfortunate uselessness'; Gorton, *Misunderstanding Financial Crises*, vii–xii; and Hodgson, 'The great crash of 2008'. According to Frydman and Goldberg in *Beyond Mechanical Markets*, the mechanical and mathematical models of macroeconomists and financial economists were particularly to blame.

[6] Offer, 'Narrow banking', p. 15.

simply supplied the ideology that was demanded by the economic and political elite. In other words, economics 'sold its soul'.

We must ask, however, whether economic historians fared any better. Notable economic historians or economists with a good knowledge of banking history did not predict the crisis. One possible explanation for this is that economic history has picked up the bad as well as the ideological habits of economics.[7] However, it is perhaps unfair to expect predictions from economic historians. To use a medical analogy, economists diagnose problems and prescribe preventive medicine, whereas economic historians are pathologists because they try to uncover what happened in the past.[8] Nevertheless, modern medicine started with pathology and medical students begin their training by examining cadavers. Similarly, this book examines the 'cadavers' of past banking crises to learn about the anatomy of banking crises and, in the process, perhaps learn something about preventive measures.

Three questions are explicitly addressed in this book. First, how often did banking crises occur in the past two centuries and how severe were they? Second, why did banking crises occur? Third, what role did the government and the Bank of England play in crises: Did they alleviate or exacerbate matters? Another question is implicitly addressed throughout the book: What insight does the history of banking stability in Britain provide about the reasons for the Great Crash of 2007–8? Although the book attempts to explain why the Great Crash occurred, it does so only in the context of two centuries of banking history. Those looking for a detailed narrative of the Great Crash should turn to the voluminous literature that it has already generated.[9]

Why should one care about banking stability?[10] As a society, we care because of the important roles of banks in the economy. First, banks provide most of an economy's money supply in the form of transaction deposits, which greatly reduces the costs of engaging in trade and exchange. Second, banks provide intermediation of funds between

---

[7] Solow, 'Economic history and economics'.

[8] I thank Cormac Ó Gráda for this analogy.

[9] See, for example, Booth, *Verdict on the Crash*; Brunnermeier, 'Deciphering the liquidity and credit crunch'; Diamond and Rajan, 'The credit crisis'; Dowd and Hutchinson, *The Alchemists of Loss*; French et al., *The Squam Lake Report*; Gorton, *Slapped by the Invisible Hand*; Johnson and Kwak, *13 Bankers*; Mian and Sufi, 'House prices'; Mishkin, 'Over the cliff'; Peston and Knight, *How Do We Fix This Mess?*; Rajan, *Fault Lines*; Schwartz, 'Origins of the financial market crisis'; Shiller, *The Subprime Solution*; and Sorkin, *Too Big to Fail*.

[10] Most scholars use the terms *banking crisis* and *financial crisis* synonymously, but some economists would also regard a currency crisis as a financial crisis. See Kaminsky and Reinhart, 'The twin crises'.

borrowers and savers. This credit intermediation ultimately facilitates investment by businesses and enables individuals to provide for their future consumption needs. Banking instability implies that these important services provided by banks are detrimentally affected, with potentially catastrophic consequences for both ordinary citizens and businesses.

A study of banking stability in the past two centuries is – in one sense – of purely historical interest. However, an historical examination of banking stability sheds light on the Great Crash because by studying the past, we understand how the banking system evolved and the origins of vulnerabilities in the banking ecosystem. Another reason that a long-run perspective is useful is that banking crises are low-frequency events. Hence, past crises are additional observations that are useful in understanding the dynamics and commonalities, as well as the basic anatomy, of banking crises. However, in looking at historical crises, one must be careful not to 'see history as a homogeneous data pool with which to test modern theories'.[11]

A benefit of focusing on only one country rather than conducting a comparative study is that a higher level of institutional detail is obtained. Furthermore, the unique methods used to measure banking stability throughout a two-century window in Britain would be extremely difficult to replicate for other economies. Of course, the downside of the single-country study is that the cross-sectional correlations and insights provided by a comparative analysis are lost. To compensate for this, a comparative analysis is utilised – whenever it is warranted – throughout the book. Nevertheless, the British case is informative about the global banking system for a number of reasons. First, for more than two centuries, Britain has been a – if not the – major player in world finance. For most if not all of the past two centuries, London has been the world's leading financial centre. Indeed, Britain has had a sophisticated and highly developed financial system longer than any other economy.

Second, it is traditionally believed that the British banking system was one of the most stable in the twentieth century. This was borne out, in particular, by the relative stability of the British banking system during the Great Depression.[12] Whereas other banking systems were collapsing and suffering panics, Britain's banking system was relatively calm, despite the substantial contraction in the wider British economy.

---

[11] Dow and Dow, 'Economic history', p. 3.
[12] Grossman, 'The shoe that didn't drop'; Capie and Wood, *Money over Two Centuries*, p. 333.

Third, central-banking practice and theory were developed mainly in Britain during the nineteenth century, notably with regard to the function of 'lender of last resort', which is believed to underpin banking stability in modern economies.[13] Britain is therefore interesting because it developed the prototype central bank and lender of last resort.

Fourth, unlike nearly all other developed nations, the United Kingdom had minimal statutory regulation of banking until 1979. Apart from Peel's Bank Charter Act (1844), which restrained bank-note issuance, no other major statutory attempts had been made to control or regulate banking. Thus, on the surface, it appears that Britain was unusual on two counts in the twentieth century: the stability of its banking system and the absence of statutory regulation for banks. Could this imply that the statutory regulation of banks and banking stability are mutually exclusive?

Fifth, as highlighted throughout this book, Britain's experience with banking stability in many cases mirrors what happened in other major economies.[14] In other words, some reasons for the rise and fall of British banking stability in the past two centuries have many parallels in other nations, particularly in the case of the Great Crash of 2007–8. As a result, the lessons and insights of this book stretch beyond the shores of Britannia.

There are, of course, risks to be avoided in a study of banking stability over the long run. One prominent risk is that of nostalgia, wherein the study of history enables one to look back fondly on the halcyon days when banking was stable. As a result of such nostalgia, one could ultimately recommend that banking should return to the way it was in the 'good old days' and that all subsequent socially optimal banking innovations that occurred during the intervening decades should be removed.[15]

Another risk of looking at the long run is that the nature of banking may have changed during the period so that banking in the nineteenth century has no similarities with banking (and, consequently, with banking crises) in the twenty-first century. One way of minimising this danger, which is adopted in this book, is to focus on commercial banks – that is, those banks that take in deposits and lend to businesses, governments and individuals. In the past two centuries, British commercial banks often

---

[13] Smith, *The Rationale of Central Banking*, pp. 8–24, 71–80.

[14] For example, the 2007–8 crisis resulted in bank failures or bailouts of major banks in Belgium, France, Germany, Iceland, Ireland, Netherlands, Spain, Switzerland and the United States.

[15] See Bhidé, *A Call for Judgment*, who, in his insightful critique of financial innovation, perhaps goes too far in recommending a return to banking as practised a half-century ago.

have changed substantially: modern banks offer a wider range of services than their ancestors, they are considerably larger in terms of scale and scope, and many of them operate across the globe. However, the two key economic functions of commercial banks in the past two centuries have not changed. First, British commercial banks have always provided a means of payment to their customers, whether in the form of bank notes or transaction deposits. Second, British commercial banks have always intermediated funds between savers, who are typically individuals, and borrowers, who are typically but not exclusively businesses.[16]

The basic argument

Banking is an intrinsically risky business, and the reason is simple: bankers lend other people's money, not their own. This creates an incentive problem because bankers get most of the benefit if the risky loans they make do well, whereas depositors, not bankers, incur most of the costs if loans go bad. Unless it is addressed, this incentive problem eventually results in unstable banking. The basic argument advanced in this book is that banking is at its most stable when one of two conditions exists, both of which address this intrinsic incentive problem at the heart of banking.

The first condition is that bank shareholders are held to account for bank failures. What does this mean? The basic idea is that when bank shareholders stand to lose substantially from a bank failure, they will ensure that their bank is properly and prudently run, thereby greatly reducing the probability of it failing in the first instance. As a result, bank depositors are assured that their deposits are safe because bankers have an incentive to ensure that they are judicious in their treatment of depositors' funds.

What can shareholders lose when their bank fails? First, shareholders can lose all of the capital they invested in the bank. Second, if their liability was not limited, shareholders could also face a call on their personal wealth in the event of bank failure. For example, bank shareholders could have unlimited liability, whereby they are liable to make good the deficit between their bank's assets and liabilities whenever it fails, down to their last penny or – in the quaint terminology of the nineteenth century – to their 'last acre and sixpence'. Alternatively, bank shareholders could

---

[16] Offer, in 'Narrow banking', argues that Victorian commercial banks, unlike modern banks, were mainly providers of liquidity to businesses and were not involved in much maturity transformation. However, although lending in this era was short term in duration, much of it was rolled over.

establish a type of 'halfway house' between pure limited liability and unlimited liability; for example, shareholders could be held liable for a defined multiple of their paid-up capital.

The second condition under which banking is at its most stable is when banks are constrained by onerous government controls. For example, banks could be required to hold a significant amount of low-risk government debt and be restricted from lending to risky or speculative sectors of the economy. Such onerous restrictions place bankers in a figurative straitjacket, which severely constrains their proclivity to take excessive risk and thereby keeps banking stable.

This book attempts to explain the stability (or otherwise) of the British banking system since 1800. To measure banking stability over the long run, an innovative approach is used. With its detailed study of bank-share prices and failure rates during a two-century period, this approach produces different results from the standard narrative accounts of British banking history, which classifies many more episodes as crises and fails to distinguish between the seriousness of various episodes of banking instability.[17]

Using this innovative approach suggests that there have been only two major banking-system crises in Britain in the past two centuries. The first major crisis was in 1825–6; the second was the Great Crash of 2007–8. In the interim, there were periods when the banking system was under stress and weak banks failed, but at no time was there a major crisis or a threat to the overall stability of the banking system. Notably, these minor crises or episodes of instability had a limited real economic effect, compared to the decreases in economic output associated with the two major crises. Indeed, some of the minor crises – in particular, those in the nineteenth century – may have had a role in strengthening banking systems because they eliminated weak and risk-loving banks.

This long-run perspective on banking stability also reveals that the severity and the scale of the 2007–8 banking crisis are unprecedented in British banking history. No previous crisis witnessed the collapse of such a large proportion of the banking system. Neither did any previous crisis necessitate such large-scale intervention by the taxpayers and the monetary authorities to save the system. No previous crisis was followed by such a steep decline in economic output, such a prolonged economic malaise, and such a large increase in public indebtedness. In other words, to quote an overused phrase, this time really does differ.

---

[17] Collins, *Money and Banking in the UK*; Baker and Collins, 'Financial crises'; Reinhart and Rogoff, *This Time Is Different*; Grossman, *Unsettled Account*; Capie and Wood, *Money over Two Centuries*.

Having identified that the UK banking system was relatively stable between 1826 and 2007, the remainder of the book addresses two principal questions: (1) Why was the British banking system crisis-free for such a long period? and (2) Why did it crash in 2007–8? A subsidiary question that the book addresses is: Why did the 1825–6 crisis happen?

Prior to 1826, the English banking system experienced frequent bouts of instability, but the crisis of 1825–6 was by far the most severe of the era. This crisis, which was purely English, occurred because banks were constrained to the partnership organisational form, which meant that they were small and therefore had inadequate capital. Scotland was able to escape the 1825–6 crisis unscathed largely because Scottish partnership law was highly flexible compared to English and Irish law. The result was that Scottish banks were more like joint-stock companies, making them more robust to economic shocks. Notably, the post-crisis reforms introduced into the English banking system in 1826 allowed banks to become more like Scottish banks in that they could be formed as joint-stock companies.

Although experiencing periodic bouts of nervousness, money-market strains and episodic bank failures, the UK banking system remained relatively stable throughout the *c.* 175 years since 1826 in that it did not experience any systemic or major crises. What explains this remarkably long period of relative stability? Briefly, the two conditions for stable banking (outlined previously) held during most of this era, with the result that banks did not take excessive risks and that the banking system was stable.

When banking incorporation law was liberalised in the mid 1820s, banks were required to have unlimited shareholder liability. This meant that when a bank failed, shareholders were liable to their last penny to repay depositors for any losses incurred as a result of the collapse. Because the unlimited liability was joint and several, the inability of some shareholders to meet their calls simply meant that wealthier and still-solvent shareholders subsequently faced larger calls. Consequently, one might expect that unlimited-liability banks would not have many wealthy shareholders. However, the voluminous evidence presented in this book suggests otherwise, and depositors typically had all of their deposits returned even when their bank failed. In addition, bank failures in this era stood as constant reminders that owners were held to account because shareholders faced calls to make good the deficit between their bank's liabilities and assets.

The incentives arising from the existence of unlimited liability constrained banks from excessive risk taking because shareholders and, more important, bank directors and managers stood to lose all of their wealth in the event of bank failure. Thus, because banks were not overextended, the banking system could withstand periodic shocks, and there were no endogenous bank-credit-fuelled asset booms followed by a crisis.

The failure of the City of Glasgow Bank in 1878, which resulted in the personal bankruptcy of most of its shareholders, was too much to bear for shareholders in other banks. Consequently, the shareholder-liability regime was diluted so that banks could adopt a halfway house between pure limited liability and unlimited liability. All British banks quickly converted to this new liability regime, under which they could choose and define exactly the extent to which shareholders were liable in the event of bank failure. In the 1880s median British bank, shareholders were liable for up to £2 for every £1 of capital held if their bank failed. Because the median bank also had a high ratio of total capital resources to deposits, this new regime still provided shareholders and managers with adequate incentives to avoid taking excessive risks. Thus, even after the demise of unlimited liability, bank shareholders continued to be held to account.

The extended shareholder liability described previously persisted in British banking until the 1950s, when there was a coordinated removal of it. However, this removal was largely symbolic because the average ratio of what shareholders were potentially liable to pay in the event of failure to total deposits in 1950 was about 3 per cent, having fallen from 33 per cent in 1900. At the same time that this decrease occurred, the ratio of capital to deposits also fell to very low levels, from 18 per cent in 1900 to 4 per cent in 1950. Both of these declines were largely a result of high inflation during the two world wars, during which deposits increased substantially without any commensurate increase in extended liability or banks' capital resources. Essentially, by the 1940s, shareholders were no longer being held to account – indeed, in the event of bank failure, they stood to lose very little. Why, then, did banks not take excessive risks? Why did banks remain stable? The answer provided in this book is that banks did not take excessive risks and remained stable because of substantial constraints placed on them by the Bank of England and the Treasury.

From 1939 until the 1970s, the Treasury adopted financial-repression policies partly to fund its high debt issuance, which had arisen as a result of fighting World War II and the cost of postwar reconstruction, and partly to guide lending towards strategic sectors and industries. These policies meant that banks were constrained, facing onerous 'requests' with regard to their liquidity ratios and their lending, which precluded them from excessive risk taking. Ultimately, financial-repression policies constrained banks from risk taking, with the result that their depositors and the financial authorities were totally unconcerned about the low

levels of bank capital. One could therefore view financial-repression policies as a substitute for shareholder capital.

Financial-repression policies in the United Kingdom were not enforced
on banks in a formal sense through statutory law; rather, British banks
participated in an informal supervisory regime that had the Bank of
England at the centre. The Treasury relayed its needs and wishes to
the Bank, which in turn relayed them to the clearing banks – that is,
the principal commercial banks.[18] The clearing banks were always sure
to align their policies to the Bank's and, by extension, the Treasury's
wishes. This informal relationship between the Bank of England and
the clearing banks had developed in the interwar period under the long
suzerainty of Governor Montagu Norman. It was held together in part by
the fact that both the banks and the Bank of England were increasingly
aware of the threat of nationalisation. The clearing banks met all of the
requests made of them either as a quid pro quo for their being allowed
to operate a cartel or because of implicit threats from the Bank or the
Treasury.

Thus, the long period of banking stability from 1826 until the interwar
period was mainly due to shareholders being held to account; from the
end of the interwar period until the 1970s, it was due to austere financial-
repression policies, which meant that banks had no capacity to engage
in risk shifting. Why then did the Great Crash of 2007–8 happen? The
simple answer is that with the end of financial repression, constraints
were gradually removed from banks and there was no attempt to return
to the pre-1939 world in which shareholders were held to account. Add
to this the perception that banks would ultimately be bailed out by the
taxpayers if they collapsed – a perception that a century of rescues of
minor banking institutions had done nothing to assuage – and one can
begin to see the malincentives facing bankers in an era when restraints
on their business activities had been removed. Although attempts were
made to constrain excessive risk taking via supervision and risk-weighted
capital-adequacy ratios, those attempts were ultimately fruitless at best
and counterproductive at worst because they may have actually created
perverse risk-taking incentives for banks.

Although Britain experienced a severe downturn in economic output
during the Great Depression of the 1930s, it is remarkable that it did
not experience a banking crisis unlike many other economies at the time.
At least three reasons are highlighted in this book that saved the British
system from experiencing a crisis during the Great Depression: (1) the

[18] Clearing banks were so called because they controlled and were members of the London
Clearing House, where cheques and other payment claims against banks were cleared.

presence of extended shareholder liability and high capital-deposit ratios, (2) the relatively large holdings of government debt by British banks, and (3) the protoregulatory role played by the Bank of England.

The simple policy choice that arises from this study of British banking stability over the long run is as follows: banks must face stringent economic regulations as they did during the era of financial repression, or bank shareholders must be held to account by making them liable for capital calls in the event of bank failure. Because the stringent regulations associated with financial repression are highly inefficient due to capital misallocation, holding shareholders to account appears to be the only viable policy choice. Such a policy would be effective only if the government made a credible commitment not to bail out errant banks in the future. But is all of this politically feasible? The final lesson from the history of British banking is that politics is the ultimate determinant of banking stability.

The 1825–6 crisis was proximately due to the existence of small, poorly capitalised banks. The reason for the existence of such banks before 1826 was the chartering privileges of the Bank of England, which restricted all other banks to the partnership organisational form and note-issuing banks to having no more than six partners. In return for providing loans to help finance government expenditure and flexibly increasing its issue of paper money during times of military emergencies, the Bank was given a monopoly of joint-stock banking in England. Ultimately, because the Bank was a vital institution that contributed to the survival of the country and its fledgling democracy, the political elite of the United Kingdom – dominated by the aristocracy and landed gentry – supported this arrangement. It also may have had a self-serving incentive to support the Bank's monopoly: this kept banks small and restricted credit to small farmers, thereby helping large landowners maintain power and control over the small farmers and their tenants.

The Great Crash of 2007–8 also had political roots. In the decade or so before the crisis, British banks and the financial system generated huge, invisible earnings for the British economy. British banks also made major contributions to gross domestic product (GDP) and GDP growth in the decade ending in 2007. This growth gave the banking system undue power and influence with politicians, making it much easier for banks to influence, manipulate and ultimately capture the regulatory authorities. The apparent success of the City was vital to government economic policy and facilitated the growth of government spending on health, education and social welfare, which enabled the Labour Government to strengthen its power base among public-sector workers and welfare recipients. The symbiotic relationship between banks and the government meant that the Financial Services Authority (FSA) was under pressure to be nonintrusive and lenient in its regulation.[19] It also meant that banks were able to take whatever risks they desired without fear of regulatory censure.

Those readers hoping for scurrilous tales of debauched bankers and aggressive bank executives will be disappointed. Ultimately, there is no room for personalities and cultures in this book because they are endogenous to the institutional environment within which banks operate. In other words, those such as banker Fred Goodwin were products of their environment and were simply reacting to the incentive structure they faced. Banking crises are ultimately not about the failures of certain individuals; rather, they are about failures in the institutional and political environment.

Structure of the book

A theory of banking instability is developed in Chapter 2, the main focus of which is on the concept of risk shifting by bankers, whereby banks increase the risk of their loan portfolio unobserved, at the expense of depositors. The scale and pervasiveness of risk shifting is a key determinant of the severity of a subsequent banking crisis. Chapter 2 suggests that risk shifting can be adequately mitigated only if shareholders are held to account through extended shareholder liability or if the government imposes stringent regulations on bank activities.

After providing an overview of the evolution of the British banking system for background and context, Chapter 3 measures banking-system stability in the past two centuries using a combination of bank-failure data and 175 years of monthly stock-price data. The data reveal that only two systemic crises occurred in British banking in the past two centuries – namely, 1825–6 and 2007–8 – and that the more recent is by far the greatest banking crisis ever experienced in the United Kingdom. In the period between these two major crises, six minor banking crises occurred (i.e., 1836–7, 1847, 1857–8, 1866–7, 1878–9 and 1974).

Chapter 4 provides narrative accounts of the major banking-system crises and the six minor crises. As part of the different accounts, the affairs of the banks that collapsed (or were bailed out by the financial authorities) during the various crises are analysed to gauge whether they were risk shifting before their failure. It is remarkable that in nearly every case of bank collapse, managers and shareholders had taken risks

---

[19] *The Failure of the Royal Bank of Scotland*, p. 261; House of Commons Treasury Committee, *Banking Crisis: Regulation and Supervision*, p. 11.

that were at the extremes of the risk-taking distribution and, in some instances, bordered on the fraudulent.

Chapter 5 outlines the evolution of bank capital and explains how the United Kingdom had a woefully capitalised banking system on the eve of the 2007–8 banking crisis. In one sense, this is the cornerstone chapter of the book because it emphasises the role of shareholders and capital in contributing to the stability of the UK banking system. Particular focus in this chapter is on the role of unlimited liability in underpinning the stability of the banking system in the nineteenth century. Chapter 5 also explores the development of reserve liability and uncalled capital following the collapse of the City of Glasgow Bank in 1878.[20] The chapter explores how this 'halfway house' between unlimited liability and pure limited liability had (unlike unlimited liability) the potential to be weakened by inflation. As discussed in Chapter 5, this occurred during World Wars I and II, with a substantial reduction in the real value of both paid-up and uncalled capital. The coordinated removal of uncalled capital, which was completed by 1958, resulted in British banks having no extra liability in the event of failure. In addition, the chapter discusses that at this time, bank capital ratios were at historically low levels. Chapter 5 then highlights how the low ebb reached in 1958 did not improve significantly during the remainder of the twentieth century, as well as how the capital position of British banking deteriorated even further from the 1990s onwards.

Chapter 6 analyses the evolution of the Bank of England's (and the Treasury's) 'firefighting' role during crises. The chapter explores the evolution of the theory and practice of last-resort lending in the nineteenth century and describes how the government cajoled and incentivised the privately owned Bank of England to act in the public good. The chapter discusses how the purpose of the lender of last resort was not to prevent overextended banks from failing; rather, it simply served to prevent large increases in demand for high-powered money from turning into a full-blown liquidity crisis. However, Chapter 6 then explores how support for banks and the banking system went beyond last-resort lending. Following the bailout of Barings in 1890, the Bank and the Treasury were reluctant to let banks fail in case the collapse of one bank endangered the overall stability of the banking system. Indeed, Chapter 6 reveals that by the 1920s, neither the Bank nor the Treasury would countenance the

---

[20] Under reserve liability and uncalled capital, shareholders' liability was set at a multiple of their paid-up capital. The main difference between the two was that the former could only be called up in the event of bank failure, whereas the latter could be called up at any time.

failure of any of the major banks. This social underwriting of bank losses has stark implications: bank depositors became relatively unconcerned, and taxpayers became concerned, about restraints on risk shifting.

Chapter 7 focuses on the relationship between bank regulation and banking stability. In essence, this chapter examines how risk shifting was restrained when the social underwriting of bank losses became an established principle and how those restraints were subsequently weakened, resulting in the 2007–8 financial crisis. Chapter 7 explores the regulations associated with the Bank of England's and the Treasury's regulation of the banking system arising from their policy to fund the huge national debt accumulated during World War II. The chapter describes how the UK banking system faced two problems when these regulations were removed: banks had extremely low levels of capital, and the United Kingdom did not have a rigorous bank-supervisory system. The solutions to these problems are explored as well as how the attempt to harmonise capital-adequacy regulation across the G-10 nations in the 1988 Basel Accord produced a deeply flawed system. This system encouraged regulatory arbitrage, created perverse risk-taking incentives, reduced diversity in the banking ecosystem and eventually resulted in the capture of the regulatory authorities by banks.

Chapter 8 considers the main policy lessons for the present from the past, without being anachronistic or unaware of historical contingencies as it does so. The unambiguous policy choice that emerges from this study of two centuries of British banking is that because risk shifting is best constrained by holding bank shareholders to account for bank losses, some type of extended shareholder liability should be reintroduced. However, as Chapter 8 elucidates, such a policy may not be possible, for banking stability is ultimately a question of political economy.

2   Banking instability and risk shifting

> The history of money, banking, and financial legislation can be inter-
> preted as a search for a structure that would eliminate instability. Expe-
> rience shows that this search failed and theory indicates that the search
> for a permanent solution is fruitless.[1]
>
> H. P. Minsky

Preamble

This chapter attempts to conceptualise and theorise the reasons why
banking becomes unstable and why banking systems experience crises.
This chapter is not about how crises should be tackled once they occur;
rather, it is about why crises occur in the first instance. It is important
to think conceptually about banking stability because it helps to organise
and interpret the historical narrative of banking stability in the United
Kindgom during the past two centuries.

The first section explains why banking instability matters by describing
how banking crises can have widespread ramifications for the economy
and even for political stability. The second section uses a hypothetical
bank to explore the traditional reasons given in the extant literature as to
why a bank might fail. It demonstrates the vulnerabilities in the nature
of banks' assets and liabilities that may make them prone to instability. The third section contends that these vulnerabilities highlighted in
the extant literature are an incomplete explanation of banking instability. Consequently, this section takes a hypothetical bank and devel-
ops a theory of banking instability based on the incentive structures of
bankers, shareholders and depositors. In particular, the concept of 'risk
shifting', which is when bankers opportunistically – and unobserved by
depositors – increase the risk of a bank's asset portfolio, is highlighted.
Risk shifting results in banking instability when the increase in asset
prices, which it induces, suddenly reverses or when an exogenous shock

---

[1] Minsky, *Stabilizing an Unstable Economy*, p. 349.

hits the banking system. The fourth section discusses potential solutions to the risk-shifting problem. Thus, as shown herein, Minksy's pessimism regarding solutions to banking stability is not shared in this book.

Why does banking instability matter?

The main implication of Modigliani and Miller's seminal 1958 paper about firm capital structure is startling: finance is irrelevant.[2] That is, what matters for the success and fluctuations of the economy is investment in real assets, not the way in which these assets are financed. In other words, banking and financial markets have no impact on the real economy. However, there is a substantial body of empirical evidence that indicates that in a causal sense, banks do matter for economic growth.[3] The importance of banks for economic growth may stem from their Schumpeterian role in financing innovation and entrepreneurship.[4] However, the importance of the banking system to the economy ultimately is demonstrated when it fails. Banking failures can impose welfare losses on society because they affect credit intermediation and the money supply. They also can result in negative externalities for the wider financial system – and may even have deleterious effects on political stability and well-being.[5]

  The most famous articulation of the effect of banking crises on the money supply is the study of the Great Depression in the United States by Friedman and Schwartz.[6] The failure of many banks during the Great Depression resulted in a contraction of the money supply as well as in the cash-to-deposit ratio, which reduced the money multiplier, thereby diminishing the effect of any reserves injected by the Federal Reserve. Because Friedman and Schwartz were advocates of the quantity theory of money, they posited that this decrease in the money supply quickly brought about a decline in national income; it also eventually led to a decline in the price level.

---

[2] Modigliani and Miller, 'The cost of capital'.
[3] Beck and Levine, 'Stock markets, banks, and growth'; Goldsmith, *Financial Structure and Development*; Levine, 'Financial development and economic growth'; Levine and Zervos, 'Stock markets, banks, and economic growth'; McKinnon, *Money and Capital*. The relationship between banking and economic growth may have an inverted U shape (Arcand, Berkes and Panizza, 'Too much finance?').
[4] Bodernhorn, *A History of Banking in Antebellum America*, ch. 2; King and Levine, 'Finance and growth'.
[5] For the effect of the crisis on self-reported well-being in the United States, see Deaton, 'The financial crisis'.
[6] Friedman and Schwartz, *The Great Contraction*.

Bernanke argued that the decline in the money supply during the Great Depression was too small to explain the entire subsequent decline in output.[7] According to Bernanke, as well as Calomiris and Mason, bank failures during the Great Depression affected the macroeconomy via a sharp contraction in credit intermediation to entrepreneurs, farmers and small businesses (i.e., a 'credit crunch').[8] In a study of forty-one countries for the period 1980–2000, Dell'Ariccia et al. found that banking crises have an effect on the real economy and that this operates through the lending channel.[9] Consistent with this evidence is that in the aftermath of the Great Crash of 2007–8, most of the major decline in output was due to a decrease in investment – the component of output that is most sensitive to a collapse of the banking system.[10]

Why does banking instability result in a credit crunch? Banks have expertise in differentiating good borrowers from bad and in preventing borrowers from engaging in moral hazard once they have received loans. The cost of credit intermediation (CCI) arises from screening, monitoring and developing long-term customer relationships and the accounting costs associated with alleviating these asymmetric information costs. Banking instability disrupts the role of banks in the credit-intermediation process, for several reasons. First, bank failures result in information and long-term relationships being destroyed, pushing up the CCI. Second, banking instability usually results in banks augmenting their capital, thereby contracting their lending. Third, because banking instability is usually associated with falling asset prices, the value of collateral decreases, resulting in an increase in the CCI and a contraction in lending.[11] This ultimately can lead to a downward spiral, in which lending shrinks because the value of collateral falls, leading to a further decrease in the value of assets, and so on.[12] Fourth, the fear of 'fire-sale' losses results in an overhang of illiquid assets, wherein banks hold on to assets in the hope that prices will recover. This increases bank demand for liquid assets, thereby reducing the funds available for lending to entrepreneurs. Fifth, depositors withdraw funds due to concerns about bank safety; in response, banks increase their reserves and liquid assets at the expense of their lending.

Although banking instability disrupts credit intermediation, it still takes place through alternative means. However, the switch away from

---

[7] Bernanke, 'Nonmonetary effects'.
[8] Calomiris and Mason, 'Consequences of bank distress'.
[9] Dell'Ariccia, Detragiache and Rajan, 'The real effect of banking crises'.
[10] Hall, 'Why does the economy fall to pieces after a financial crisis?'
[11] Bernanke, Gertler and Gilchrist, 'The financial accelerator'.
[12] Kiyotaki and Moore, 'Credit chains'.

banks greatly increases the CCI. This increase is compounded if the banking crisis is accompanied by substantial deflation, which erodes the value of collateral and raises the real burden of repaying debts.[13] According to Bernanke, this credit-crunch scenario not only explains the depth of the Great Depression in the United States but also its duration because it takes time to create new or reestablish old credit channels.[14]

As witnessed during the Great Crash of 2007–8 and earlier episodes, banking instability can be followed by sovereign-debt crises.[15] The transmission mechanism can be due to contingent liability, in which a government assumes responsibility for the large debts of private banks.[16] It also can be due to a currency crash if the sovereign has extensive foreign-currency debts.[17] Alternatively, collapsing revenues in the aftermath of a systemic banking crisis can result in substantial increases in government debt to possibly unsustainable levels.[18]

Banking instability also can result in political instability.[19] If a banking crisis results in a decline in GDP, a stalling of economic growth, and widespread unemployment and austerity, the populace may turn on its political leaders, as it did in Indonesia after the 1997 Asian financial crisis. Instability also can arise from government actions taken to save the banking sector. For example, government measures to save the banking system can result in transfers of wealth from taxpayers to banks and from savers to creditors. In addition to the detrimental effect of crises on the macroeconomy, these transfers can result in social agitation and widespread political unrest.

Empirical attempts to measure the costs of banking crises typically focus on the direct costs of resolving the crisis as well as the welfare costs of the crisis, which are typically proxied by output losses.[20] The cost estimates for post-1970 banking crises are substantial. For example, Hoggarth et al. found that the average output losses arising from episodes of banking instability in the last quarter of the twentieth century are on the order of 15 to 20 per cent of annual GDP.[21] Similarly, Laeven and Valencia's study of post-1970 crises estimates median output losses for crises in the 1970–2006 and 2007–9 periods at 19.5 and

[13] Bernanke and Gertler, 'Agency costs'.
[14] Bernanke, 'Nonmonetary effects', p. 272.
[15] Reinhart and Rogoff, 'From financial crash to debt crisis'.
[16] Diaz-Alejandro, 'Good-bye financial repression'.
[17] Kaminsky and Reinhart, 'The twin crises'.
[18] Reinhart and Rogoff, 'The aftermath of financial crises'.
[19] de Bromhead, Eichengreen and O'Rourke, 'Right-wing political extremism'.
[20] Laeven, 'Banking crises'.
[21] Hoggarth, Reis and Saporta, 'Costs of banking system instability'.

24.5 per cent of GDP, respectively.[22] In addition, the median direct fiscal costs as a percentage of GDP for these two periods are 10.0 and 4.9, respectively.[23] Given the considerable costs, we need to understand why banking becomes unstable in the first place.

Why do banking systems become unstable?

The traditional textbook explanation of the evolution of modern banking begins with bankers providing a safekeeping function for specie (i.e., coined precious metal).[24] Then, through experimentation, innovation and imitation, a scenario arises in which bankers issue bank notes that are redeemable for specie and they develop cheques to facilitate the exchange of deposits. Such banks are merely warehouses because deposits are backed 100 per cent by bank reserves. Consequently, except for theft or State expropriation, such banks are stable because note-holders, cheque-holders and depositors are always guaranteed to get their funds. However, such banking systems are costly because there is a substantial opportunity cost associated with holding a 100 per cent specie reserve. In essence, 100 per cent reserve banks provide a payments function, but they are not engaged in intermediating funds from savers to borrowers – that is, intermediating finance from those who have funds but no productive opportunities to those who have productive opportunities but no funds.

Financial innovation and experimentation resulted in bankers discovering that they did not need to hold anywhere near a full reserve to service deposit withdrawals and the redemption of bank notes. Bankers could hold a fractional reserve, lend some of the deposits to entrepreneurs and invest the remainder in securities. A typical bank might have a balance sheet similar to the one shown in Table 2.1.

We now have two questions to answer. First, according to the extant literature, what would cause this hypothetical bank to fail? Second, would there be negative externalities for the banking system arising from this failure? In answering these questions, we must think about the vulnerabilities for this bank on the asset and liability sides of its balance sheet.

On the liability side of the balance sheet, this bank faces the threat of a bank run. Because deposit contracts have a first-come-first-served redemption clause, any suspicion that banks cannot meet future withdrawals will result in rational depositors rushing to withdraw their deposits. Because this rush will quickly exhaust the bank's specie reserves,

[22] Laeven and Valencia, 'Resolution of banking crises'.
[23] Laeven and Valencia, 'Resolution of banking crises', p. 22.
[24] See White, *The Theory of Monetary Institutions*, pp. 1–19.

Table 2.1 *A hypothetical bank balance sheet*

Assets	(£ million)	Liabilities	(£ million)
Reserves	5	Notes in circulation	10
Interbank deposits	4	Demand deposits	30
Securities	19	Nontransaction deposits	30
Loans	66	Borrowings	22
Other assets	6	Capital	8
	100		100

the bank will have to raise extra reserves by selling off its marketable securities or perhaps by borrowing specie from other banks. One problem that our hypothetical bank might face in selling off its marketable securities is that the market for such securities becomes less liquid because the bank is trying to offload them quickly. In other words, the bank may experience fire-sale losses. This bank also may find that competing banks are reluctant to lend to it because (1) the presence of a run may make the interbank market suspicious of this bank's solvency, (2) the presence of a run makes banks generally more cautious, and (3) banks with surplus reserves may fear that future liquidity is going to evaporate; consequently, they may hoard their surplus reserves. Because loan portfolios are extremely illiquid, any attempt to sell them may result in substantial losses to the selling bank. This scenario may provide a rationale for a lender of last resort, who will provide the liquidity in times of need by lending against temporarily illiquid assets.

What triggers a bank run in the first place? In the Diamond and Dybvig model of bank runs, the no-bank-run equilibrium is fragile, with runs being triggered by runs observed at other banks, bad earnings reports, negative macroeconomic news or sunspots.[25] Because none of these variables (other than the last one) is integrated into the Diamond and Dybvig model, bank runs in their model are not triggered by the real economy but rather by random factors and irrational behaviour on the part of depositors.[26] However, depositors may run a bank not in anticipation of its being run by other depositors but rather because of a fear that a real economic event will impair the assets of a bank and its ability to repay depositors.

Can banks 'run-proof' themselves? They could change the nature of the contract so that deposits are not payable on demand and are not

---

[25] Diamond and Dybvig, 'Bank runs'.
[26] Dowd, *The State and the Monetary System*, p. 17.

subject to the sequential-service constraint. However, an institution with this type of contract would not resemble an historical or contemporary bank. Although banks can discourage runs by lending prudently and holding sufficient reserves and other liquid assets, they cannot be made totally run-proof. Paradoxically, these features of the deposit contract may actually function to enhance stability because the threat of bank runs encourages bankers to operate their bank prudently.[27] If a run threatens, banks can temporarily close or suspend the convertibility of their deposits to stave off a run. This may, however, merely delay the inevitable collapse of the bank.

Bank runs can be contagious, spilling over from unhealthy onto healthy banks and resulting in potentially substantial social-welfare losses. Runs can be contagious due to irrationality and pure panic on the part of depositors. They also can be contagious due to asymmetric information – that is, depositors do not have the information to distinguish between healthy and unhealthy institutions. Runs also can be contagious due to network externalities, whereby the interconnectedness of the banking system through the interbank and derivatives markets, for example, gives one institution the capacity to affect other healthy banks.

Our hypothetical bank also is potentially vulnerable on the asset side of the balance sheet. If the value of its securities or loans decreases by more than £8 million, the bank is technically insolvent and depositors face the risk of losing some of their money. Indeed, if depositors or other creditors anticipate that a bank's assets are going to fall in value, they will run the bank, thereby precipitating its rapid and costly demise.

Why might the value of bank assets fall? One possibility is that the economy experiences an exogenous shock, which results in a decrease in asset values. Some shocks, such as natural disasters and military subjugation, may trigger a substantial decline in asset values that potentially could wipe out banks. Although they reduce asset values, supply or other economic shocks should not create a problem for the hypothetical bank if it had been acting prudently at the time. In one sense, we can compare banking stability with the structural stability of buildings in earthquake-prone cities. Buildings in these cities are constructed to withstand seismological activity up to a certain limit. It is similar with the hypothetical bank: the managers would know the size and frequency of past economic shocks, with the result that their asset- and liability-management policies would consider this information to be able to withstand future shocks.

Could banks be their own cause of instability? According to Minsky, banking is 'a disruptive force that tends to induce and amplify

[27] Calomiris and Kahn, 'The role of demandable debt'.

instability'.[28] In his view, bank managers have a tendency to increase leverage ratios without a decrease in the perceived security of bank earnings. This induces bank customers to increase their leverage, which in turn results in speculative and Ponzi financing and in an increased probability of economic instability. When the inevitable crash comes, both asset prices and the value of collateral fall, which is followed by a depletion of bank capital and solvency difficulties for banks. In this situation, there is no exogenous cause of a financial crisis; banks are endogenous destabilisers, given that the built-in procyclicality of the banking system makes it vulnerable to crises. Minsky's theory raises more questions than it answers. Why do bank managers and banks increase leverage and risk in the first place? Why cannot depositors place constraints on the risks that banks take? Why do not banks and economic agents adapt their behaviour, given their awareness of this inherent procyclicality?

For Kindleberger, the decline in bank-asset values that triggers banking crises is usually the result of the bursting of asset-price bubbles.[29] Speculation in an asset fuels a bubble because mania, irrationality and 'herding' on the part of investors drive asset prices to unsustainable levels. Banks have a role in financing (and thus contributing to) these bubbles for they provide the funds to buy the assets and take overvalued assets as collateral. When the inevitable price reversal occurs, the value of bank assets can fall quite substantially depending on their exposure to the asset class that experienced the bubble.

The extant literature is not in complete agreement with the idea that banks are inherently vulnerable to instability. For a small minority of economists, banking instability is a result of government intervention or bad government policies. For example, according to Selgin, 'despite frequent claims to the contrary, fractional-reserve banking systems are not inherently fragile or unstable. The fragility and instability of real-world banking systems is not a free-market phenomenon, but a consequence of legal restrictions'.[30] Similarly, Dowd argued that 'the *sine qua non* of bank runs is outside (i.e., state) interference in the monetary system'.[31] Other government policies that could undermine bank stability include the presence of deposit-insurance schemes and taxpayer bailouts, which result in a moral-hazard problem whereby banks take on greater risk as depositors and other creditors exert less effort in monitoring and disciplining banks.[32] As described throughout this book, the historical record

---

[28] Minsky, *Stabilizing an Unstable Economy*, p. 255.
[29] Kindleberger, *Manias, Panics and Crashes*.   [30] Selgin, 'Legal restrictions', p. 456.
[31] Dowd, *The State and the Monetary System*, p. 23.
[32] Benston and Kaufman, 'The appropriate role of bank regulation'; Flannery, 'Deposit insurance'; Kareken and Wallace, 'Deposit insurance and bank regulation'; Selgin, 'Legal restrictions'.

of banking stability in Britain lends little in the way of support to this view of the causes of banking instability.

Risk shifting and banking instability

The vulnerabilities described previously alone are unsatisfactory explanations as to why banking systems become unstable because, in some ways, they are proximate causes. In addition and more important, they ignore the incentive structures of bankers, owners and depositors. Therefore, in this section, we develop a more complete theory: one that encapsulates the behaviour of bank owners and managers, who ultimately make the decisions about a bank's exposure to risk. Ultimately, as discussed herein, the unique and special nature of bank assets and liabilities means that both managers and shareholders have a crucial role in determining the stability of their bank and, thus, the overall banking system.

Because most modern banks are limited-liability joint-stock corporations, we begin by assuming that the hypothetical bank in Table 2.1 has this organisational form. We initially assume that the owners of the bank are also its managers (i.e., there is no separation of ownership from control) and thus no agency problems.

Bank-loan portfolios are opaque in that depositors, at any given time, do not know their true value.[33] They are opaque for at least two reasons. First, bank borrowers place a high value on discretion; they do not want sensitive information about their investment projects released into the public domain in case doing so benefits competitors or potential competitors. This implies that banks must not release the full details of a loan into the public domain, enabling depositors to value a bank's loan portfolio. Second, if banks release private information about their borrowers, they lose some of the return on their proprietary investment in information. The opacity of the loan portfolio means that depositors – even in a fully competitive environment – are unable to discipline banks for excessive risk taking. In addition, the opacity of the loan portfolio means that it is a highly fungible or plastic asset that is easy to shift, unobserved, into riskier loans. This is known as 'risk shifting'.

If it is assumed that depositors are fully rational, they will know that the bank has an incentive to shift risk and will accordingly adjust their expectations to reflect the true risk-adjusted value of the bank's loan portfolio. As a consequence, they will demand a higher compensatory risk premium from the bank. In this case, all of the agency costs of debt are borne by the bank's owners rather than its depositors. However, if depositors are less than fully rational, the benefits from risk shifting

---

[33] Bhattacharya, Boot and Thakor, 'The economics of bank regulation', p. 761.

accrue to the bank, whereas the cost is partially borne by depositors in the sense that they get a lower risk premium than was warranted by the potential riskiness of the loan portfolio.[34]

In a world full of rational depositors, the ability of banks to engage in risk shifting might result in depositors demanding a prohibitive compensatory risk premium unless they receive a credible commitment that their bank would not engage in risk shifting. Without such a commitment, there might be a substantial underprovision of banking services. However, it could be that depositors have no alternative but to deposit with a bank if they want access to a payments system or if financial markets are segmented. Thus, even in a world in which depositors are fully rational, banks may be able to shift risk.

Risk shifting, by definition, occurs unobserved by depositors. However, risk shifting by an individual bank or a set of banks can be exposed when a real or monetary shock hits a banking system. The exogenous shock causes asset values to fall and borrowers to default on loans; eventually, banks that engaged in large-scale risk shifting declare insolvency or are run by depositors who realise that their bank is about to default. Risk shifting also can be exposed when asset prices collapse after a bank-fuelled increase in asset prices above their fundamental values. The decrease in asset prices could push banks into default or cause them to be run, ultimately resulting in their default. Such an asset-price bubble typically would require a substantial extension of credit by a large proportion of the banking system, resulting in a systemic banking collapse rather than the failure of a single institution or set of institutions. Thus, in this scenario, banking instability is endogenous rather than exogenous. Indeed, such endogenously produced crises will be larger in scale and cause severe problems for the real economy.

A possible solution to the risk-shifting propensity of banks is for them to commit to holding 100 per cent reserves against deposits. This would remove any temptation for banks to engage in risk shifting with depositors' funds. It also means that banks would always have sufficient funds to meet deposit withdrawals and therefore would never experience bank runs because they no longer operate on a fractional reserve. However, this is not how modern banks evolved; they have an intermediation function as well as a payments function. Banks may have good reasons to operate with a fractional reserve. First, holding depositor funds in the form of reserves incurs huge opportunity costs, which are ultimately borne by depositors. Second, holding depositor funds in the form of reserves means that the bank is not diversified. Furthermore, although a bank can

---

[34] Jensen and Meckling, 'Theory of the firm', p. 334; Stiglitz, 'Credit markets', p. 135.

insure its physically held reserves against fire or theft, it cannot insure them against government expropriation.

Eminent economists, including Friedman, Miller, Tobin and Fisher, advocated that banks be required to hold 100 per cent reserves against deposits.[35] Even Hayek briefly entertained the idea.[36] However, these so-called narrow banking policies are not without problems. First and foremost, the imposition of a 100 per cent reserve requirement would simply transfer the risk-shifting problem onto other near-bank institutions that would arise in response to this regulation.[37] Second, such a regulation would increase the transaction costs of intermediation, making credit more costly.

Another possible solution to the risk-shifting problem is for depositors to monitor banks. Competition between banks would enable depositors to discipline them if their monitoring uncovers risk-shifting behaviour, for they would be able to punish errant banks by simply switching their deposits.[38] There could be, however, a free-riding problem with this monitoring solution, with the result that there is an underinvestment in monitoring. However, the sequential-service feature of demand deposits provides incentives for those who choose to invest in information, thereby alleviating the free-riding problem.[39] In other words, those who invest in information will be first in the queue to withdraw their funds. We would expect large depositors to invest more in monitoring than other depositors. In addition, depositors could delegate monitoring to outside or third-party monitors so as to prevent the duplication of monitoring effort. Perhaps auditors or credit-rating agencies could perform this function.

Although the free-riding problem can be minimised, there are two fundamental problems with the monitoring solution that make it ineffective in preventing risk shifting. First, as discussed previously, a bank's loan portfolio is opaque, which implies that depositors or their third-party monitors cannot obtain the necessary information about the constituents of the portfolio needed to value it. Although depositors or their third-party monitors can collect information on the liquidity, capital positions, and value of marketable securities of a bank, they will not be able to discover enough to assess the value and risk of the bank's loan portfolio.

---

[35] Allen, 'Irving Fisher'; Friedman, *A Program for Monetary Stability*; Miller, 'Do the M+M propositions apply to banks?'; Tobin, 'A case for preserving regulatory distinctions'; Wallace, 'Narrow banking'.
[36] White, 'The evolution of Hayek's monetary economics'.
[37] Diamond and Dybvig, 'Banking theory'.
[38] England, 'Agency costs and unregulated banks'.
[39] Calomiris and Kahn, 'The role of demandable debt', p. 497.

Second, in the last period of the contractual relationship, monitoring does not constrain banks because there are no negative consequences for a bank that risk shifts. Although depositors may not know when the last period occurs, banks have an incentive to risk shift whenever the present value of future revenue streams is less than the present value of risk shifting. An increase in discount rates can easily cause such a scenario to arise.

Yet another possible solution to the risk-shifting problem is for banks to invest in brand-name capital. Klein's seminal work on this issue argued that a bank can invest in brand-name capital through, for example, advertising, reputation building and erecting impressive buildings.[40] Because such expenditure is asset-specific, it acts to ensure that a brand-name-type bank operating in a competitive environment will not risk shift if the present value of its future net-income stream is greater than the present value that it derives from risk shifting. In a competitive equilibrium, the value of the bank's asset-specific investment equals the present value of the bank's net-income stream. The present value of a bank's future net-income stream may be larger if there are entry barriers into banking. The existence of this franchise value potentially reduces the probability of risk shifting.[41]

Free-banking models ultimately rely on Klein's brand-name-capital concept. Unlike Klein, free bankers argue that banks are kept in check by the contractual requirement to redeem notes and deposits for a precious commodity at a previously agreed rate of exchange.[42] Although automatic reflux – whereby notes and cheques return to the issuing bank primarily via the clearing system and must be redeemed on presentation with a precious commodity – puts a check on the overexpansion of a bank's liability issue, it does not prevent banks from engaging in risk shifting. Indeed, free bankers admit that safer banks can send costly confidence-bolstering signals of their sound financial health to their note-holders and depositors through asset-specific investments in the form of impressive bank edifices and publicity.[43]

Brand-name-capital solutions are viable only when it is assumed that banks operate in the context of an infinite horizon. However, under the assumption of a finite horizon, the investment in brand-name capital becomes worthless in the last period and banks will risk shift. As a consequence, rational depositors are unwilling – at any interest rate – to hold

[40] Klein, 'The competitive supply of money'.
[41] Demsetz, Saidenberg and Strahan, 'Banks with something to lose'.
[42] Selgin and White, 'How would the invisible hand handle money?'
[43] White, *Free Banking in Britain*, p. 7.

the deposits of a brand-name-type bank in the last period. Thus, the bank will cheat in the penultimate period and, through a process of backwards induction, we can deduce that depositors will refuse to hold the liabilities of a brand-name-type bank in any period, including the first period. Although it may be uncertain when the last period will occur, we can justify the assumption on the basis that given a sufficiently high rate of time discount, banks will risk shift. Notably, no less an authority than Charles Goodhart also recognised that brand-name or reputational capital is useful only if contractual relationships are infinite or if there is a low rate of time discount.[44]

Capital may have a role in mitigating risk shifting because the more capital owners put into the bank relative to deposits, the lower is the likelihood of the bank engaging in risk shifting because the owners stand to lose their investment when loan defaults occur. Conversely, the less capital the owners put into a bank, the greater is the likelihood of risk shifting. For example, the hypothetical bank in Table 2.1 is relatively highly leveraged, with only eight pence of every pound lent to borrowers coming from owners, which means that most of the downside of high risk taking is borne by depositors rather than shareholders.

If banks carry relatively low amounts of capital, then a series of loan losses can quickly deplete the owners' investment. Once the capital is depleted, the owners' incentive will change because they now have nothing to lose. Indeed, they may have an incentive to 'gamble for resurrection'. Consequently, to assure depositors that they will not engage in risk taking, bank owners must contribute relatively large amounts of capital and invest it in very low-risk assets. The size of the capital buffer must be such that a bank will still have substantial capital resources even after suffering loan losses. The opportunity cost of having to hold large amounts of idle funds may be prohibitive for many bankers.[45]

Another potential weakness with capital is that it can be covertly dispersed to owners in the last period through an extraordinary dividend, for example. The bank then can engage in risk shifting because owners no longer have much downside risk. This ability to extract capital may be possible if the bank is a private company. However, if the bank is a public company, a covert extraction of capital may not be possible due to company law and the requirement to publish financial reports.

---

[44] Goodhart, *The Evolution of Central Banks*, pp. 60–4.

[45] Admati and Hellwig, *The Bankers' New Clothes*, p. 99, argue that capital can be used to fund loans and that it does not have to be held in idle funds. However, for capital to be credible to depositors, a large proportion of it must be held in low-risk securities.

Thus far, we assume that banks are private companies with limited liability and that there is no separation of ownership from control (i.e., there are no agency problems). However, if banks are public companies with dispersed ownership, then there is a potential agency problem, which may add to the cost of equity capital. Bank managers may have an incentive to act other than in the best interests of shareholders; in other words, they may have an incentive to engage in risk shifting at the expense of both depositors and shareholders. Although the presence of debt may alleviate the agency problem in most firms, the nature of banking (as outlined herein) means that debt does not discipline managers.[46] Indeed, the agency costs of bank equity may be such that banks find it difficult to raise sufficient capital to credibly assure depositors that they will not risk shift.

Risk shifting, shareholder liability and regulation

A bank's propensity to risk shift is aggravated when its owners enjoy limited liability.[47] Limited liability exacerbates the unique problems facing a banking firm in two ways. First, *ceteris paribus*, a more efficient contract design is to always assign liability to the side of the contract that incurs the least cost in obtaining information (i.e., the bank owners). Second, *ceteris paribus*, efficient contract design also implies that liability should always be assigned to the side of the contract that is the least risk averse. Deposits are highly liquid because they are relatively short term and, in other respects, are more easily convertible into cash than other assets. Therefore, it is reasonable to assume that a typical depositor is highly risk averse, whereas a typical bank owner is not.

If the owners of a private bank were to have joint and several unlimited liability, this might provide depositors with a credible commitment that the bank would not risk shift. Joint and several unlimited liability implies that each owner is liable to cover the debts of the bank down to their very last penny, irrespective of whether other owners make a contribution to covering the bank's debts. The credibility of the commitment depends on three conditions. First, if owners had low wealth (i.e., if all of their wealth were tied up in the bank), the unlimited-liability commitment would become de facto limited. In addition, if the wealth of owners were extremely illiquid or in a fungible form, depositors might be wary of the commitment. This implies that depositors would pay close attention to

---

[46] On the role of debt in alleviating agency problems, see Jensen, 'Agency costs of free cash flow'.

[47] Hickson and Turner, 'Free banking and the stability'.

the wealth of bank owners. Second, the credibility of the commitment depends on whether owners can precommit to not dump their ownership stake before a bank enters bankruptcy, which is done by inserting a clause into the bank's constitution or articles to prevent such an action. Because such a clause could be easily eliminated at the most expedient time (i.e., when a bank is in financial distress), the credibility of unlimited liability ultimately depends on whether the legal system prevents such opportunistic dumping. Third, the greater the number and variety of owners, the greater is the commitment to depositors because a bank with few homogeneous owners could begin risk shifting if the owners' wealth experienced a shock. In addition, the wealth of a small number of owners may be insufficient to cover loan losses.

If the bank were a public corporation, this could render the unlimited-liability commitment more credible because ownership would be diversified among several heterogeneous individuals. In essence, a bank with multiple wealthy owners would have extensive resources backing its deposits. The potential problem with joint-stock unlimited-liability banks is threefold. First, can the equilibrium of wealthy bank shareholders be preserved if bank stock can be sold or transferred? Second, given that liability is joint and several, how can bank shareholders ensure that co-owners have sufficient wealth? Third, facing the potential loss of all of their wealth, how can shareholders ensure that bank managers prudently operate the bank?

It is commonly accepted that if stock is transferable without restrictions, unlimited liability quickly becomes de facto limited as stocks are transferred to impecunious investors.[48] Consequently, economists have hypothesised two mechanisms through which unlimited liability can be sustained. First, each incumbent owner with a vote on new-member acceptance could engage in costly verification of all applicant owners and regular monitoring of existing co-owners to ensure that they each had enough wealth to meet their contribution in the event of bankruptcy.[49] Verification and monitoring costs could be minimised by restricting share transfers to a pool of individuals who have a minimum level of wealth.[50]

Second, owners could be held legally liable for what was deemed a suitable period after they sold their shares for any *pro rata* shortfall in assets

[48] Woodward, 'Limited liability', p. 602.
[49] Carr and Mathewson, 'Unlimited liability as a barrier to entry', p. 769; Jensen and Meckling, 'Theory of the firm', p. 331; Winton, 'Limitation of liability', p. 490.
[50] Carr and Mathewson, 'Unlimited liability', p. 769; Woodward, 'Limited liability', p. 606.

required to cover liabilities in the event of a bankruptcy occurring.[51] Nevertheless, there is a possible serious problem with the feasibility of this solution: shareholders faced with an increasing prospect of bankruptcy could always collectively renege on any post-sale extended-liability commitment to creditors by selling their shares to impecunious investors before default. Consequently, creditors – realising the ineffectiveness of such a commitment – would respond by demanding a sufficient compensatory risk premium. Thus, it might be optimal to legally enforce such commitments for a uniform specified period to prevent shares from being dumped when firms are under financial stress.

However, there remains the problem associated with any imposed fixed-term period of post-sale extended liability: stockowners will always be inclined to sell their ownership share to less wealthy investors in the boom period of the business cycle, when there seems to be little likelihood of default during the post-sale liability period. However, depositors would demand increases in the risk premium to compensate them for the reduction in the overall wealth backing the bank's shares. Thus, within the context of a longer-term horizon, it is in the interest of the firm to vet sales to avoid wealth reduction. Consequently, it is only when a firm suffers extreme financial stress, when the prospect of bankruptcy is greatly increased, and when the propensity of shareholders is to collectively dump their ownership that legally enforced post-sale extended liability is required.

We can easily comprehend how the costs associated with applicant-owner verification could dramatically reduce the liquidity of shares. However, this verification could be delegated to a firm's directors, who could control entry to the shareholding membership, thereby ensuring that the aggregate wealth of the shareholding constituency is not diluted. Notably, this policy is not a solution with co-owners monitoring one another and verifying each applicant owner; it is simply a control mechanism operated by the directors.

This discussion raises the following related questions: How can shareholders be confident that directors will exclude low-wealth shareholders? How can shareholders be confident that directors will not engage in excessive risk taking, thereby endangering the personal wealth of shareholders? The directors would have adequate incentives to circumspectly vet applicant owners if the directors themselves were among the wealthiest owners. The wealthiest owners would have the greatest incentives of any owner to exclude low-wealth individuals from membership because the former would be most likely to be pursued through the courts by

---

[51] Woodward, 'Limited liability', p. 606; Winton, 'Limitation of liability', p. 500.

depositors in the event of default.[52] For this same reason, we would expect the wealthiest owners to participate in the governance of the bank – they have the most to lose in the event of their bank failing. Indeed, these owners may even operate the bank more conservatively than other owners would desire.

Ultimately, the question arises as to whether the cost of equity capital for unlimited-liability banks would be prohibitive. First, the need for director vetting may impair the transferability and liquidity of bank stocks, thereby increasing the premium paid on equity capital. Second, and more fundamentally, investors will need compensation for the risk that they may lose all of their wealth. Counterbalancing this risk, the conservative nature of bank management arising from the wealthiest shareholders' participation in a bank's governance would tend to lower substantially the agency costs of equity capital. In addition, the existence of capital held beyond the bank implies that shareholders would not have to deposit so much capital in the first instance, with the result that the opportunity costs of holding idle funds should be lower for unlimited-liability banks. With regard to returns, the security provided by unlimited liability should result in a lower interest rate being paid on deposits, which would increase a bank's profitability.

There is an entire spectrum of liability regimes between pure limited liability and joint and several unlimited liability that a bank might adopt. Crucially, joint and several unlimited liability is undefined ex-ante, whereas with lesser forms of extended liability, a shareholder's liability is defined ex-ante. Extended shareholder liability could simply be a fixed multiple of paid-up capital (e.g., double liability), or it could be that shares are partially paid, with an unpaid proportion callable in the case of bank failure.[53] Such regimes, by their nature, are *pro rata* rather than joint and several. In other words, once owners have paid the entire unpaid portion on their shares or their multiple of paid-up capital, they would not be liable if other owners are unable to pay their portion; whereas with joint-and-several-unlimited-liability regimes, owners are liable for what their co-owners cannot pay. This implies that with anything less than joint and several unlimited liability, lower externalities will be imposed on owners by the admission of low-wealth shareholders into a bank. However, there are no near-zero externalities because the absolute amount that an owner must pay out in the event of bank failure will be a function of the wealth of the co-owners. Nevertheless, the limitation of liability may

---

[52] Hickson and Turner, 'Trading in the shares', p. 952.
[53] For example, a bank share could have a nominal value of £10 and a paid-up value of £3, which means that shareholders are liable for the remaining £7 unpaid on the share.

dramatically reduce the incentive of wealthy owners to actively participate in the management of the bank; hence, the professional manager
arises, who would have few incentives to circumspectly conduct the vetting role.[54] However, as long as professional managers own shares that
constitute a substantial proportion of their wealth, they will have an
incentive to vet circumspectly and ensure that only those with adequate
wealth become owners of the bank's stock.

Regulation also may have a role in reducing the level of risk shifting by
banks. Using the hypothetical bank in Table 2.1, it appears that a regulator could take several actions to prevent risk shifting. On the liability
side of the balance sheet, a regulator could compel the bank to hold a
certain amount of capital, which could be linked to the size of its deposit
issue or the riskiness of its assets. Regulations could also be imposed that
constrain the ability of banks to overexpand their liability issue.

On the asset side of a bank's balance sheet, reserve requirements –
which require banks to hold a certain proportion of their deposits in
the form of reserves (i.e., central-bank money or a precious commodity
such as gold) – could be imposed. Such requirements would operate
against the tendency of banks to hold insufficient reserves, and they also
would limit the amount of deposits that banks have to lend and invest,
thereby reducing the ability of banks to risk shift. Regulators also could
require banks to invest a certain proportion of their asset portfolio in safe
government bonds, which again limits the ability of banks to risk shift.
Of course, governments may impose such requirements to help finance
their deficits at a low cost, and such bonds may not be safe. Regulators
also could restrict banks to investing none or only a certain proportion of
their asset portfolio in real estate and stocks. Given the historical volatility
of these asset classes, it could be relatively easy for banks to risk shift by
investing in them. Similarly, regulators may restrict the amount that can
be lent on the security of real estate.

Regulators also may be concerned with restricting risky off-balance-
sheet activities such as investment banking and security issuance and
trading. Because these risky activities are extremely volatile, banks easily
could divert assets towards them as part of a risk-shifting strategy.

Regulations must be enforced if they are to be credible. Consequently,
to ensure that it is complying with regulation, the hypothetical bank in
Table 2.1 would have to send regular reports to the regulator and then
would be subject to periodic (and possibly random) examination by the
regulator. Furthermore, the regulator will need the authority to discipline
the bank if it fails to comply with the regulations.

---

[54] Acheson and Turner, 'The impact of limited liability'.

Concluding comments

In this chapter, we suggest that banking stability matters for the economy. We also establish that a banking firm is intrinsically unstable because managers can easily risk shift due to the opacity and plasticity of a bank's asset portfolio. This means that rational depositors may demand a prohibitively large risk premium. Banks may be able to solve this problem by holding sufficient capital, but this might prove to be very costly for bank shareholders. Two other possible solutions, both of which were mooted, could potentially prevent banks from risk shifting: (1) bank shareholders carry extended liability, which provides shareholders and managers with a disincentive to risk shifting; and (2) a government or government-appointed regulator places and enforces constraints on banks that aim to prevent them from risk shifting.

These two solutions do not mean that banks will not fail, but they should ensure that banks as a whole do not risk shift, thereby avoiding a systemic crisis. Are there circumstances under which a banking system might experience a systemic crisis even though it operated in a political environment in which property rights are protected and secure, underpinned by extended shareholder liability? One circumstance might be when such banks are constrained by law to have a small pool of owners. As highlighted herein, such banks are vulnerable to shocks to owners' wealth, which might result in their risk shifting. In addition, a few owners may not have sufficiently deep collective pockets to survive a large exogenous shock to their bank.

Systemic banking crises also can occur in a system in which banks are regulated. First, for various reasons, regulators may have systematically failed to enforce regulations or may have been captured by those they regulate. Second, regulations may have been diluted over time or become no longer appropriate, or banks may have innovated so as to engage in regulatory avoidance. Consequently, risk shifting occurs en masse and results in credit-fuelled speculation that eventually unravels as a result of either an endogenous implosion or an exogenous shock to the economy. As a result, banks suffer major loan losses and a crisis ensues.

Thus far, we largely ignore the relationship between the industrial structure of banking and banking stability.[55] In one sense, the theory outlined herein applies equally to all types of market structure because risk shifting will occur whether one bank dominates the market or the

---

[55] A good introduction to this literature is provided by Berger et al., 'Bank competition'; Boyd and De Nicoló, 'The theory of bank risk taking'; and Martinez-Miera and Repullo, 'Does competition reduce'.

market is competitive. An oligopolistic banking structure creates franchise value in that a bank enjoys monopolistic profits today and into the future. However, franchise value suffers from a last-period problem, whereby at some stage, the present value of the future cash flows from the franchise to managers and shareholders is less than the present value of risk shifting.

The theory outlined in this chapter, however, has implications for bank size, which is closely related to the industrial structure of banking. First, the larger the bank, the greater is the potential upside and downside from risk shifting. Second, small banks may be more vulnerable to collapse due to the inadequacy of their capital resources.

In the remainder of this book, the risk-shifting concept provides a framework in which to analyse the historical experience with banking stability in Britain. In particular, the book describes how episodes of banking instability are associated with the absence of checks on risk shifting, whereas stable banking is associated with the existence of checks on risk shifting, such as extended shareholder liability and stringent regulation of bank activities.

3   The evolution of British banking structure and stability since 1800

It's awful – why did nobody see it coming?[1]

Her Majesty Queen Elizabeth II

Introduction

In this chapter, we measure and assess the stability of the British banking system from 1800 to the present, using a combination of bank-failure data and bank-stock prices. The main finding from this analysis is that there have been two major or systemic banking crises in the past two centuries: 1825–6 and 2007–8. In the interim, there were several minor or nonsystemic crises.

However, before we examine the stability of the banking system, we need to understand how the structure of British banking has evolved since 1800, for at least three reasons. First, we need background and context if we are going to examine the stability of the banking system. Second, the structure of the banking system may have a bearing on its stability and vice versa. Third, the two ways that we have to assess banking stability require us to comprehend the basic evolution of UK banking structure. Thus, the following section describes and explains how the UK banking system evolved. The two subsequent sections explore the stability of the British banking system since 1800 and the effect of banking instability on the real economy.

The development of the British banking system

At the time of the Great Crash of 2007–8, Britain's banking system was dominated by a small number of banks that had branches not only throughout the United Kingdom but also subsidiaries around the globe.

---

[1] This was a question regarding the banking crisis asked during Her Majesty's visit to the London School of Economics, *Daily Telegraph*, 5 November 2008.

However, two centuries earlier, the United Kingdom had literally hundreds of banks, all of which had a limited geographical reach. How did this transformation happen? To fully understand the evolution of the UK banking system, we must recognize the fact that it evolved from separate systems in England and Wales, Scotland, and Ireland.

Established in 1694, the Bank of England was the first joint-stock bank in Britain. The monopoly powers of the Bank were strengthened in Acts passed in 1697, 1707 and 1708 that restricted note issuing to the Bank of England and partnerships of six or fewer members.[2] During the eighteenth century, the number of these partnership banks grew steadily, with slightly more than three hundred banks by 1800. By 1813, after a huge growth phase during the Napoleonic Wars, there were 761 partnership banks in England.[3]

These partnership banks were the subject of much debate and controversy during the early part of the nineteenth century, particularly in regard to the perceived overissue of bank notes.[4] Furthermore, by the early 1820s, many commentators were blaming the frequent bouts of banking failures on the Bank of England's monopolistic position and the concomitant weak state of the partnership banks.[5] Consequently, a large majority of Parliamentarians supported the passage of the Banking Copartnership Act in 1826.[6] This Act is noteworthy because it was the first piece of legislation in England that permitted business organisations to constitute freely on the joint-stock principle. Despite a suggestion that banks be allowed to limit their liability, bank owners remained liable without limit.[7] According to William Clay, M.P., the Bank – wishing to preserve its monopoly status – would have opposed the passage of the legislation if other banks had been granted limited liability.[8] Although its consent was not required, the Bank's power gave it undue influence over Parliament at that time.[9] The influence of the Bank on the Banking Copartnership Act (1826) also is evident in the provision to allow joint-stock banks to issue notes only if they were located outside a 65-mile radius of the Eleanor Cross at Charing Cross (i.e., for legislative purposes, the nominal centre of London).

---

[2] 8 & 9 Wm. III, c.20, s.28; 6 Anne, c.22, s.9; 7 Anne, c.7, s. 61. The 1697 Act was relatively unsuccessful in achieving its aims (Richards, *The Early History of Banking*, p. 147).
[3] Pressnell, *Country Banking*, p. 127.
[4] Viner, *Studies in the Theory of International Trade*, chaps. 3 and 4.
[5] Thomas, *The Rise and Growth*, p. 58.
[6] 7 Geo. IV, c.46. See Harris, *Industrializing English Law*, p. 214.
[7] Hunt, *The Development of the Business Corporation*, p. 50.
[8] W. Clay, *Speech of William Clay*, pp. 14 and 43.   [9] Turner, 'The last acre and sixpence'.

At the beginning of the nineteenth century, the Bank of Ireland, which had been granted a charter in 1783 in return for investing its £600,000 capital in government securities, was the dominant Irish bank. The charter granted the privileges of incorporation and limited liability and also resulted in a dominant note-issuing position in Ireland by constraining other note-issuing banks to an upper limit of six partners.[10] According to the 1804 Irish Currency Report, there were only eleven private banks in the entire country in 1800.[11] By 1804, however, there were forty private banks operating in Ireland. This increase was associated with the large expansion of the Irish currency derived from suspending the convertibility of Bank of Ireland notes into specie.[12] During the next fifteen years, the number of private banks fluctuated; however, on the eve of the 1819–20 Irish depression, there were thirty-one private banks in operation. In 1820, sixteen of those banks failed or suspended payment.

There were several legislative responses to the 1820 crisis, culminating in the enactment of the Banking Copartnership Regulation Act (1825), which permitted the establishment of joint-stock banks – as long as they did not issue notes within 50 Irish miles (i.e., 65 statutory miles) of Dublin.[13] This meant that banks could freely form as joint-stock firms with no restrictions on the transfer of their shares, but their shareholders had joint and several unlimited liability. The passing of this joint-stock legislation opened the way for the development of large commercial banks in Ireland.

The Bank of Scotland originally had been granted a monopoly of public banking in Scotland for a twenty-one-year period, but this monopolistic privilege was not renewed. In 1727, the Royal Bank of Scotland was incorporated by the state, followed by the British Linen Bank in 1746. These three banks had charters granted by the state, which bestowed on them the privileges of incorporation. However, unlike in England and Ireland, other Scottish banks did not face a six-partner restriction. Furthermore and more fundamentally, because the Scottish commercial-law system closely resembled those of its civil-law Continental trading partners, the partnership banks in Scotland enjoyed the privilege of a separate legal personality. This allowed these banks to separate ownership from control, enabling them to develop a managerial hierarchy, which in turn

---

[10] Hall, *The Bank of Ireland*, pp. 35–6.
[11] Hall, *The Bank of Ireland*, p. 14; Fetter, *The Irish Paper Pound*, pp. 73–4.
[12] Turner, 'Irish contributions', p. 221.
[13] 6 Geo. IV, c.42. Earlier attempts to amend the Irish banking system included the Bank of Ireland Restriction Act, 1821 (1 & 2 Geo. IV, c.72) and the Irish Banking Act, 1824 (5 Geo. IV, c.73).

facilitated transferable stock.[14] As a result, these Scottish partnership banks were effectively quasi-joint-stock companies with unlimited liability, which is why Scotland did not need to pass the equivalent of the 1826 Banking Copartnerhip Act.

The establishment of the Commercial Bank of Scotland (1810), the National Bank (1825) and the Aberdeen Town and Country Bank (1825) opened an era of nationally branched joint-stock banking. Although these banks had unlimited liability, they were significantly larger than the partnership banks in terms of owners and number of branches. Uncertainty regarding the legality of these concerns was eliminated by legislation passed in 1826, which confirmed their legal status as joint-stock companies with unlimited shareholder liability by permitting joint-stock banks to sue and be sued in the name of designated company officers.[15]

The liberalisation of banking incorporation law in the mid 1820s freed entrepreneurs to form joint-stock banks across all parts of the British Isles. However, the liability of the shareholders of these banks was unlimited. As shown in Table 3.1, the early to mid 1830s witnessed a rapid expansion of joint-stock banking in all three countries but primarily in England and Wales, where the number of banks increased substantially. At least two factors contributed to this promotional boom in joint-stock banking. First, the passage of the Bank of England Privileges Act (1833) removed legal doubts about the establishment of nonissuing joint-stock banks within the 65-mile radius of London.[16] Second, there was an increase in general economic activity, with widespread speculation in railways. This rapid expansion of joint-stock banking, however, came to a halt in 1837, following several high-profile failures, including the Northern and Central Bank and the Agricultural and Commercial Bank of Ireland as well as an investigation from 1836 to 1838 by Parliamentary select committees into the governance and regulation of joint-stock banks.[17]

For about two decades after the 1830s, few new joint-stock banks developed in any of the three parts of the United Kingdom. This may have been partly because the market was already saturated, but it may

---

[14] Acheson, Hickson and Turner, 'Organizational flexibility'; Brown, *Early Scottish Joint-Stock Companies*, p. 5; Campbell, 'The law and the joint-stock company', p. 143; Christie, 'Joint-stock enterprise'; Clark, *A Treatise on the Law of Partnership and Joint-Stock Companies*, p. 2.

[15] 7 Geo. IV, c.67. See Munn, *The Scottish Provincial Banking Companies*, p. 85; and Freeman, Pearson and Taylor, 'Different and better'.

[16] 3 & 4 Will. 4, c.98.

[17] Select Committees on Joint Stock Banks (P.P. 1836, IX; P.P. 1837, XIV; P.P. 1838, VII).

Table 3.1 *Joint-stock banks in Britain, 1826–1899*

	1826	1830	1839	1849	1869	1889	1899
England & Wales							
State-chartered bank	1	1	1	1	1	1	1
Unlimited-liability joint-stock banks	3	14	117	113	73	2	0
Limited-liability joint-stock banks	–	–	–	–	41	102	81
Ireland							
State-chartered bank	1	1	1	1	1	1	1
Unlimited-liability joint-stock banks	3	3	8	8	7	0	0
Limited-liability joint-stock banks	–	–	–	–	1	8	8
Scotland							
State-chartered banks	3	3	3	3	3	3	3
Unlimited-liability joint-stock banks	5	5	13	16	9	0	0
Limited-liability joint-stock banks	–	–	–	–	0	7	8

Sources: Thomas, *Rise and Growth*, pp. 656–62; *Banking Almanac and Yearbook*, 1850, 1870, 1890, 1900.
Notes: The National Bank of Ireland is counted as one bank even though it is reported as three separate banks in the *Banking Almanac and Yearbook* until the mid 1850s. The figures for Scotland from 1826 to 1849 include several provincial banks that were quasi-joint-stock companies.

have been due primarily to the enactment of two pieces of legislation in 1844 that erected barriers to entry.[18]

The Bank Charter Act (1844), together with its Scottish and Irish equivalents that had as their rationale the control of the money supply, prevented any new banks from issuing bank notes.[19] In Scotland, the 1844 and 1845 Acts resulted in the sudden termination of projects to develop new banks.[20]

The Joint Stock Bank Act of 1844 was passed to exclude English banks from the general incorporation act passed in the same year.[21] This legislation was extended in the Joint Stock Banks (Scotland and Ireland) Act of 1846 to Scotland and Ireland.[22] These two Acts specified that each new bank with more than six partners must obtain a charter or

[18] See Barrow, *The Emergence of the Irish Banking System*, p. 188; and Thomas, *Rise and Growth*, p. 400.
[19] Bank Charter Act (1844) – 7 & 8 Vict. c.32; Bank Notes (Scotland) Act (1845) – 8 & 9 Vict. c.37; and Bankers (Ireland) Act (1845) 8 & 9 Vict. c.38. Sections 10 and 12 of the Bank Charter Act applied across the United Kingdom as a whole.
[20] Checkland, *Scottish Banking*, pp. 456–8.
[21] 7 & 8 Vict. c.113. See Harris, *Industrializing English Law*, p. 282; and Hunt, *The Development of the Business Corporation*, p. 96.
[22] 9 & 10 Vict. c.75.

Table 3.2 *Joint-stock bank branches and shareholders, 1844–1899*

	1844	1859	1879	1899
England and Wales				
Branches				
Mean	5.0	5.6	12.3	56.9
Maximum	92	105	155	283
Shareholders				
Mean	234.7	249.8	611.9	1,878.5
Maximum	1,000	1,114	4,960	13,390
Scotland				
Branches				
Mean	18.2	43.4	88.2	96.4
Maximum	52	99	129	143
Shareholders				
Mean	834.3	780.6	1,474.4	2,159.0
Maximum	1,695	1,393	2,061	3,325
Ireland				
Branches				
Mean	14.7	21.6	55.0	73.4
Maximum	38	49	116	132
Shareholders				
Mean	424.6	556.8	1,949.4	2,996.8
Maximum	913	1,000	4,500	6,000

Sources: Turner, 'Wider share ownership', p. 177; *Banking Almanac and Yearbook* 1845, 1860, 1880, 1900.
Notes: Branch and shareholder numbers were not reported for some banks in some years. This was particularly the case for small English banks. The English figures exclude the Bank of England, the Irish figures exclude the Bank of Ireland and the 1859 figures for Scotland exclude the three public banks.

letters patent to conduct business. Each charter could not be for more than twenty years' duration and was subject to numerous and onerous chartering stipulations.[23]

Table 3.2 shows that in 1844 and 1859, the joint-stock banks that formed in the three parts of the United Kingdom had different characteristics. Scottish and Irish banks tended to be larger than English banks in terms of both shareholder constituency and branch networks, which extended across substantial geographical areas. The branch networks of the average English provincial bank tended to be concentrated

[23] 7 & 8 Vict. c.113, section 6.

in one town or city; only two English banks had sizeable networks in 1844: the National Provincial Bank of England with ninety-two branches, and the London and County Joint Stock Bank with thirty-six branches. These two banks had branches in London and the provinces, unlike other London banks that, despite large shareholder numbers, tended to branch within the city.

The Limited Liability Act was passed in 1855 and then repealed soon after but was subsequently reenacted in 1856 as the Joint Stock Companies Act.[24] Although banks were initially excluded from the provisions of this legislation, limited liability for banking companies was legislated for in two bills passed in the late 1850s.[25] As shown in Table 3.1, by 1869, there were forty-one joint-stock limited-liability banks in England, one in Ireland and none in Scotland. Notably, most of the English limited-liability banks in 1869 were new ventures, with only seven established banks converting from unlimited liability. By 1889, the banking structure of Ireland and Scotland was much as it had been in the 1850s (see Table 3.1). However, the banks in these two countries had grown substantially, as evidenced by the major increase in branch networks and shareholder constituencies (see Table 3.2). English banking structure also was relatively unchanged in 1889; however, as with Irish and Scottish banks, the average branch network and shareholder base had grown.

General conversion to limited-liability status did not occur until confidence in unlimited-liability joint-stock banks was undermined, following the failure of the City of Glasgow Bank in October 1878. Because the majority of this bank's shareholders were bankrupted by its failure, other bank shareholders exerted great pressure to move to limited liability.[26] Subsequently, the Companies Act was passed in 1879 to aid the conversion of the old and established joint-stock banks to limited liability.[27] After the passage of this legislation, banks quickly converted to limited liability. As shown in Table 3.1, by 1899, only two unlimited-liability joint-stock banks were left in the entire United Kingdom, and they disappeared by the beginning of the twentieth century.

In 1899, however, the banking systems of Ireland and Scotland resembled those from a half-century earlier in that the number of joint-stock banks had remained relatively constant. The banks in these two countries were comparatively large and had substantial national branch

---

[24] 18 & 19 Vict. c.133; 19 & 20 Vict. c.47.   [25] 20 & 21 Vict. c.49; 21 & 22 Vict. c.91.

[26] 'Banking Capital and Limited Liability', *The Bankers' Magazine,* September (1882), p. 717. See also Sayers, *Lloyds Bank,* p. 222.

[27] 42 & 43 Vict. c.76. See Crick and Wadsworth, *A Hundred Years of Joint Stock Banking,* p. 33.

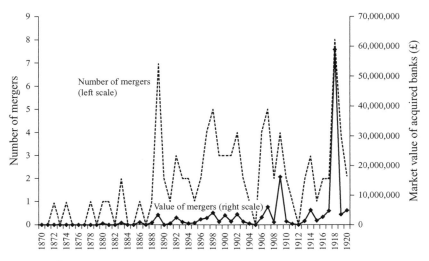

Figure 3.1 UK joint-stock bank mergers, 1870–1920
Sources: Mergers are from *Bankers' Almanac and Year Book,* 1931/32,
'Amalgamations and other changes among banks in the United Kingdom'. The market values of acquired banks are from relevant issues of
the *Investor's Monthly Manual,* 1870–1920.
Notes: The number of bank mergers in the *Bankers' Almanac and Year
Book* differs slightly from the number in Sykes, *The Amalgamation Movement,* pp. 195–6. The market values of acquired banks are the total value
of the acquired bank's shares in the month before the merger. Market-
value data were not available for twenty-seven acquired banks because
they were too small to be quoted in the *Investor's Monthly Manual.*

networks. However, as shown in Table 3.1, there was a rationalisation
in the number of English banks during the same period, primarily due
to amalgamations.[28] As a result, by 1899, an average English bank had
approximately fifty-seven branches (see Table 3.2).

As shown in Figure 3.1, which provides merger frequency and the
value of mergers between 1870 and 1920, bank mergers became increasingly common from the late 1880s onwards. In the 1890s and for most
of the first decade of the 1900s, most mergers were between London-
based banks and small English provincial banks. The banks merged primarily for reasons of diversification because there was generally little
overlap in the branch networks of the two merging entities. However,
the 1909 merger of the London and County Joint Stock Bank and the

[28] See Sykes, *The Amalgamation Movement.*

Table 3.3 *Bank mergers in 1918*

Acquiring bank	Acquired bank	Value of acquired bank (£'000s)	Name of merged entity
Martin's Bank	Bank of Liverpool	5,158	Bank of Liverpool and Martin's (name changed to Martin's Bank in 1928)
Lloyds Bank	Capital and Counties	4,725	Lloyds Bank
London City and Midland	London Joint Stock Bank	18,160	London Joint City and Midland Bank (name changed to Midland Bank in 1923)
London County and Westminster Bank	Parr's Bank	10,675	London County Westminster and Parr's Bank (name changed to Westminster Bank in 1923)
Barclays Bank	London Provincial and South Western Bank	8,917	Barclays Bank
National Provincial Bank of England	Union of London and Smiths Bank	7,490	National Provincial and Union Bank of England (name changed to National Provincial Bank in 1924)

Sources: Merger information is from *Bankers' Almanac and Year Book*, 1931/32, 'Amalgamations and other changes among banks in the United Kingdom'. The market values of acquired banks are from relevant issues of *Investor's Monthly Manual*, 1870–1920. Name-change information is from Orbell and Turton, *British Banking*.

Note: The market values of acquired banks are the total values of the acquired bank's shares in the month before the merger.

London and Westminster Bank differed markedly in dimension (see Figure 3.1) and nature: this merger concerned two large banks, both of which had a major presence in London.[29] Five of the six mega-mergers that occurred in 1918 (see Table 3.3) were similar, between already-large banks, which had a similar branch network in terms of geographical area. From these 1918 mergers, the 'Big Five' banks emerged: Barclays, Lloyds, Midland, National Provincial and Westminster.

[29] Gregory, *The Westminster Bank*, vol. 2, p. 2.

Until 1917, the amalgamation movement was mostly confined to the English banking system.[30] However, from 1917 onwards, large English banks started to acquire Scottish and Irish banks. What was to become the Midland Bank acquired the Belfast Bank in 1917 and what was to become the Westminster Bank acquired the Ulster Bank in the same year.[31] Although the share capital of these banks was acquired by the English parent bank, the Belfast Bank and Ulster Bank both maintained their separate corporate identities; they could have lost their profitable note-issuing privileges if they had been assimilated into the parent bank.

Following the takeover of the two Irish banks, Lloyds in 1918 acquired the National Bank of Scotland, Barclays absorbed the British Linen Company in 1919 and, in the same year, the Midland took over the Clydesdale Bank and later the North of Scotland Bank in 1923. All of these banks operated as independent institutions, possibly as a nod to Scottish national sentiment but also because they would have had to surrender their note-issuing privilege if they had become part of the parent bank.[32]

As shown in Table 3.4, as a result of these amalgamations, the share of deposits of the top five banks increased from 24.7 to 39.8 per cent between 1900 and 1915 and to 79.4 per cent by 1921.[33] Similarly, the share of branches of the top five banks increased from 21.9 to 78.5 per cent between 1900 and 1921. In terms of shareholders, the average constituency of the top five banks increased from 8,364 in 1900 to 53,304 in 1921.

The large mergers of 1918 resulted in the government setting up the Treasury Committee on Bank Amalgamations, chaired by Lord Colwyn. This committee stated that the main reason for opposing further amalgamations was that any more mergers would reduce competition as well as create the possibility of a money trust, wherein a few individuals ultimately control the country's banking system.[34] The recommendation of the committee was that, given the importance of banking, government control of future amalgamations was required. As a quid pro quo for no

[30] Two mergers had occurred in Scotland in 1907: the Caledonian Banking Company with the Bank of Scotland and the Town and Country Bank with the North of Scotland Bank (Checkland, *Scottish Banking*, pp. 507–10).

[31] The other northern Irish bank, the Northern Bank, remained independent despite affiliation negotiations with Barclays Bank in 1919–20 and with Lloyds Bank in 1926 (Holmes and Green, *Midland*, p. 237).

[32] Munn, *Clydesdale Bank*, pp. 155–6.

[33] This differs for two reasons from the 1920 figure of 65.5 per cent given by Capie and Rodrik-Bali in 'Concentration in British banking'. First, the 1921 figures exclude southern Irish banks because by this time, partition had occurred. Second, in the figures for 1921, deposits of independent but wholly owned subsidiaries are counted as deposits of the parent bank.

[34] *Report of the Treasury Committee on Bank Amalgamations*, p. 6.

Table 3.4 *The rise of national banks in Britain, 1900–1930*

	1900	1905	1910	1915	1921
PANEL A: Statistics on Top Five Banks					
Average shareholder constituency of top five banks	8,364.8	15,269.0	17,101.6	21,808.8	53,304.8
Average branch network of top five banks	245.4	346.6	467.0	669.0	1,311.0
Top five banks' share of UK bank shareholders (%)	21.8	26.6	35.6	39.4	81.9
Branches of top five banks/total branches in United Kingdom (%)	21.9	19.8	32.5	39.9	78.5
Top five banks' share of UK deposits (%)	24.7	28.7	36.7	39.8	79.4
PANEL B: Top Five Banks by Deposits (Rank)					
Barclays Bank	5	5	5	5	2
Lloyds Bank	3	1	1	2	3
London, City and Midland Bank	4	3	3	1	
London Joint Stock, City and Midland Bank					1
London and County Joint Stock Bank	2	4			
London County and Westminster Bank			2	3	
London County Westminster and Parr's Bank					4
National Provincial Bank of England	1	2	4	4	
National Provincial and Union Bank of England					5

Sources: Banking Almanac and Yearbook 1900, 1905, 1910, 1915, 1921; Goodhart, *The Business of Banking*, pp. 417–566.

Notes: The top five banks in Panel A are defined as those with the largest deposit base. The London County and Westminster Bank was formed by the merger of the London and County Joint Stock Bank and the London and Westminster Bank in 1909. The London Joint Stock, City and Midland Bank was formed by the merger of the London, City and Midland Bank and the London Joint Stock Bank in 1918. The National Provincial and Union Bank of England was formed by the merger of the National Provincial Bank of England and the Union of London and Smiths Bank in 1918. The London County Westminster and Parr's Bank was formed by the amalgamation of Parr's Bank with the London County and Westminster Bank in 1918. The figures for 1921 exclude southern Irish banks but include those banks that the Big Five wholly owned as independent entities: Barclays Bank (Union Bank of Manchester and British Linen Company); Lloyds Bank (National Bank of Scotland); London Joint, City and Midland (Belfast Bank and Clydesdale Bank); London County and Westminster (Ulster Bank); and National Provincial and Union Bank of England (Coutts Bank).

legal barriers to mergers, the Big Five banks accepted informal control of future mergers by the Treasury and the Bank of England.[35] The ultimate effect of the Colwyn committee was that the Big Five banks could not merge *inter se* and that they required express permission from the Treasury and the Bank to merge with smaller banks.[36]

As shown in Table 3.5, the Big Five banks dominated British banking in 1931, with the other nine independent banks listed in the table being geographically peripheral. The banking structure outlined in Table 3.5 remained mostly unchanged until the 1950s, other than the merger of the Manchester and County Bank (which had been restyled as the County Bank in 1934) with the District Bank in 1935 and the full assimilation by Barclays of the Union Bank of Manchester. In the 1950s, the structure of Scottish banking was rationalised by a series of amalgamations, which reduced the number of Scottish banks from eight to five.[37]

The opposition of the Treasury and the Bank of England towards mergers by any of the Big Five with other banks lasted until 1962, when the National Provincial Bank, the smallest of the Big Five, was given permission to merge with the District Bank. Then, in 1965, the Midland acquired the Northern Bank, which was the one remaining independent Northern Irish bank.[38] In 1967, the National Board on Prices and Incomes reported that the authorities would not stand in the way of further amalgamations if they resulted in rationalising wasteful branch networks.[39] Subsequently, the most significant change to the banking landscape in a half-century occurred when the National Provincial Bank and Westminster Bank – the two smallest of the Big Five banks – announced in January 1968 that they had been given official approval to merge and form the National Westminster Bank. Some time after this

---

[35] Ackrill and Hannah, *Barclays*, p. 70.

[36] For example, Barclays Bank was given permission to merge with the Union Bank of Manchester and the British Linen Bank in 1919 (Ackrill and Hannah, *Barclays*, p. 71) and Midland was given permission to merge with the North of Scotland Bank in 1923 (Holmes and Green, *Midland*, pp. 162–3). The only other major acquisition in this era was the Bank of England–orchestrated merger of the Manchester-based Williams Deacon's Bank with the Royal Bank of Scotland in 1930 (Anon., *Williams Deacon's*, pp. 158–9).

[37] Checkland, *Scottish Banking*, pp. 642–4. In 1950, the Midland Bank merged its two Scottish affiliates, the Clydesdale Bank and the North of Scotland Bank, to form the Clydesdale and North of Scotland Bank (this name was shortened to Clydesdale Bank in 1963). The Bank of Scotland merged with the Union Bank of Scotland in 1955. In 1959, the Commercial Bank of Scotland merged with the National Bank of Scotland, which was wholly owned by Lloyds Bank. The merged entity changed its name to the National Commercial Bank. Lloyds Bank held a 36.6 percent stake in the bank.

[38] In 1970, the Northern Bank was merged with the Belfast Bank, which was also owned by the Midland Bank (Simpson, *The Belfast Bank*, pp. 342–8).

[39] Winton, *Lloyds Bank*, p. 195.

Table 3.5 *British banking in 1931*

Bank	Parent company	Share of deposits (%)	Branches	Shareholders
Midland Bank		17.46	2,129	75,493
Lloyds Bank		16.07	1,950	65,000
Barclays Bank		15.77	2,125	57,094
National Provincial Bank		13.46	1,380	40,000
Westminster Bank		13.43	1,085	86,000
Martin's Bank		3.45	569	16,769
Royal Bank of Scotland		2.32	247	4,992
District Bank		2.32	397	9,677
Commercial Bank of Scotland		1.53	351	7,600
Bank of Scotland		1.50	247	4,707
National Bank of Scotland	Lloyds Bank	1.49	181	–
Williams Deacon's Bank	Royal Bank of Scotland	1.47	202	–
Clydesdale Bank	Midland Bank	1.39	201	–
Union Bank of Scotland		1.34	210	4,670
British Linen Bank	Barclays Bank	1.27	206	–
North of Scotland Bank	Midland Bank	1.00	159	–
Ulster Bank	Westminster Bank	0.99	115	–
Union Bank of Manchester	Barclays Bank	0.82	170	–
Coutts Bank	National Provincial Bank	0.81	1	–
Manchester and County		0.78	189	3,368
Northern Bank		0.65	188	4,255
Belfast Bank	Midland Bank	0.63	86	–
Isle of Man Bank		0.11	9	409

Source: Bankers' Almanac and Year Book, 1931/32.

merger, both Barclays and Lloyds were given permission to merge with Martin's Bank, which accepted the Barclays' higher offer.

Thus, the events of 1968 resulted in a more concentrated banking system, with four instead of six banks dominating affairs: Barclays, Lloyds, Midland and National Westminster. A similar move towards greater concentration also took place in Scotland.[40] By 1970, Scotland had three banks – the Bank of Scotland, the Clydesdale and the Royal Bank of Scotland – and the big London clearing banks held minority stakes in two of them and fully owned the third. As a result of all of this consolidation, the Big Four banks plus their subsidiaries had 72.1 per cent of the sterling-deposit market for nonbank UK residents in 1972.[41]

From the 1960s onwards, UK banks faced a host of new competitive pressures. On the business lending and deposit side, they faced stiff competition from overseas banks that were establishing London branches.[42] They also faced competition on the deposit side of their business from the rapidly expanding building-society sector and the foray of the Trustee Savings Bank (TSB) into commercial banking after its 1986 flotation on the stock market.[43]

Building societies were mutual savings institutions that emerged in the late eighteenth century to help their members build or buy their own homes. The building-society movement grew rapidly in the interwar and post-1945 eras, almost simultaneously with the rise of homeownership. Such was the growth of the movement that by the 1960s, the savings deposits of building societies were slightly more than half the size of total bank deposits.[44] Following continued growth, the sector was deregulated in the 1986 Building Societies Act, which allowed building societies to convert from their mutual status to public companies.[45] The Act also permitted building societies to engage in business lending and to raise funds from the wholesale money markets. Only one major building society, the Nationwide, did not demutualise.[46]

In response to these growing competitive pressures, the Big Four clearing banks developed different strategies. Three of the Big Four focused on building global banks, whereas Lloyds focused mainly on the UK

---

[40] In 1969, the Royal Bank of Scotland merged with the National Commercial Bank. In the same year, the British Linen Bank (wholly owned by Barclays Bank) merged with the Bank of Scotland, and Barclays Bank acquired a 35 per cent stake in the merged entity.

[41] House of Commons, *Committee to Review the Functioning of Financial Institutions, Evidence on the Financing of Industry and Trade*, p. 123.

[42] In 1965, there were 104 overseas banks in the United Kingdom, with deposits of £4,553 million versus the £10,622 deposits of domestic banks. See Alhadeff, *Competition and Controls in Banking*, p. 219.

[43] The growth of building societies from 1945 to 1980 was mainly due to the growth of homeownership and the fact that building societies totally dominated this market (Reid, *Abbey National Conversion*, p. 12).

[44] Cleary, *The Building Society Movement*, p. 275.   [45] 1986 Eliz. II, c.53.

[46] In 1989, the Abbey National was the first to demutualise, followed by the Cheltenham and Gloucester in 1994 and the Alliance and Leicester, the Halifax, the Northern Rock, and the Woolwich in 1997. The Bradford and Bingley, in 2000, was the last of the big societies to demutualise.

retail market. This strategy led to its merger with TSB in 1995 to form Lloyds-TSB. In the case of the Midland, its forays into overseas markets – most notably, its acquisition of Crocker Bank of California in 1980 – and its inability to cope with competition in the domestic market meant that it posted large losses from 1980 onwards.[47] Such was the weakness of the Midland that its acquisition by HSBC in 1992 was inevitable. In retreating from aspects of global wholesale banking, Barclays refocused on the domestic market by acquiring the Woolwich, a recently demutualised building society, in 2000. However, the National Westminster's retreat from global banking had left it vulnerable to a takeover, with potential acquirers coming from the most unlikely of places. Both the Bank of Scotland and the Royal Bank of Scotland were keen to acquire the National Westminster, with the latter making the successful bid in 2000. After its failure to acquire the National Westminster, the Bank of Scotland merged in 2001 with the Halifax – one of the largest demutualised building societies – to form HBOS.

Thus, on the eve of the Great Crash of 2007–8, the British commercial-banking system was dominated by nine banks, four of which were former building societies. As shown in Table 3.6 – which includes the nine major clearing banks as well as the only large national building society – the top five banks dominated UK banking, followed by the Nationwide and four former building societies.

How stable was the British banking system?

Thus far, this chapter outlines the evolution of the British banking system from 1800 to the eve of the Great Crash. The system evolved from a plethora of small regional partnership banks to one in which a small number of global financial institutions dominated the system. The remainder of this chapter assesses the stability of this system during the past two centuries.

How do we assess whether a banking crisis has taken place? Because attempts to answer this quantitatively in the long run are notoriously difficult, scholars typically use a narrative approach and various criteria to determine whether a banking crisis has occurred. For example, Grossman defines it as including one of three elements: (1) a high proportion of banks failed; (2) the failure of an especially large bank; or (3) failures of the type described in (1) and (2) were prevented by direct government assistance to struggling banks, ranging from bank holidays to bailouts.[48] Reinhart and Rogoff proffer a broader definition; that is, a banking crisis

---

[47] Rogers, *The Big Four British Banks*, p. 177.   [48] Grossman, *Unsettled Account*, pp. 58–9.

Table 3.6 *Distribution of deposits, assets and employees of the major domestic deposit-taking institutions, 2006*

	UK-group employees	% Share of deposits among major deposit takers	% Share of assets among major deposit takers
Royal Bank of Scotland	135,000	26.65	23.10
Barclays Bank	62,400	17.81	26.43
HSBC	79,127	15.77	11.69
HBOS	74,252	14.69	15.67
Lloyds-TSB	74,079	9.76	9.16
Nationwide	15,622	5.61	3.02
Abbey National (owned by Santander)	19,277	4.61	5.09
Northern Rock	5,936	1.86	2.68
Alliance and Leicester	8,315	1.70	1.79
Bradford and Bingley	3,174	1.54	1.20

Sources: Annual reports for 2006; British Bankers' Association, *Annual Abstract of Banking Statistics*, 2007.
Notes: Major deposit takers consist of the Major British Banking Groups as defined by the British Bankers' Association and the Nationwide, which is the only remaining large building society with a national network. The deposits and assets are based on entire banking groups, not only their UK group operations.

is marked by two types of events: (1) bank runs that lead to closure, merging or a public-sector takeover of one or more financial institutions; and (2) the closure, merging, takeover or government assistance of an important financial institution or group of institutions.[49]

The narrative approach is eschewed in this study for several reasons. First, bank failures alone do not necessarily mean that the banking system is unstable. This point is illustrated by the failures in Ireland of the Tipperary Bank (in 1856) and Munster Bank (in 1885), in which there was no discussion of a banking crisis by contemporaries or subsequent scholars.[50] In fact, sporadic bank failures actually may promote overall stability of the banking system because they act as a device that encourages banks to be prudent in the first place.[51] For example, in the case of the English banking system, scholars suggest that banks in the nineteenth century learned to become more prudent as a result of observing

[49] Reinhart and Rogoff, *This Time Is Different*, p. 10.
[50] Ó Gráda, 'Moral hazard and quasi-central banking' and 'The last major Irish bank failure'.
[51] Calomiris and Kahn, 'The role of demandable debt'.

occasional bank collapses.[52] In addition, bank failures may remove the riskiest institutions, making the overall banking system more robust.

Second, bank failures may indicate that a shock has occurred in the money markets and therefore may be a useful way to identify pressure in them, but the failures alone do not necessarily mean that the banking system is unstable. Third, including investment and merchant banks in the definition of banking crises is probably not helpful, least of all in an historical context, because they are neither directly linked to the money supply (via deposits) nor directly involved in credit intermediation.

Schwartz differentiated between real and pseudo-financial crises.[53] She defined a real financial or banking crisis as a scramble for high-powered money arising from a fear that the means of payment will not be available at any price. A pseudo-financial crisis in her lexicon was a situation wherein the authorities intervene under the guise of preventing a financial crisis from occurring but where there would not have been a crisis even if the authorities had failed to intervene. Schwartz's definition was influenced by her monetarist leanings and was overly focused on the monetary functions of banks. However, credit provision is an equally important function of banks. Notably, under Schwartz's strict definition, the events of 2007–8 cannot be considered a banking crisis because there was no scramble for high-powered money.

We do not want to regard banking crises in a binary manner; rather, we want to determine whether there has been a major or systemic crisis by assessing the extent or scale of banking instability. The main methods used to measure banking stability are movements in both bank-share prices and in bank-share prices relative to the overall stock market. Using bank-stock prices enables us to determine whether the failure of banks affected other institutions. It also helps us to determine the depth of a crisis when direct government intervention prevents a bank or banks from failing. The scale of banking instability is measured first by using the failure rate of commercial banks. Although this is subject to several of the criticisms discussed previously, it serves as an approximate measure of stability, particularly in the early period in which banks were partnerships and share prices therefore are not available.

In an attempt to measure the failure rate of UK banks, we focus solely on commercial banks that raise money from retail depositors and lend to companies and individuals. As a result, merchant and investment banks are excluded from this measure. In addition, this measure ignores foreign and colonial banks that are registered as companies in London because,

[52] Collins, *Money and Banking in the UK*, pp. 84–5; Baker and Collins, 'Financial crises'.
[53] Schwartz, 'Real and pseudo-financial crises'.

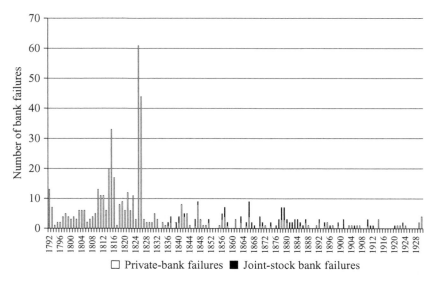

Figure 3.2 UK bank failures, 1792–1930
Sources: Bank failures from 1792 to 1826 are from Acheson, Hickson and Turner, 'Organizational flexibility', p. 521. Bank failures from 1826 to 1930 are based on information from the *Bankers' Almanac and Year Book*, 1931/32, pp. 279–330.
Notes: The *Bankers' Almanac and Year Book* provides details on banks that failed, suspended payment, or went into liquidation. Because this source does not report whether liquidations were voluntary or involuntary, it is assumed that all liquidations were due to failure unless Orbell and Turton in *British Banking* imply that a particular liquidation was voluntary. It also is assumed that all banks that suspended payment failed. The figures before 1826 exclude Ireland because there is little offered in the way of reliable data.

historically (and even in the present), these banks always conducted most of their business outside of the United Kingdom. For example, many of the Australian banks that collapsed in 1893 were registered as companies in the United Kingdom, but they were Australian institutions that simply raised capital on the London stock market.[54]

Figure 3.2 shows the annual number of bank failures in the United Kingdom from 1792 to 1930. After 1930, privately orchestrated or state bailouts mean that banks no longer fail per se (see Chapter 6). As shown in Figure 3.2, many bank failures occurred before 1826 but relatively few

[54] Hickson and Turner, 'Free banking gone awry'.

afterwards. However, the arrival of joint-stock banking resulted in much larger banks, meaning that one joint-stock bank collapse had a greater effect than the failure of ten or more private and partnership banks. Of note from the post-1826 data is that bank failures peak in some years that were traditionally identified as crises in the extant literature (e.g., 1847, 1866, 1878 and 1914) but not in others (e.g., 1836–7 and 1890).

To gain perspective on the scale of bank collapses, a failure rate was calculated using the following two methods for the years identified by Reinhart and Rogoff as crisis years: (1) the number of commercial bank failures divided by the number of commercial banks and (2) the capital of failed commercial banks divided by the total capital of commercial banks. Because partnership and private banks were small relative to joint-stock banks, we excluded private-bank failures from the failure rate after 1826. This makes little difference because after 1826, few of the total number of private banks failed (see Figure 3.2).[55] For example, the failure rates of private banks in the years identified as crises by Reinhart and Rogoff are as follows: 2.2 per cent in 1847, 1.6 per cent in 1857–8, 1.4 per cent in 1866–7, and 2.3 per cent in 1878–9.[56]

As shown in Table 3.7, other than in 1825–6, the bank failure rate never rose above 10 per cent during the pre-1914 crises that Reinhart and Rogoff identify. Indeed, after 1825–6, the failure rate never rose above 5 per cent, and the capital-weighted failure rate exceeded 5 per cent only in 1857 – principally as a result of the failure of the Western Bank of Scotland.

Reinhart and Rogoff identify four banking crises in the United Kingdom in the 1914–2006 period: 1974, 1984, 1991 and 1995. Although no UK commercial banks failed in any of these episodes, other types of institution collapsed. In 1974, several secondary banks failed. These institutions had raised funds in the wholesale money markets and used them to make property and consumer-finance loans. In fact, the UK commercial banks, coordinated by the Bank of England, provided £1,300 million of liquidity support and loans to these secondary banks.[57] In 1984, Johnson Matthey Bankers, the banking subsidiary of Johnson Matthey plc, experienced difficulties and was taken over by the Bank of England after a failed attempt to coordinate a private-sector rescue; however, this bank was not

---

[55] In 1850, there were 266 private country banks alone; see Dawes and Ward-Perkins, *Country Bankers of England and Wales*, pp. 11–12.

[56] Bank failures from 1826 to 1930 are based on information from the *Bankers' Almanac and Year Book*, 1931/32, pp. 279–330. The numbers of private banks in existence before each crisis were obtained from the list of private banks in England and Wales in the *Banking Almanac*, 1847, 1857, 1866 and 1878.

[57] Reid, *The Secondary Banking Crisis*, p. 192.

Table 3.7 *Bank failure rates in Britain, 1800–1914*

	Failure rate (%)	Capital-weighted failure rate (%)
1810	1.6	–
1815–17	7.0	–
1825–6	18.4	–
1836–7	3.7	–
1847	0.7	*c.*1.0
1857–8	3.2	9.4
1866–7	4.2	4.1
1878–9	4.2	3.9
1890	0.0	0.0
1914	0.0	0.0

Sources: Bank-failure rates for 1800–1826 are from Acheson et al., 'Organizational flexibility', p. 521. Bank failures from 1826 to 1930 are based on information from the *Bankers' Almanac and Year Book*, 1931/32, pp. 279–330. The number of UK banks from 1836 onwards is from Thomas, *Rise and Growth*, pp. 656–62, and various issues of the *Banking Almanac*. The paid-up capital to calculate the capital-weighted failure rate was obtained from various issues of the *Banking Almanac*.

Notes: The pre-1826 figures exclude Ireland and the three chartered Scottish banks. The later years include all Scottish and Irish banks but exclude all private banks and discount companies. The capital-weighted failure rate simply divides the paid-up capital of failed banks by the paid-up capital of the entire UK banking system.

a commercial bank. The Bank of Credit and Commerce International (BCCI), a large international bank with offices in London, collapsed in 1991; however, this institution also was not a commercial bank. In 1995, Barings failed, following losses accumulated by one of its traders, Nick Leeson; however, this bank was an investment rather than a commercial bank.

Ultimately, the Great Crash of 2007–8 should be set against this background of a long period – that is, since 1878 – without any major commercial-bank failures. In early 2008, Northern Rock, one of the ten deposit takers that dominated British commercial banking (see Table 3.6), was nationalised by the UK government. Then, in September 2008, the troubled Alliance and Leicester Bank was taken over by Santander, the large Spanish bank that already owned Abbey National. The Bradford and Bingley was nationalised and Lloyds-TSB took over HBOS. Within a matter of weeks, Lloyds-TSB and the Royal Bank of Scotland received huge injections of capital from the British government, making it the largest owner of these banks. In total, six of the nine major UK banks were effectively insolvent in 2008 and, in terms of total assets, 51.8 per cent of the British banking system required a government bailout (see Table 3.6); this does not include the immense central bank and regulatory support required by the remainder of the system.[58]

The second and superior method of assessing the scale of banking instability is to use the price of bank stocks and the price of bank stocks relative to the market.[59] Because joint-stock banking commenced in the mid 1820s and only began to succeed in the early to mid 1830s, particularly in London, there are few joint-stock bank-share prices before 1830. Monthly share prices for all Scottish and Irish banks were obtained from 1830 onwards and for all of the major London banks, as well as London and provincial banks, from 1834 onwards. Because most English provincial banks were small concerns, their share prices were not reported systematically and comprehensively until the 1860s. However, monthly share prices were obtained for most English provincial banks from 1869 onwards.

Monthly share-price data were obtained for the period 1965–2010 from *Thomson Reuters Datastream,* supplemented by data from Bureau van Dijk's *OSIRIS* database. Data for the period 1830–1965 were hand-collected from several sources. First, share-price data for English banks for the period 1834–68 were obtained from the *Course of the Exchange*. Second, Scottish bank-share prices for the period 1830–34 were obtained from the *Course of the Exchange*; for the period 1835–67, they were acquired from *The Scotsman* newspaper. Third, Irish bank-share prices for the period 1830–67 were collected from the *Course of the Exchange*, the *Belfast Newsletter* and the *Northern Whig*. Fourth, share-price data for all UK banks for the period 1869–1929 were acquired from the *Investor's Monthly Manual*. Fifth, monthly share prices for the period 1930–64 were hand-collected from *The Times*, with share prices for the Bank of Scotland for the period 1930–38 and Royal Bank of Scotland for 1930 from *The Scotsman* because they were not reported in *The Times* during those periods.

As shown in Table 3.8, the number of banks in the returns series closely follows the evolution of the UK banking system as described in the previous section. The dramatic increase in the number of banks in 1870 is due to the addition of English provincial banks to the returns series rather than any fundamental change to the banking system. For the sake of robustness, the returns series is calculated without these banks and also

---

[58] This is in terms of 2006 assets, which were obtained from *Thomson ONE Banker Analytics.*
[59] Reinhart and Rogoff, *This Time Is Different*, p. 8.

Table 3.8 *Number of banks in returns series, 1830–2007*

Year	Number of banks in returns series
1830	8
1840	20
1860	23
1870	108
1890	97
1910	51
1920	25
1930	9
1950	9
1970	6
1990	7
2007	8

for only the London banks and the London and provincial banks. Because these adjustments have little effect on the returns series, the results for the entire sample of banks are reported. Due to the amalgamation process, the number of banks in the returns series declines during the first three decades of the twentieth century so that by 1930, only nine banks remain.

After the data were adjusted for stock splits and capitalisation changes, log returns were used to construct the returns series; the average return was unweighted, which means that each bank has an equal weight in the returns series. Because a returns series consisting of large London-based banks produces a similar series to that including all banks, the absence of value weighting does not affect the substantive findings (Figures 3.3 and 3.4 and Table 3.9). Delisting returns in the event of bank failure are not set to zero because bank failures are rare events and stock prices typically fall before a bank fails. In addition, including delisting returns makes little difference to the average return due to the sheer number of banks in existence during the period when banks were allowed to fail. More fundamentally, we are more interested in examining how the banking system responds as a whole to bank failures rather than in precise measures of portfolio returns for bank stocks.

Three features are readily apparent from Figure 3.3, which plots monthly stock returns for UK banks from 1830 to 2010. First, there is significantly more volatility in bank-stock returns after the 1950s; however, this is also true of the overall stock market. Second, the severity of the 2007–8 crisis, placed in context of the previous 180 years, is readily

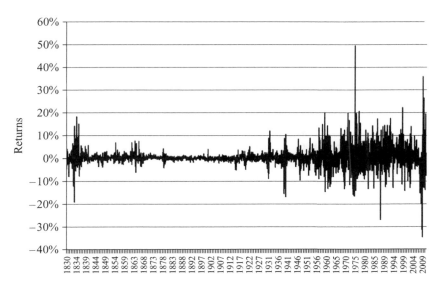

Figure 3.3 Monthly returns on UK bank stocks, 1830–2010
Source: See text.
Notes: The closure of the London Stock Exchange for five months at the end of 1914 explains why there were no returns for these months.

apparent: this was a crisis unlike any other that had previously occurred. Third, as Figure 3.3 highlights, there are no substantial negative returns during the so-called crises that occurred between 1830 and 1914.

Figure 3.4 examines annual returns on bank stocks and compares them to a value-weighted capital appreciation for the overall stock market. This value-weighted series of annual returns was obtained by splicing together the following series: the Acheson et al. index for the period 1830–70, the Grossman index for the period 1871–1913, the *Banker's Magazine* index for the period 1914–33, the Actuaries General Index for the period 1933–62, and the Financial Times Stock Exchange (FTSE) All-Share Index for the period 1962–2010.[60]

Figure 3.4 shows that none of the pre-1914 episodes of instability are associated with substantial negative annual returns on bank stocks. Indeed, there were no negative annual returns in 1836–7 or in 1890. The

[60] Acheson, Hickson, Turner and Ye, 'Rule Britannia!'; Grossman, 'New indices'. The *Banker's Magazine* index and Actuaries General Index were supplied by the *Global Financial Database* in 2000. The FTSE All-Share Index was obtained from *Thomson Reuters Datastream.*

Table 3.9 *Banking instability in Britain, 1830–2010*

Crisis years	Worst month returns (%)	Returns on bank stocks in crisis period (%)	Returns on bank stocks from year before to year after crisis (%)	Returns on market from year before to year after crisis (%)	Excess of bank returns over market returns from year before to year after crisis (%)
1836–7	September 1836 (−4.59)	11.76	30.58	32.46	−1.88
1847	October 1847 (−3.18)	−12.15	−15.50	−17.90	2.39
1857–8	June 1858 (−2.58)	−2.19	4.53	14.59	−10.05
1866–7	August 1867 (−3.43)	−16.18	−16.30	−1.28	−15.02
1878–9	November 1878 (−4.00)	−13.39	−10.22	20.25	−30.46
1890	February 1890 (−0.76)	1.97	2.69	−1.88	4.58
1914	July 1914 (−2.22)	0.67	−17.06	−14.04	−3.02
1931	November 1931 (−8.82)	−24.88	0.28	−45.42	45.70
1974	September 1974 (−16.32)	−62.85	−5.40	−8.05	2.65
1984	June 1984 (−13.04)	26.17	53.61	44.54	9.07
1991	December 1991 (−6.18)	22.30	63.65	6.47	57.17
1995	February 1995 (−3.59)	40.33	55.30	45.25	10.05
2007–8	October 2008 (−35.90)	−80.32	−78.04	−18.00	−61.60

Sources: See text.
Notes: The 'crises' in this table are those identified by Reinhart and Rogoff, *This Time is Different*. The year 1931 also is included given that it was the height of the Great Depression.

episodes of 1847, 1857–8, 1866–7, 1878–9 and 1914 all resulted in moderate to small negative annual returns. Other than in 1847, bank stocks fell more than the overall market during these episodes of instability.

In the post-1914 era, there are four years in which bank stocks fell by more than 20 per cent: 1931, 1974, 2002 and 2007–8. In 1931, the overall market fell by more than bank stocks and, in 2002, the decline in bank stocks was almost matched by the market. This suggests that

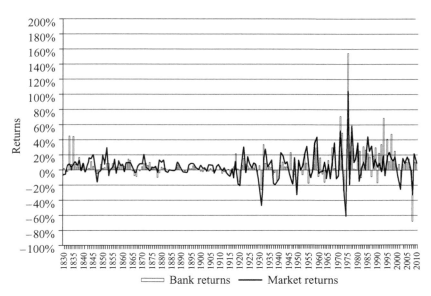

Figure 3.4 Annual returns on UK banks and the stock market, 1830–2010

Source: See text.

Notes: Because the London Stock Exchange was closed for five months at the end of 1914, the price from 30 July 1914 is used as the end-of-year price for 1914.

in both years, the decline in bank stocks reflects problems in the wider economy. Notably, in the case of 1931, the United Kingdom – unlike many other economies at the time – did not suffer a banking crisis.[61] Why UK banking remained stable at this time is addressed at several points throughout the remainder of this book.

In 1974, the 62 per cent fall in bank stocks was almost equalled by the overall market, which fell by 54 per cent. In addition, as shown in Figure 3.4, there is in 1975 an immense recovery in the market for bank and other stocks, suggesting that the decline in bank stocks in 1974 was due more to wider economic problems than to a particular problem with banks.

The 2007–8 crisis clearly stands out as the worst crisis in the 180 years covered in Figure 3.4. Bank stocks fell by nearly 80 per cent, whereas the overall market fell by only 30 per cent. Because the Royal Bank of Scotland, HSBC and Barclays Bank constituted 10.96 per cent of the

---

[61] See Billings and Capie, 'Financial crisis'.

FTSE All-Share Index in August 2007, the market for nonbank stocks fell considerably less than 30 per cent.[62]

The third column in Table 3.9 lists the returns on bank stocks during the entire crisis period, and the fourth column lists them from one year before to one year after the crisis period. This analysis allows us to determine whether the crisis resulted in a major shock to bank-share prices that subsequently recovered. The last column lists the extent to which returns on bank stocks fell below those of the overall market from one year before to one year after the crisis. As clearly shown in Table 3.9, the 2007–8 crisis is by far the greatest crisis, regardless of which measure we consider: that is, returns during the crisis period, returns from one year before to one year after the crisis, or returns relative to the market.

The evidence in Table 3.9 also suggests that returns on bank stocks from one year before to one year after the 1890, 1931, 1984, 1991 and 1995 episodes were positive, as were returns relative to the market, which suggests that banking crises did not occur in these years. The small difference in returns on bank stocks relative to the market in 1914 also implies that this episode should not be considered a banking crisis.

Table 3.9 also reveals some notable things about the classic nineteenth-century episodes of instability. First, bank stocks did not fall during the 1836–7 episode, although the excess of the returns on bank stocks over the market returns is slightly negative. Second, the returns on bank stocks during the 1847 episode and from one year before to one year after the crisis are negative and substantial, but the relative returns for the 1847 episode are positive. Third, in 1857–8, 1866 and 1878, the relative returns and returns on bank stocks during the crisis episodes are all negative. Fourth, the returns data for 1878–9 reveal a 13.39 per cent fall in bank stocks. This decline occurred between October and December of 1878, and the overall market fell by a similar level during that period. However, the overall market rebounded in 1879, whereas the market for bank stocks did not, which explains the substantial negative excess returns of bank stock compared to the market.

The 1974 crisis is interesting in that bank stocks plummeted, but so did other stocks. The recovery of bank stocks in 1975 was such that the return on bank stocks from one year before to one year after the crisis was positive. In addition, as shown in Table 3.9, the returns relative to the market for this episode are positive.

[62] This figure, which refers to 31 August 2007, is from a FTSE 100 Index Factsheet. Available at http://www.ftse.com/Indices/UK_Indices/Downloads/FTSE100_Index_Factsheet.pdf, accessed 23 May 2012.

Taking together the failure-rate data and the returns data, it is evident that there were two major systemic crises during the past two hundred years: one occurring in 1825–6 and the other in 2007–8. Although similar metrics to compare these two episodes are not available, it appears that the 2007–8 collapse is by far the most severe banking crisis that the United Kingdom ever experienced. What about the other episodes that previous scholars identified and labelled as crises? The failure-rate and stock-return data suggest that the episodes in 1836–7, 1847, 1857–8, 1866–7, 1878–9 and 1974 can be considered minor crises of varying degrees of severity, with the crisis of 1836–7 probably the least severe and a borderline case as to whether it is even a minor crisis.

Based on the evidence from bank stocks, it is difficult to categorise the events of 1890, 1914, 1984, 1991 and 1995 as banking crises.[63] Nevertheless, it could be that government intervention or central-bank assistance prevented crises from occurring during these episodes. For example, the private-sector bailout of Barings in 1890, which was coordinated by the Bank of England, and the Bank's takeover of JMB in 1984 may have prevented crises from occurring on both occasions. However, in both cases, the returns on bank stocks in the month before the Bank's intervention suggest that these were not serious threats to the banking system – that is, bank stocks fell by only 0.05 per cent in November 1890 and rose by 1.78 per cent in September 1984.

In the summer of 1914, the breakdown of European capital markets and a foreign-exchange crisis resulted in UK banks facing severe liquidity pressures in the money markets, which were aggravated by aggressive liquidity hoarding by commercial banks. The Bank of England at first was unable to address this crisis due to the need to maintain gold convertibility. However, the liquidity crisis was averted by an extension of the usual Bank Holiday (3 August) by four days and an issue of Treasury notes rather the usual policy of suspending gold convertibility.[64] This episode was a currency rather than a banking crisis.

Banking stability and the real economy

This section analyses the effects of these major banking (1825–6 and 2007–8) and minor crises (1836–7, 1847, 1857–8, 1866–7, 1878–9 and 1974) on the wider economy to determine an additional measure of their severity. Indeed, in one sense, this may be the best way to assess whether a banking crisis has occurred. We first review GDP estimates to assess

[63] Notably, Sayers, *Lloyds Bank*, p. 206, refers to 1890 as a 'shudder rather than a crash'.
[64] Sayers, *The Bank of England*, vol. 1, pp. 74–6.

Table 3.10 *Real GDP before, during and after major and minor banking crises, 1830–2010*

Crises	Average annual change in decade before crisis (%)	Change in year before crisis (%)	Average annual change during crisis (%)	Change in year after crisis (%)
1825–6	1.9	6.4	−4.2	8.4
1836–7	2.4	5.3	0.5	5.6
1847	2.3	7.0	−2.5	6.3
1857–8	1.8	4.7	0.2	4.2
1866–7	2.3	4.5	−0.3	3.3
1878–9	2.6	0.5	−0.7	7.9
1974	3.4	7.6	−1.0	−0.5
2007–8	3.0	2.9	1.3	−4.9

Sources: Pre-1830 data are from Broadberry and van Leeuwen, 'British economic growth'. Data for 1830–70 are from Mitchell, *British Historical Statistics*, pp. 836–7. Data for 1870–1913 are from Solomou and Weale, 'Balanced estimates of UK GDP'. Data for 1948 onwards are from *Office for National Statistics* and are available at http://www.ons.gov.uk/ons/datasets-and-tables/data-selector.html?cdid=YBHH&dataset=md&table-id=1.1.

the effects, if any, of the major and minor banking crises, but we also examine bankruptcy rates and anecdotal evidence about the effect of the crises on the wider economy.

The effect of the 1825–6 crisis on merchants and businesses was twofold, in that the money supply fell and merchants found it difficult to raise funds because many bills were refused for discount and surviving banks contracted their lending.[65] Bankruptcies increased significantly in December 1825; in 1826, they were at least double the average annual bankruptcy rate for the period 1822–32.[66] As shown in Table 3.10, the economy grew substantially in 1824; however, during the crisis, there was a sharp decline in GDP. Indeed, of all of the episodes listed in Table 3.10, the 1825–6 crisis was associated with the steepest decline in GDP during the actual crisis episode.

The minor banking crisis of 1836–7 had relatively little effect on the real economy. Bankruptcies in 1836 and 1837 did not differ much from the average annual bankruptcy rate for the period 1832–42.[67] As shown in Table 3.10, there was high economic growth in 1835; although

[65] *The Times*, December 8, 1825, p. 2; Pressnell, *Country Banking*, p. 491.
[66] Gayer, Rostow and Schwartz, *The Growth and Fluctuation*, vol. 1, p. 205; Neal, 'The financial crisis of 1825', 69.
[67] Gayer, Rostow and Schwartz, *The Growth and Fluctuation*, vol. 1, pp. 265 and 296.

this fell slightly in 1836–7, the average growth rate in the crisis years was still positive. Notably, there was a substantial rise in GDP in 1838.

The minor banking crisis of 1847 also probably had little effect on the real economy. Mercantile bankruptcies began to increase in the summer of 1847 and, in the first quarter of 1848, the number of bankruptcies was higher than in any previous quarter since recordkeeping began. The contraction of GDP in 1847 is unsurprising, given the poor harvests in 1846, the effects of the Irish potato famine and the failure of numerous corn and wheat merchants. Nevertheless, economic growth rebounded substantially in 1848, as shown in Table 3.10.

Following the 1857–8 crisis, the number of bankruptcies – which had averaged 1,445 per annum in the previous five years – was 2,014 in 1857 and 2,116 in 1858.[68] As shown in Table 3.10, GDP growth slowed during the 1857–8 crisis; however, unlike all other nineteenth-century crises, GDP did not contract either during the crisis or in the year after it. Consequently, although the 1857–8 crisis was one of the greatest in terms of the size-adjusted bank-failure rate, it appears to have had little effect on the overall UK economy. According to Laurence Robertson, the Royal Bank of Scotland's chief cashier, the depressed state of trade in the months following the Western Bank failure was due to stagnation that necessarily followed a period of overtrading. It was not attributable to the collapse of banks or a credit crunch because creditworthy businesses in need of funds were still able to obtain them.[69]

The minor banking crisis of 1866 was not immediately followed by an increase in the number of bankruptcies, but they increased substantially between 1867 and 1869.[70] As shown in Table 3.10, real GDP growth averaged -0.3 per cent during 1866 and 1867, rising by 0.8 per cent in 1866 and falling by 1.3 per cent in 1867. However, real GDP increased by 3.3 per cent in 1868 and, between 1868 and 1871, real GDP growth averaged 4.7 per cent.

In terms of the wider economic effects of the 1878–9 crisis, bankruptcies in England and Wales – which had averaged 950.6 per annum in the previous five years – rose to only 1,084 and 1,156 in 1878 and 1879, respectively.[71] However, liabilities of bankruptcies in England and Wales totaled £9.3 million in 1878, compared to an average of £4.3 million in the previous five years. Given that Scottish banks were the focus of the crisis, it is not surprising that the situation in Scotland was

---

[68] Mitchell, *British Historical Statistics*, p. 695.
[69] Anon., *The Western Bank Failure*, p. 36.
[70] Mitchell, *British Historical Statistics*, p. 695.
[71] Mitchell, *British Historical Statistics*, p. 695.

much worse: bankruptcies, which had averaged 429.8 in the previous five years, were 717 and 1,077 in 1878 and 1879, respectively.[72] These figures reveal only part of the story, for banking historians paint a bleak picture of the stresses on industry across Scotland, South Wales and parts of England as a result of the 1878 crisis.[73] The difficulties faced by industry are reflected in the 2.2 per cent contraction of GDP in 1879. However, as shown in Table 3.10, GDP rebounded in 1880.

The minor banking crisis of 1974 affected secondary banks but had relatively little effect on the wider economy. The numbers of bankruptcies in England and Wales, which had averaged 4,109 in the period 1969–73, were 5,191 and 6,676 in 1974 and 1975, respectively. These bankruptcy figures are reflected in the GDP growth figures for 1974 and 1975 (see Table 3.10). However, the decline in GDP can be attributed mostly to the oil shock and problems associated with high inflation rather than the relatively minor problems of the secondary-banking sector.

The 2007–8 crisis was unlike previous crises in that it had a major and long-lasting effect on the economy. In terms of the wider economy, the numbers of company and individual insolvencies in Great Britain – which in the period 2002–6 had averaged 14,374 and 67,978, respectively – averaged 16,785 and 139,950, respectively, in the period 2007–11.[74] These figures suggest that it is individuals rather than companies that have suffered as a result of the 2007–8 crisis. The crisis also has been associated with a credit crunch, arising from the needs of banks to shrink their balance sheets and recapitalise. The effects on the wider economy are reflected in the GDP figures listed in Table 3.10, which reveal that real GDP fell almost 5 per cent in 2009. From its height in the first quarter of 2008 to its depth in the third quarter of 2009, real GDP fell 6.6 per cent. Even after the crisis, growth was both low and negative in several quarters of 2011 and 2012. Overall, the collapse in GDP associated with the 2007–8 crisis is the worst of any banking crisis in the United Kingdom, notwithstanding the bailout and the government's fiscal largesse. Indeed, to put this in perspective, the fall of 4.90 per cent in real GDP in 2009 is similar to the fall in real GDP in 1931 and 1944 (i.e., 4.97 and 4.85 per cent, respectively). The fall in GDP in 2009 may not provide a true reflection of the economic cost of the 2007–8 crisis because the output losses from this crisis might be permanent; therefore, the economic cost in the long run may prove to be massive.

[72] Mitchell, *British Historical Statistics*, p. 695.

[73] Clapham, *The Bank of England*, vol. 2, p. 309; Crick and Wadsworth, *A Hundred Years of Joint Stock Banking*, pp. 102 and 397; Holmes and Green, *Midland*, p. 61.

[74] Data from The Insolvency Service, available at http://www.insolvencydirect.bis.gov.uk/ otherinformation/statistics/201205/uksa/index.htm.

It is significant that the two largest declines in GDP during the banking crises listed in Table 3.10 are associated with the two major crises. The wider economic effects of the 2007–8 crisis are unprecedented and mark it as a totally different type of banking crisis in terms of scale. None of the minor crises is associated with a major fall in real GDP; where GDP does fall, as in 1974, other more important causes are contributing to the decline.

Concluding comments

This chapter describes how the British banking system has evolved since 1800. There have been two dominant trends in this period. First, the banking system moved from having numerous participants in the nineteenth century to a position in the twentieth century in which the banking industry is highly concentrated. Second, the banking systems in the different parts of the United Kingdom have become increasingly integrated since 1914.

Using failure-rate data and relative returns on bank stocks, this chapter measures the stability of the banking system since 1800. It also explores the real effects of banking crises. The primary result of this analysis is that the Great Crash of 2007–8 is by far the greatest banking crisis that the United Kingdom has ever experienced. Indeed, based on the evidence presented in this chapter, it is one of only two episodes since 1800 that could be classified as major or systemic banking crises: 1825–6 and 2007–8. The British banking system was relatively stable in the period between these two crises, with only minor episodes occurring. The remainder of this book is devoted primarily to explaining why these two major crises occurred and why the banking system was relatively stable in the interim period.

This chapter raises the following question: How is the structure of the banking system related to its stability? Chapter 2 concluded that from a theoretical perspective, there may not necessarily be a connection between the two. Consistent with this, the two major and systemic crises occurred in two different structures – that is, banking had a competitive structure in 1825–6, whereas it had an oligopolistic structure in 2007–8. Although the banking system was stable in the interim, it was transformed in this period from a highly competitive system to one in which five banks dominated the market – which further supports the view that banking structure and stability are not necessarily correlated.

4   Major and minor British banking crises
    since 1800

Each separate panic has had its own distinctive features, but all have resembled each other in occurring immediately after a period of prosperity, the hollowness of which it has exposed. So uniform is this sequence, that wherever we find ourselves under circumstances that enable the acquisition of rapid fortunes, otherwise than by plodding industry, we may almost be justified in auguring that the time for panic is at hand.[1]

D. Morier Evans

Introduction

The previous chapter established that there were major banking crises in the United Kingdom in 1825–6 and 2007–8 and that in the interim period, there was a series of what we termed minor crises (i.e., 1836–7, 1847, 1857–8, 1866–7, 1878–9 and 1974). In this chapter, we develop narrative accounts of these major and minor crises. The main reasons for doing so are twofold.

First, we need a qualitative idea of the extent and scale of these crises to confirm (or otherwise) the results from the quantitative measures of stability developed in Chapter 3. In particular, we explore how each crisis developed and analyse anecdotal evidence of its severity. In addition, to understand why they failed, we examine the major institutions that experienced difficulties or failed during each crisis episode.

Second, we want to examine the possible triggers for and precursors to each crisis. Because easy monetary and credit conditions and speculation are important elements of both the Kindleberger and Minsky explanations for crises, we examine monetary and credit conditions in the run-up to each crisis and also consider whether speculation in assets of various types preceded each crisis.[2]

---

[1] Evans, *The History of the Commercial Crisis*, p. 1.
[2] Minsky, *Stabilizing an Unstable Economy*; Kindleberger, *Manias, Panics and Crashes*.

1825–1826

With the end of the Napoleonic Wars and in preparation for the resumption of gold convertibility, the Bank of England began to contract its note issue, thereby ushering in a period of deflation that resulted in a 32.6 per cent decline in the composite price index between 1818 and 1822.[3] The economic contraction also was severe, with nominal GDP falling by 13.9 per cent in those years.[4] However, following a deliberate easing of monetary conditions and a concomitant expansion of credit, the economy began to recover in 1822.[5] The aim of this policy was to relieve the distress of agricultural interests, which had been exerting continued pressure on the government.[6]

The easing of monetary and credit conditions had several sources. First, in April 1822, the government extended the right of country banks to issue small notes (i.e., under £5) until 1833, a right that it was assumed had been about to disappear under the terms of the Resumption of Cash Payments Act of 1819.[7] Second, under pressure from the Prime Minister, Lord Liverpool, the Bank of England reduced its discount rate in June 1822 from 5 to 4 per cent, where it remained until December 1825.[8] Third, the government was buying and retiring its long-term debt, thereby injecting money into the economy.[9] Fourth, the government in 1823 lowered the long-term interest rate in the economy by converting £135 million of 5 per cent bonds to 4 per cent bonds, and in 1824 it converted £80 million of its 4 per cent bonds to 3.5 per cent bonds.[10]

The Bank of England independently assisted the government in its policy of monetary and credit easing. It did so by increasing its note issue by 25 per cent between February 1822 and February 1825, at a time when it was reducing its holdings of gold bullion (Table 4.1). In addition, in May 1823, the Bank began to purchase the Dead Weight Annuity, which was created to pay for naval and military pensions and

---

[3] O'Donoghue, Goulding and Allen, 'Composite price index'.
[4] Broadberry and van Leeuwen, 'British economic growth'.
[5] *Committee of Secrecy on the Bank of England Charter*, P.P. 1831–32 VI, Evidence of William Ward, qq. 1981–3, 2015, John Richards, q. 5107.
[6] *Committee of Secrecy on the Bank of England Charter*, P.P. 1831–32 VI, Evidence of William Ward, q. 2015, Samuel Gurney, q. 3760; Pressnell, *Country Banking*, pp. 487–8; Clapham, *An Economic History of Modern Britain: The Early Railway Age*, p. 264.
[7] Clapham, *An Economic History of Modern Britain: The Early Railway Age*, p. 264.
[8] Hawtrey, *A Century of Bank Rate*, p. 14.
[9] Neal, 'The financial crisis of 1825', p. 60.
[10] *Committee of Secrecy on the Bank of England Charter*, P.P. 1831–32 VI, Evidence of J. Horsley Palmer, q. 606.

Table 4.1 *Bank of England notes in circulation and securities and bullion held, 1821–1826*

	Circulation (£ million)	Securities (£ million)	Bullion (£ million)
August 1821	20.295	18.475	11.233
February 1822	18.665	15.478	11.057
August 1822	16.609	17.290	10.097
February 1823	18.392	18.319	10.384
August 1823	19.231	17.467	12.658
February 1824	19.736	18.872	13.810
August 1824	20.132	20.904	11.787
February 1825	20.753	24.951	8.779
August 1825	19.398	25.106	3.634
February 1826	25.467	32.918	2.459
August 1826	21.563	25.083	6.754

Source: *Committee of Secrecy on the Bank of England Charter*, P.P. 1831–32 VI, Appendix 5.

which the government had failed to sell to the public.[11] As a result of these actions, the Bank's holdings of securities increased by 62 per cent between February 1822 and August 1825 (see Table 4.1).

Several witnesses before the 1832 *Committee of Secrecy on the Bank of England Charter* were of the belief that the monetary easing of the Bank and the government was at the root of the 1825–6 crisis.[12] It is not surprising that George W. Norman, a director at the Bank of England from 1821 until 1872, argued that the Bank's monetary easing was in no way responsible for the panic of 1825–6.[13] However, Thomas Tooke argued that, given the reduction in interest as a result of the government's debt refinancing, the Bank should have reduced rather than increased its note issue in 1824.[14] He also argued that the Bank's purchases of securities added to the spirit of speculation.[15]

---

[11] By February 1825, the Bank was holding more than £5 million of these annuities; see *Committee of Secrecy on the Bank of England Charter*, P.P. 1831–32 VI, Appendix 6.

[12] *Committee of Secrecy on the Bank of England Charter*, P.P. 1831–32 VI, Evidence of Vincent Stuckey, q. 1186; Samuel J. Loyd, q. 3466; George Grote, q. 4646; John Easthope, q. 5795.

[13] *Committee of Secrecy on the Bank of England Charter*, P.P. 1831–32 VI, Evidence of George W. Norman, q. 2557.

[14] *Committee of Secrecy on the Bank of England Charter*, P.P. 1831–32 VI, Evidence of Thomas Tooke, qq. 3852, 3857.

[15] *Select Committee on Banks of Issue*, P.P. 1840 IV, Evidence of Thomas Tooke, q. 3762.

Table 4.2 *Country-bank-note circulation, 1821–1826*

	Stamp duty paid on all notes	Stamp duty paid on notes under £1. 1s.	Burgess return of the issues of 122 country banks	Gayer et al.'s estimate of country-bank-note issue stamped (£ million)
1821	53,654	34,600	100.0	n/a
1822	66,957	45,158	94.9	4.3
1823	62,178	38,615	94.7	4.5
1824	65,051	39,694	102.5	6.7
1825	93,272	51,028	109.9	8.8
1826	114,913	63,309	n/a	1.5

Source: Committee of Secrecy on the Bank of England Charter, P.P. 1831–32 VI, Appendix 99; Evidence of Henry Burgess, q. 5165. Gayer, Rostow and Schwartz, *Growth and Fluctuation*, vol. 1, p. 206.

Note: The Burgess return is simply an average of 122 country-bank-note issues in July each year. The returns are in an index form.

Although English country banks were heavily criticised for overissuing their notes, the evidence on this is contradictory, with the Burgess returns suggesting a 7.2 per cent increase in note issues between 1824 and 1825, whereas the stamp-duty evidence suggests that the increase in the country-bank-note issue was closer to 50 per cent (Table 4.2). Burgess rather implausibly suggests that the difference can be explained by the fact that banks at this time were replacing their old notes and that many newly stamped notes were not issued.[16] A more likely explanation is that the Burgess sample of 122 banks may not have been representative and the banks may have under-reported their note issues to Burgess.[17] Other evidence before the *Committee of Secrecy on the Bank of England Charter* suggested that there had been a considerable expansion of the country-bank-note issue.[18]

Although some witnesses before the 1832 *Committee of Secrecy on Bank of England Charter* did not think that the easing of monetary and credit conditions described previously had had any effect on speculation or asset prices, the majority opinion was otherwise and that the expansion

[16] *Committee of Secrecy on the Bank of England Charter*, P.P. 1831–32 VI, Evidence of Henry Burgess, qq. 5484–5. See also *The Times*, 13 December 1825, p. 2.

[17] *Committee of Secrecy on the Bank of England Charter*, P.P. 1831–32 VI, Evidence of Henry Burgess, qq. 5152–9.

[18] *Committee of Secrecy on the Bank of England Charter*, P.P. 1831–32 VI, Evidence of George W. Norman, q. 2666; William Beckett, q. 1392; and John Wilkins, q. 1638.

of the country-bank-note issue was particularly to blame.[19] Speculation in Latin American loans and shares of joint-stock companies, not to mention insurance and mining companies, took place in the stock exchange in 1824 and 1825.[20] In addition, there was a promotional boom in joint-stock companies, with 624 companies floated in 1824 and 1825.[21] Between joint-stock companies and foreign loans, £42.9 million of capital was raised on the London market in 1824 and 1825 – a remarkable amount given that the entire market value of the London equity market in December 1825 was £43.6 million.[22]

The first portents of the crisis came in autumn 1825 with the failure of banks in Devon and the west of England. Then, at the beginning of December, Pole, Thornton and Company – a major London bank that had invested money in risky securities – faced a series of runs and eventually collapsed.[23] This was followed by the collapse of a leading Yorkshire bank and a series of runs on and failures of country banks. After the stoppages of London and country banks on 14 December, there were few locations in England where the 'stoppage of local banks had not occurred or was not feared hourly'.[24] Many of the banks that stopped payment reopened eventually, but in December alone, thirty country banks were bankrupted, with thirty-three more entering bankruptcy in the first three months of 1826.[25] At the same time as these bankruptcies, banks all over England and Wales faced severe runs.[26]

The crisis of 1825–6 was so severe that virtually every English country bank approached the Bank of England for assistance. Such was the perilous state of affairs that William Huskisson, President of the Board of Trade, stated that England 'was within four-and-twenty hours of a state of barter'.[27] This statement may have been hyperbole, but witnesses before

---

[19] *Committee of Secrecy on the Bank of England Charter*, P.P. 1831–32 VI, Evidence of William Ward, q. 1992; Jeremiah Harman, q. 2330; George W. Norman, q. 2667; John Richards, q. 5019; and Thomas Tooke, q. 3852, 3911. For a contrary opinion, see evidence of Samuel Gurney (q. 3763).

[20] *Committee of Secrecy on the Bank of England Charter*, P.P. 1831–32 VI, Evidence of Thomas Tooke, q. 3849. See Neal, 'The financial crisis of 1825', pp. 62–4, for the yield on foreign loans and a stock price index.

[21] English, *A Complete View*, p. 30.

[22] English, *A Complete View*, pp. 30, 42; Acheson, Hickson, Turner and Ye, 'Rule Britannia'.

[23] *Committee of Secrecy on the Bank of England Charter*, P.P. 1831–32 VI, Evidence of J. Horsley Palmer, q. 606.

[24] Pressnell, *Country Banking*, p. 487.

[25] *Committee of Secrecy on the Bank of England Charter*, P.P. 1831–32 VI, Appendix 101.

[26] *The Times*, December 20, 1825, p. 2, carries a list of reports from regional newspapers on the severity of runs in its area. See also *The Times*, 16 December 1825, p. 2.

[27] Stuckey, 'Thoughts on the improvement', p. 424.

the 1832 committee stated that the entire credit system and economy in December 1825 was within a few days of collapsing.[28]

1836–1837

Although there was no great expansion of the note issue by the Bank of England or other banks in 1836, it appears that money was circulating rapidly, and the creation of new joint-stock banks resulted in an expansion of deposits and credit.[29] In terms of speculative activity, other than the many joint-stock banks established in the period 1834–6, many new railway companies also were promoted; Parliament authorised fifty-nine new railways, which represented about £36.4 million in capital.[30] However, neither bank nor railway shares experienced a substantial asset-price reversal at this time.[31]

In the summer of 1836, as a belated response to the substantial drain of gold that it had experienced, the Bank of England twice raised its bank rate, from 4 to 5 per cent. At the same time, the Bank refused to discount any bill that bore the name of a joint-stock bank.[32] The subsequent pressure in the money market towards the end of 1836 and into early 1837 exposed the weaknesses of two large newly established joint-stock banks: the Agricultural and Commercial Bank of Ireland (A&C) and the Northern and Central Bank of England (NCBoE).

Following its inception in May 1834, the A&C rapidly expanded its branch network throughout Ireland so that before its collapse, it had a total of forty-five branches and sub-branches.[33] In response to a series of runs in October 1836, the A&C called on its shareholders to increase the paid-up capital of the bank by £157,000.[34] The A&C also asked the Bank of Ireland to discount some of its bills; however, after meeting requests on 10 and 11 November, the Bank of Ireland declined to discount bills on the next day and continued to do so because it did 'not feel itself warranted to make any advances on the security proposed'.[35] Following the refusal of the Bank of Ireland and the Bank of England to discount its loans, and coupled with its inability to raise enough capital from

---

[28] *Committee of Secrecy on the Bank of England Charter*, P.P. 1831–32 VI, Evidence of John Richards, q. 5006, and Jeremiah Harman, q. 2262.

[29] Clapham, *The Bank of England*, vol. 2, p. 149; Thomas, *Rise and Growth*, p. 297.

[30] *The Economist*, 4 October 1845, p. 949.

[31] Gayer, Rostow and Schwartz, *Growth and Fluctuation*, vol. I, p. 375; Acheson, Hickson, Turner and Ye, 'Rule Britannia'.

[32] Clapham, *An Economic History of Modern Britain: The Early Railway Age*, p. 515.

[33] *Select Committee on Joint Stock Banks*, P.P. 1837 XIV, Evidence of James Dwyer, q. 2688.

[34] *Select Committee on Joint Stock Banks*, P.P. 1837 XIV, Evidence of James Dwyer, q. 2723.

[35] Bank of Ireland, Court of Directors Transactions, 10–14 November 1836.

shareholders, the A&C suspended payments on 14 November.[36] Despite several revival attempts, the A&C was liquidated; however, depositors and note-holders were eventually paid in full.[37]

The NCBoE also commenced business in 1834, with an extensive network of forty branches and sub-branches radiating out from its Manchester headquarters.[38] Another similarity with the A&C was that the NCBoE had numerous owners: 1,204 shareholders in 1836.[39] Unlike the A&C, however, the NCBoE had extensive paid-up capital; by 1836, it had issued 71,860 £10 shares, all of which were fully paid.

After the evidence of Cassels (i.e., the NCBoE's London agent) was published in August 1836, the NCBoE had difficulty rediscounting in the London money market, a situation that was compounded by the Bank of England's refusal to discount any bill that bore an NCBoE endorsement. Because the NCBoE had no unpaid capital, it was unable to call on shareholders to meet its funding problems.[40] Even after receiving assistance from the Bank of England, the bank closed its doors in November 1836 and entered liquidation; however, neither the Bank's nor the NCBoE's note-holders and depositors lost anything.

Why did these two large banks fail? Although inexperience and mismanagement may be offered as explanations, the available evidence suggests that they were aggressive risk takers, and they even may have occasionally engaged in fraudulent behaviour.[41] There also were governance problems, with large advances being made to directors and their friends, as well as directors borrowing from the banks to pay for their shares.[42]

1847

The three years preceding the 1847 commercial crisis had seen substantial economic growth, with GDP growing by 5.4, 5.3 and 7.0 per cent in 1844, 1845 and 1846, respectively.[43] In addition, there had been a large inflow of gold into the United Kingdom, arising from the abundant

---

[36] The call on shareholders raised only £23,000 of a possible £157,000.
[37] *Select Committee on Joint Stock Banks*, P.P. 1838 VII, Evidence of James Pim, qq. 596–97, and Jeremiah Dunne, qq. 1382–83.
[38] *Select Committee on Joint Stock Banks*, P.P. 1836 IX, Appendix 41.
[39] *Select Committee on Joint Stock Banks*, P.P. 1836 IX, Appendix 64; Hickson and Turner, 'The genesis of corporate governance'.
[40] *Select Committee on Joint Stock Banks*, P.P. 1837 XIV, Evidence of J. W. Gilbart, q. 1930.
[41] Hickson and Turner, 'The genesis of corporate governance', 185; Thomas, *Rise and Growth*, p. 286.
[42] *Select Committee on Joint Stock Banks*, P.P. 1837 XIV, Appendix IV; Thomas, *Rise and Growth*, pp. 276, 283–5.
[43] Mitchell, *British Historical Statistics*, pp. 836–7.

harvests of 1842, 1843 and 1844. This resulted in historically low market discount rates of almost 2 per cent in 1843 and 1844 and in the Bank of England's accumulation of a large bullion reserve.

The Bank Charter Act came into operation in September 1844.[44] This Act was an attempt to make the paper currency operate like a purely metallic currency; as a result, the Bank of England was split into two separate departments.[45] On the day that the Act came into effect, the Bank – realising that it had a large bullion reserve – took advantage of its new-found freedom and immediately dropped its discount rate for bills from 4 per cent to the then-historic low of 2.5 per cent.[46]

These low interest rates were followed by what has become known as the 'Railway Mania'. In 1844 and 1845, more than a thousand railways were promoted, and a value-weighted index of railway stock prices doubled between January 1843 and August 1845.[47] This index fell sharply in the last quarter of 1845 and continued to fall for the remainder of the decade, to 67 per cent below its market peak by 1850.[48] Recent evidence suggests that the Railway Mania originated in a combination of political failures and investor myopia.[49]

In addition to the discovery of potato blight, there was a poor harvest in the autumn of 1845. The subsequent importation of grain from abroad resulted in a contraction of Bank of England notes along with a contraction in its bullion reserve. To prevent reserves from contracting further, the Bank increased its discount rate to 3 per cent on 16 October and to 3.5 per cent on 6 November; both increases negatively affected the market for railway stocks.[50]

Although money-market pressures eased during the first half of 1846, the failure of the potato crop and the poor harvest of that year resulted in the importation of substantial amounts of grain. As a result, the Bank's reserves fell from £9.4 million at the beginning of January 1847 to £3.0 million at the end of April, and its holdings of bullion fell from £15.0 million to £9.3 million.[51] As a consequence of these declines, the Bank increased its discount rate from 3 to 3.5 and then to 4 per cent in January 1847. A further increase from 4 to 5 per cent came in April 1847, and

---

[44] 7 & 8 Vict. c.32.
[45] The issue department was concerned with issuing notes and ensuring that the Bank had adequate bullion to back its note issue. The banking department was essentially to act as other commercial banks did.
[46] Thomas, *Rise and Growth*, p. 433.   [47] Campbell, 'Myopic rationality'.
[48] Campbell, 'Myopic rationality'.
[49] Campbell, 'Myopic rationality'; Campbell and Turner, 'Dispelling the myth of the naive investor'.
[50] Evans, *The Commercial Crisis*, p. 18.   [51] Thomas, *Rise and Growth*, p. 438.

the Bank also began to ration its discounting and lending.[52] The money markets came under further pressure as railway shareholders attempted to raise the money necessary to pay calls on the unpaid portion of their shares.[53] During the summer of 1847, the pressure on the money markets increased; many corn merchants experienced difficulties as a result of the unexpected decline of more than 50 per cent in the price of wheat and corn in a matter of a few months.

Mercantile failures continued unabated during September 1847, including those of three Bank of England directors who were subsequently disqualified from office. The 'Week of Terror' from 16–23 October resulted in several banks suspending payments and well-run Scottish banks looking for accommodation from the Bank. At the end of the week, the Prime Minister and Chancellor of the Exchequer sent the Bank of England a relaxatory letter indemnifying it from breaking the Bank Charter Act, which was enough to ease concerns in the money markets.

The city of Newcastle experienced banking difficulties before and during the Week of Terror. During the money-market pressures in the spring of 1847, the North of England Joint Stock Banking Company failed. This bank had been established in 1832 but, after its failure, it transpired that heavy losses had been incurred in the first five years of business such that the original paid-up capital of £340,955 had all but disappeared.[54]

The failure of the North of England Joint Stock Banking Company raised suspicions about other banks in the region, undermining public confidence from the spring of 1847 onwards. On 21 October 1847, during the Week of Terror, the Newcastle, Shields and Sunderland Union Joint Stock Bank suspended payment. At a special meeting of shareholders, William Woods, one of the largest shareholders, was appointed to chair a shareholder committee that had a remit to turn the bank around. The deficiency between the bank's assets and liabilities was approximately £80,000, which was met by calls totalling £20 on each share.[55] The bank eventually reopened in 1849.

Three other notable banks temporarily suspended business in 1847.[56] First, the Royal Bank of Liverpool suspended payment at the start of

---

[52] There is a view that the Bank should have increased its discount rate much sooner than it did; see Hawtrey, *A Century of Bank Rate*, p. 21; and *Secret Committee of the House of Lords on Causes of Commercial Distress*, P.P. 1847–8 I, Evidence of James Morris and H. J. Prescott, qq. 2661–2.

[53] *Secret Committee of the House of Lords on Causes of Commercial Distress*, P.P. 1847–8 I, Evidence of James Morris and H. J. Prescott, q. 2674.

[54] Philips, *A History of Banks*, p. 333.   [55] Philips, *A History of Banks*, p. 324.

[56] *Secret Committee of the House of Lords on Causes of Commercial Distress*, P.P. 1847–8 I, Evidence of C. Turner, q. 991.

the Week of Terror, despite having received £300,000 from the Bank of England on the security of good quality bills.[57] This bank had been so mismanaged as to have advanced £520,000 (i.e., 84 per cent of its capital) to one individual.[58] Nevertheless, it resumed business on 1 December 1847. Second, the small Liverpool Banking Company also was temporarily suspended at this time, but it called up funds from shareholders to help it through its funding difficulties.[59] Third, the North and South Wales Bank, with significant operations in and connections to Liverpool, was wrongly accused by a London newspaper of having suspended trading. Subsequent runs following the false report resulted in its temporarily suspending payment. After an injection of capital from shareholders and with the support of its customers, the bank reopened in early 1848.[60]

The crisis of 1847, like that of 1836–7, was a money-market crisis. However, this time, the pressures felt in the money markets appear to have reflected the fear (imaginary or otherwise) that the Bank Charter Act restricted the Bank of England as a lender of last resort.[61] According to contemporaries, the 1847 crisis appears to have created fewer problems for banks than the crisis of 1836–7.[62] The 1847 crisis was viewed by contemporaries as a commercial or a mercantile rather than a banking crisis – hence, its appellation as the 'commercial crisis'. At no time in 1847 was the soundness of the banking system ever questioned.[63]

1857–1858

The 1857–8 crisis has been described as the first global financial crisis.[64] There were at least three previous developments that, according to the report of the Select Committee on the Bank Acts, contributed to the scale of the crisis.[65] First, the discovery of gold in California resulted in a huge monetary stimulus, with an £80.7 million increase in the European stock of bullion between 1851 and 1856.[66] Second, there was a remarkable

---

[57] *Secret Committee of the House of Lords on Causes of Commercial Distress*, P.P. 1847–8 I, Evidence of James Morris and H. J. Prescott, q. 2645.

[58] *Secret Committee of the House of Lords on Causes of Commercial Distress*, P.P. 1847–8 I, Evidence of James Morris and H. J. Prescott, q. 3223.

[59] Thomas, *Rise and Growth*, p. 444.

[60] Crick and Wadsworth, *A Hundred Years of Joint Stock Banking*, pp. 184–5.

[61] Gayer et al., *Growth and Fluctuation*, p. 326.

[62] *Secret Committee of the House of Lords on Causes of Commercial Distress*, P.P. 1847–8 I, Committee Report, p. vii.

[63] Thomas, *Rise and Growth*, p. 444.

[64] Clapham, *Bank of England*, vol. 2, p. 226; Kindleberger, *Manias, Panics and Crashes*, p. 129.

[65] *Select Committee on the Bank Acts*, P.P. 1858, LXXVIII, Committee Report, p. v.

[66] *Select Committee on the Bank Acts*, P.P. 1858, LXXVIII, Committee Report, p. iv.

increase in UK exports – which doubled in value in the decade before the crisis – particularly those to the United States, which constituted about one quarter of the United Kingdom's £122 million in exports in 1856.[67] Third, between 1847 and 1857, the deposits of the London joint-stock banks quintupled to £43.1 million, with a substantial proportion of those deposits ultimately loaned to merchants.[68]

As the autumn of 1857 approached, there were no warning signs to the Bank of England or the public of what was about to unfold.[69] On 15 September, the first of a series of bad news stories arrived from the United States: the value of its railroad securities had fallen substantially, with implications for the United Kingdom because the country held about £80 million of US stocks and bonds at the time.[70] Then, during the following weeks, news came of numerous bank suspensions up and down the Atlantic coast. For example, 62 of 63 New York banks suspended payment, and it is estimated that a total of 1,415 US banks suspended payment during the 1857 panic.[71] Consequently, UK firms that were heavily engaged in American trade began to fail, which had repercussions for their banks. UK banks, particularly those based in Liverpool and Glasgow – two cities with extensive mercantile links to the United States – began to experience a drain of gold. As a result, the Bank of England raised the bank rate to 6 per cent on 8 October, to 7 per cent on 12 October, to 8 per cent on 19 October and to 9 per cent on 9 November.

The first bank to fail was the Liverpool Borough Bank on 27 October 1857. Then, on 9 November, the Western Bank of Scotland failed and the bank rate was immediately increased to 10 per cent. On 11 November, the City of Glasgow Bank temporarily suspended payment. By 12 November, market discounting had almost ceased because several major bill brokers were in trouble. Consequently, as in 1847, the Chancellor of the Exchequer wrote a letter to the Governor of the Bank of England temporarily suspending the Bank Charter Act on condition that the bank rate remained at 10 per cent. The final bank to fail was the Northumberland and Durham District, which closed in late November 1857.

However, the crisis was essentially over by the middle of December 1857 and the bank rate went down to 8 per cent, with the result that the temporary suspension of the Bank Charter Act came to an end. The bank rate was reduced even more during subsequent weeks: by 11 February

---

[67] *Select Committee on the Bank Acts*, P.P. 1858, LXXVIII, Committee Report, pp. iii, viii.
[68] Evans, *The History of the Commercial Crisis*, pp. 32–3.
[69] *Select Committee on the Bank Acts*, P.P. 1858, LXXVIII, Committee Report, p. vii.
[70] *Select Committee on the Bank Acts*, P.P. 1858, LXXVIII, Committee Report, p. viii.
[71] Notably, very few banks ultimately failed; see Calomiris and Schweikart, 'The panic of 1857'.

1858, it was at 3 per cent. According to *The Economist*, 'there was never a more severe crisis nor a more rapid recovery'.[72]

Three major banks failed in 1857. The first failure, the Liverpool Borough Bank (established in 1836), occurred in the city that was most heavily exposed to American trade and shipping. Having accumulated bad debts in the preceding decades, this bank was in difficulty before the onset of the commercial crisis.[73] These bad debts ultimately had been hidden from shareholders, in that securities for loans were overinflated in value and bad debts were not properly accounted for.[74] When the bank failed, two former managing directors were in debt to it.[75] The bank ultimately failed because its managers had taken too many risks that were not checked and monitored by the bank's directors.[76]

The largest bank to fail in 1857 was the Western Bank of Scotland (established in 1832), which had Scotland's largest branch network at the time. Its collapse resulted in a call on its 1,280 shareholders for £1,089,577, a figure that was inflated by about £300,000 because the bank owned 1,671 of its own shares.[77] The call also may have been exacerbated by the fact that some shareholders of the Western Bank had borrowed £988,487 on the security of their shares.[78] This was a common practice of early joint-stock banking in Scotland, but it ultimately reduced the capital of any bank that experienced difficulties.[79]

The Western Bank had a well-known reputation for taking high risks: it had experienced difficulties in 1834, was threatened with exclusion from the Scottish note-exchange system in 1837 and had required liquidity support totalling £300,000 from the Bank of England during the 1847 crisis. After its failure, it became apparent that the bank had been discounting and rediscounting aggressively and had held low amounts of secondary reserves.[80] In addition, it had a concentrated lending portfolio, with loans totalling slightly more than £1.6 million to four Glasgow mercantile houses that failed during the 1857 crisis; this sum represented more than the bank's paid-up capital.[81] Creditors of some of the four

---

[72] *The Economist*, 5 January 1858.

[73] *Select Committee on the Bank Acts*, P.P. 1858, LXXVIII, Evidence of J. Dixon, q. 4200.

[74] *Select Committee on the Bank Acts*, P.P. 1858, LXXVIII, Appendix 18. This fictitious accounting resulted in a civil case against one of the bank's directors (*The Times*, 28 August 1858, p. 7; 21 October 1858, p. 5; 29 January 1859, pp. 7–8).

[75] *Select Committee on the Bank Acts*, P.P. 1858, LXXVIII, Appendix 18 and Evidence of J. Dixon, qq. 4250–1.

[76] *Select Committee on the Bank Acts*, P.P. 1858, LXXVIII, Committee Report, p. xvii.

[77] *Select Committee on the Bank Acts*, P.P. 1858, LXXVIII, Appendix 21, p. 460.

[78] Anon., *The Western Bank Failure*, p. 70; Anon., *How to Mismanage a Bank*, p. 17.

[79] Acheson and Turner, 'Investor behavior'.

[80] Anon., *The Western Bank Failure*, p. 14.   [81] Anon., *The Western Bank Failure*, p. 59.

failed mercantile houses received dividends of only one or two shillings on the pound.[82] Furthermore, the Western Bank of Scotland had been actively involved in financing overseas trade, particularly the US primary products market. Although some scholars blamed the Western Bank's failure on the unwillingness of Edinburgh banks to help it through the crisis,[83] the failure was ultimately one of governance, with many directors oblivious to the dubious state of the bank's accounts.[84]

The Northumberland and Durham District Bank was the final major bank to collapse in the 1857 crisis. This failure occurred primarily because of a series of substantial loans, backed by completely inadequate security, to the Derwent Iron Company.[85] At the time of the bank's closure, the loans to this company totalled £947,000 – that is, 158 per cent of the bank's paid-up capital. It appears that Jonathan Richardson, who was the 'moving-spring of the whole bank . . . the person who managed everything' – although not an owner of the Derwent Iron Company – held the royalties on the minerals that the company worked.[86] The deficit between the bank's assets and liabilities was met by a call of £35 per share on its 407 owners, with several owners liable for more than £35,000.[87]

In terms of severity, the 1857 crisis was one of the greatest nineteenth-century crises. The three banks that collapsed were all weak institutions that had been taking excessive risks for a long time; the shock from across the Atlantic simply exposed their inherent weaknesses. However, there was never any threat of a systemic collapse, and many banks were unaffected by the crisis.[88] The collapse of the Northumberland and Durham District Bank did not lead to runs on other banks in the region.[89] Although Scottish banks faced a general run the day after the Western Bank's closure, the Scottish banking system as a whole was never in any danger.[90] As for the other two Glasgow-based banks, the City of

---

[82] Anon., *The Western Bank Failure*, p. 59.

[83] Tamaki, *The Life Cycle*, p. 69; Campbell, 'Edinburgh bankers'.

[84] Anon., *The Western Bank Failure*, pp. 43, 70.

[85] *Select Committee on the Bank Acts*, P.P. 1858, LXXVIII, Committee Report, p. xix, and Evidence of K. D. Hodgson, qq. 3456–7.

[86] *Select Committee on the Bank Acts*, P.P. 1858, LXXVIII, Evidence of K. D. Hodgson, qq. 3458.

[87] Philips, *A History of Banks*, p. 344. See *The Times* 26 May 1858, p. 7, for the major shareholders.

[88] Clapham, *Bank of England*, vol. 2, p. 231; Crick and Wadsworth, *A Hundred Years of Joint Stock Banking*, p. 66. The Wolverhampton and Staffordshire Bank suspended payment following the Western Bank's collapse, but it resumed business within a few weeks (Holmes and Green, *Midland*, p. 40).

[89] *The Times*, 27 November 1857, p. 5.

[90] Crick and Wadsworth, *A Hundred Years of Joint Stock Banking*, p. 389.

Table 4.3 *End-of-month share prices (£) of Scottish banks, 1857–1858*

	Bank of Scotland	British Linen	Caledonian	City of Glasgow	Clydesdale	Commercial	National	North of Scotland	Royal Bank of Scotland	Union Bank of Scotland
September 1857	193.0	218.5	3.85	13.50	13.60	241.5	193.0	5.50	137.0	105.0
October 1857	188.0	216.0	3.85	11.85	13.25	240.0	190.0	5.50	134.0	100.0
November 1857	187.0	215.0	3.75	n/a	12.00	232.0	182.5	5.50	135.0	89.0
December 1857	188.6	210.0	3.35	n/a	11.35	219.0	179.5	5.95	140.0	71.5
January 1858	183.0	210.0	3.60	7.25	12.00	220.0	171.0	5.25	137.0	75.0
February 1858	190.0	214.5	3.60	8.60	12.35	224.0	183.0	5.25	137.5	81.0
March 1858	193.0	217.0	3.80	8.60	13.00	225.0	184.2	5.60	143.0	90.0

Source: Share price lists are from *The Scotsman*.
Note: These prices are the last reported prices of each month. Share prices are not available for the City of Glasgow Bank in November and December because of its suspension.

Glasgow Bank reopened within five weeks of its suspension and the Union Bank of Scotland survived the crisis, albeit with support from Edinburgh banks and the Bank of England.[91] As shown in Table 4.3, only the shares of these two Scottish banks experienced substantial declines during the crisis, and even the Union Bank's share price had mostly recovered by March 1858.

1866–1867

In terms of monetary and credit conditions, the run-up to the 1866 crisis was one of an increasing bank rate, from 3 per cent in June 1865 to 8 per cent in January 1866, caused by an internal demand for gold and an external demand driven by European governments preparing for war.[92] The bank rate was eased to 7 per cent in February and then to 6 per cent in March; however, by this stage, the 'financial community had been worked up into a state of extreme apprehension'.[93] The crisis of 1866, therefore, was unlike its nineteenth-century predecessors in that it was not preceded by a large monetary expansion.

GDP grew by 4.5 per cent in 1865. Part of this growth was a result of an increase in Britain's exports, which were responding to the increased postbellum US demand for British goods. In addition, industrial activity

[91] Tamaki, *Life Cycle*, p. 73.
[92] Clapham, *An Economic History of Modern Britain: Free Trade and Steel*, p. 375.
[93] Hawtrey, *A Century of Bank Rate*, p. 82.

in Britain had been high between 1863 and 1865 due to investment in increased railway mileage and to the incorporation boom that had followed the complete liberalisation of incorporation law in the Companies Act of 1862.[94] After the crash of May 1866, it was demonstrated that many company flotations – particularly those of finance and investment companies – were of a dubious nature.[95] Many of the newly established finance companies loaned money at high rates of interest to other limited-liability companies, taking low-quality securities. These companies were also instrumental in financing the activities of railway contractors, who were actively working on an immense addition to the nation's railway mileage. This led Thompson Hankey at the Bank of England to suggest that much money-market paper was closer to a mortgage than a bill.[96] In effect, the finance companies were pseudo-banking companies that created and rediscounted bills of exchange and other credit instruments.[97]

One of the most prominent financial-company flotations was the partnership of Overend and Gurney, London's leading discount house and a competitor of the Bank of England, which incorporated as a limited-liability company and floated its shares in July 1865.[98] At the time of its flotation, Overend, Gurney and Co. was insolvent by at least £4.2 million, having engaged in inappropriate business in the first half of the 1860s.[99] However, the bad assets had been segregated into a separate account, which was backed by a guarantee of the partners' personal fortunes. Nevertheless, the company's shares did well, being at a premium of £10 in October 1865. In January 1866, however, several of the newly created finance companies were experiencing difficulties. First, the trouble of the railway contractors in the early months of 1866 meant that the companies that were financing them also experienced pressure.[100] Second, the shareholders of finance companies were not paying calls on shares and were attempting to sell their shares to avoid paying the calls.[101] Many of the finance companies created in the 1860s had issued shares with a low proportion of paid-in capital, with the intention of making calls on shareholders as the company expanded but also leaving a proportion uncalled as a buffer to protect their depositors.[102] However,

[94] 25 & 26 Vict. c.89.
[95] Hunt, *The Development of the Business Corporation*, pp. 153–4.
[96] Cottrell, 'London's first big bang', p. 75.   [97] Chubb, 'The Bank Act'.
[98] King, 'The extent of the London discount market'.
[99] *The Economist*, 16 June 1866, pp. 697–8.
[100] Anderson and Cottrell, 'Another Victorian capital market', 613.
[101] Taylor, *Creating Capitalism*, p. 179.
[102] Acheson, Turner and Ye, 'The character and denomination of shares'.

this arrangement became problematic because many investors of limited means had been tempted to invest in these companies.[103]

The collapse of the Joint Stock Discount Company at the end of January precipitated the onset of severe problems for discount and finance companies. The market for their shares began to be so stressed that by the beginning of May 1866, the shares of finance companies were being sold at any price that could be obtained.[104]

During the first four months of 1866, Overend, Gurney and Co. also experienced a fall in its share price – from £21.50 at the end of December to £12.25 immediately before its collapse.[105] It simultaneously suffered a slow drain of deposits in those months, estimated at its close to be £4.6 million.[106] When it closed on 10 May, the deficit between assets and liabilities was approximately £5 million, and many of the creditors were banks that had deposited balances with it.[107] The next day, 11 May, became known as 'Black Friday' because of the sheer, violent panic that descended on the money markets. On 12 May, the Chancellor wrote a letter that indemnified the Bank of England if it infringed the Bank Charter Act; within a week, this 'psychological palliative' had brought the panic to an abrupt end.[108] According to Clapham, unlike previous crises, the panic of 1866 appears to have been psychological and not based on real or monetary phenomena[109]; whereas *The Economist* regarded the panic as induced by the undermining of confidence in suppliers of credit by the failure of an important financial institution.[110]

Overend, Gurney and Co. ultimately failed because it had taken too many risks in the late 1850s, a period of 'hothouse' growth. The firm made considerable advances to companies of questionable creditworthiness on the basis of dubious security. According to the liquidation figures, it made advances to thirteen borrowers totalling £3.5 million, which were worth only an estimated £711,500 by the time the partnership converted to a limited-liability company.[111]

As a result of the firm's collapse, the Gurney family lost most of its wealth and the company's shareholders faced substantial calls on their shares. One shareholder claimed that he (with other shareholders) was not liable to pay his unpaid capital because he had been fraudulently

[103] Hunt, *The Development of the Business Corporation*, p. 155.
[104] *The Times*, 1 May 1866, p. 12.
[105] *The Times*, 28 December 1865; 29 March 1866; 10 May 1866.
[106] *The Economist*, 16 June 1866, p. 698.
[107] *The Economist*, 2 March 1867, p. 234; Holmes and Green, *Midland*, pp. 43–5.
[108] Clapham, *Bank of England*, vol. 2, p. 266.
[109] Clapham, *Bank of England*, vol. 2, p. 266.
[110] *The Economist*, 23 June 1866, pp. 730–1.
[111] *The Economist*, 24 November 1866, p. 1361.

induced to take shares in the company when it converted from a partnership to a limited-liability company in 1865. The House of Lords ruled against this shareholder on 15 August 1867, thereby underpinning the rights of creditors to claim unpaid capital.[112] According to *The Times* editorial, had the House of Lords not done so, many joint-stock companies would have faced runs by their creditors and ultimate ruination.[113] In a subsequent case, the directors of Overend, Gurney and Co. were cleared of knowingly and fraudulently deceiving their investors.[114]

The first British commercial bank to fail was Barned's Banking Company Ltd., on 18 April 1866.[115] Barned's had incorporated as a limited-liability company only eight months before and, as with Overend, Gurney and Co., it had been formed to take over an existing partnership – that is, the banking business of J. Barned and Co. The similarities did not cease there because it appears that the bank was not in great financial health before it was floated. After it failed, shareholders commenced legal action (which proved unsuccessful) against Charles Mozley and Lewin Barned Mozley, two of the original partners of J. Barned and Co. and who subsequently became directors of the new limited-liability bank.[116] The shareholders of Barned's Banking Co. Ltd. had to pay a call of £40 per share on the bank's unpaid capital to cover the substantial deficit between the bank's assets and liabilities, and it appears that the creditors were never fully paid.[117]

The first joint-stock bank to fail after the collapse of Overend, Gurney and Co. was the English Joint Stock Bank Ltd., on 11 May 1866. This bank began as the South Eastern Banking Company Ltd. in January 1864 and quickly developed a large branch network, with twenty-seven branches, £200,000 of paid-up capital and approximately 485 shareholders by 1865. As part of its liquidation, calls of £8 per share on the bank's unpaid capital were made on shareholders, meaning that the average shareholder had to pay £329.[118] The bank's creditors were paid in full. Three directors and Samuel Finney, the general manager, were tried for attempting to defraud shareholders by issuing false accounts and statements. Although the evidence to prosecute the three directors was insufficient, Finney was tried in a criminal court for his part in

---

[112] *The Times*, 16 August 1867, p. 7; *The Economist*, 17 August 1867, p. 817.
[113] *The Times*, 17 August 1867, p. 9.   [114] *The Economist*, 25 December 1869, p. 1522.
[115] *The Manchester Guardian*, 21 April 1866, p. 4. Several colonial and overseas banks that had been established in London in the post-1862 promotional boom failed in 1866.
[116] *The Times*, 10 December 1869, p. 8.
[117] *The Manchester Guardian*, 24 December 1866, p. 4; *The Times*, 10 December 1869, p. 8.
[118] *The Observer*, 30 May 1869, p. 7.

the fraud.[119] It also appears that the directors attempted to support the bank's share price from about November 1865 onwards by using the bank's own funds to buy its shares.[120]

The next joint-stock bank to fail was the Bank of London (established in 1855), on 24 May 1866. With a paid-up capital of £400,000, this bank had made a number of large and imprudent advances; for example, the Atlantic and Great Western Railway defaulted on a £500,000 loan.[121] Just before its collapse, the Bank of London reached an agreement to transfer its business to the Consolidated Bank Ltd. However, due to legal difficulties regarding the preferential treatment of creditors, the Consolidated had to rescind the agreement and temporarily enter into voluntarily liquidation. Nevertheless, the Consolidated was solvent and reopened in June 1866.[122] All of the creditors of the Bank of London were repaid and its shareholders received £4.25 per share.[123]

By far the largest bank to fail in the 1866 crisis was the Birmingham Banking Company (established in 1829). It was the senior bank in the West Midlands and had safely negotiated previous crises.[124] When it closed on 14 July 1866, its liabilities were £1.8 million against a paid-up capital of £280,000. The bank was subsequently reconstructed under the 1862 Companies Act as a limited-liability company, and it reopened for business in August 1866.

The Birmingham Banking Company failed because of mismanagement and failures in governance, which resulted in a debt of £75,000 by the bank's previous manager and substantial loans to five of its directors.[125] Through their attorneys, the directors of the Birmingham Banking Company issued a letter stating that (1) they did not know how bad things had been in terms of the bank's assets; (2) directors had not been dumping their shares before the bank's closure – some directors had even been buying shares; (3) seven of the bank's twelve directors had not borrowed from the bank; and (4) the directors as a group had loaned the bank £75,000 to see it through its difficulties.[126]

The Preston Banking Company (established in 1844) suspended payment on 19 July 1866 following a run on it, which may have been triggered by depositor fears following the closure of the Birmingham

---

[119] *The Times*, 8 June 1869, p. 10.   [120] *The Times*, 20 April 1869, p. 12.

[121] Gregory, *The Westminster Bank*, vol. 2, p. 63.

[122] Gregory, *The Westminster Bank*, vol. 2, pp. 57–62.

[123] Gregory, *The Westminster Bank*, vol. 2, p. 64.

[124] Holmes and Green, *Midland*, p. 47.

[125] Crick and Wadsworth, *A Hundred Years of Joint Stock Banking*, p. 69.

[126] HSBC Archives, 16.F.02, Press Cuttings Relating to Birmingham Banking Company.

Banking Company five days earlier.[127] This bank had made substantial loans totalling £400,000 to two businesses that subsequently failed due to the cotton famine.[128] Because the bank's paid-up capital was only £100,000, this concentrated lending was the ultimate source of its difficulties.[129] Nevertheless, within five weeks, the bank had increased its paid-up capital to £239,000 and had resumed business.[130]

The last casualty of the 1866 panic was the Royal Bank of Liverpool (also known as the Liverpool Royal Bank), which had been founded in 1836 and had suspended payments during the 1847 crisis. This bank failed on 21 October 1867 essentially because it had advanced extraordinary amounts to two firms that became insolvent.[131] In addition, not only were the two paid directors heavily in debt to their bank for sums that they could not repay; a brother of the bank's manager also could not repay his large debt to the bank.[132]

1878–1879

Unlike the previous crises of the nineteenth century, the crisis of 1878–9 was not preceded by an expansion of credit, speculative activity or a joint-stock promotion boom. In fact, Britain was at the beginning of the 'Great Depression', a prolonged period of deflation lasting from 1873 to 1896.[133] Also, unlike most other banking crises, the 1878–9 crisis was preceded by low economic growth, with GDP in the year before the crisis growing by only 0.5 per cent.

The central event of the 1878–9 crisis was the failure of the City of Glasgow Bank (CGB) in October 1878. By the mid 1870s, the CGB was a prominent bank with 123 branches (i.e., the third largest network in the United Kingdom) and had amassed £8,489,000 in deposits. Such was the extent of the failure that one commentator at the time called it 'a calamity so unlooked for, so huge and disastrous, that it riveted men's gaze and made their hearts stand still and we shall all remember it to our dying day as a landmark in the history of our generation.'[134] Almost eighty years after the event, a son of Howard Lloyd (of Lloyds Bank)

---

[127] *The Manchester Guardian*, 20 July 1866, p. 3.
[128] Orbell and Turton, *British Banking*, p. 442.
[129] *The Manchester Guardian*, 20 July 1866, p. 3.
[130] Orbell and Turton, *British Banking*, p. 442.
[131] *The Manchester Guardian*, 21 October 1867, p. 7.
[132] *The Manchester Guardian*, 12 November 1867, p. 5.
[133] See Saul, *The Myth of the Great Depression*.   [134] Wilson, *Banking Reform*, p. 46.

recalled as one of his earliest childhood memories the 'sense of anxiety and depression' occasioned by the CGB failure.[135]

When the CGB came under pressure in the money markets in late summer of 1878, it was urged to retire some of its acceptances, but other banks refused to assist it.[136] On 30 September 1878, a meeting in Edinburgh of the general managers of other Scottish banks received a communication from the CGB directors indicating that its annual report, published three months earlier, had been falsified. The CGB directors closed their bank on the following day and, on 3 October, independent accountants were appointed to examine the bank's books. The report of those accountants, published on 18 October, found that although the bank's paid-up capital of £1 million and shareholder reserves of £450,000 had been exhausted, the remaining deficit between the bank's assets and liabilities to the public was a staggering £5,190,983, 11 shillings 3 pence.[137] To put this loss in perspective, it was approximately 4 per cent of Scottish GDP and about 0.45 per cent of British GDP for 1878.[138]

The next day, 19 October, the directors, manager and secretary of the bank were arrested and charged with fraud. At their trial, Robert Stronach, the bank's general manager, and Lewis Potter, one of the bank's directors, were found guilty of falsifying the bank's balance sheets; they each were given an eighteen-month prison sentence.[139] Five other directors were found guilty of publishing balance sheets that they knew to be false; as a result, were imprisoned for eight months.[140]

Why did the CGB fail so spectacularly? From its inception, the CGB had been aggressive in expanding its branch network and deposit base.[141] The bank's asset-management strategy was dissimilar to that of other banks in that it (1) held relatively low amounts of secondary reserves in the form of saleable securities, (2) had engaged heavily in international financing via the discount market, and (3) had invested heavily in an American railroad and land in New Zealand.[142] The bank's risk-loving asset-management policy also was apparent from its concentrated loan portfolio, with almost 45 per cent of its loans in the hands of three

---

[135] Sayers, *Lloyds Bank*, p. 211.   [136] Kerr, *History of Banking in Scotland*, p. 294.

[137] Couper, *Report of the Trial*, p. 2.

[138] Scottish GDP based on Crafts, 'Regional GDP in Britain', p. 58.

[139] Couper, *Report of the Trial*, p. 463.

[140] Couper, *Report of the Trial*, p. 463; Rosenblum, 'The failure of the City of Glasgow Bank', p. 291.

[141] Checkland, *Scottish Banking*, p. 469; French, *Unlimited Liability*, p. 8; Kerr, *History of Banking in Scotland*, p. 295.

[142] Checkland, *Scottish Banking*, pp. 470–1; French, *Unlimited Liability*, p. 8.

borrowers and insufficient collateral attached to many of the loans.[143] Ultimately, the risky profile of the CGB can be traced to its governance structure: the directors of the bank had a limited stake in it and several owed it large sums of money.[144]

In banking circles, the CGB was viewed with suspicion and regarded as a risky institution.[145] Rait comments that unlike the Western Bank, which had failed in 1857, 'the City of Glasgow Bank was never highly esteemed outside the circle of its dupes and seems to have been a long-continued fraud'.[146] According to Clapham, the Bank of England had never trusted the CGB.[147]

Notably, the impact of the CGB failure on the Scottish banking system was mitigated by the action of the other Scottish banks.[148] Not only did they resolve at once to accept CGB's notes, they also allowed its depositors (except those who were shareholders) to transfer their deposits, some of which would be made immediately available.[149]

The Caledonian Banking Company, a bank that had a branch network in the north of Scotland, had the misfortune to be the registered owner of four CGB shares at the time of its failure; Caledonian had taken the shares as security against an advance. On realising this fact, the Caledonian's shareholders are said to have started selling their shares because joint and several unlimited liability meant that they were ultimately liable for the CGB debts. This caused the Caledonian's share price to fall from £7.63 at the end of September 1878 to £2.00 by November of that year. In response to the concern that shares might be transferred to 'men of straw', the liquidators of the CGB forced the Caledonian to stop trading on 5 December 1878 and to begin the winding-up process.[150] However, the bank reopened in June 1879, having paid £11,000 in calls on its four CGB shares.

The only other major bank to fail in 1878–9 was the West of England and South Wales District Bank, which by the time of its failure had approximately 1,800 shareholders, 42 branches and £4.8 million in deposits. Its liquidators estimated that the deficit between its assets and liabilities was about £400,000, with its paid-up capital of £750,000 and

---

[143] Checkland, *Scottish Banking*, p. 470.
[144] Acheson and Turner, 'The death blow to unlimited liability'.
[145] Wilson, *Banking Reform*, p. 52; Saville, *Bank of Scotland*, p. 421. See also *The Bankers' Magazine*, Nov 1878, p. 917. The same was true of many investors (Acheson and Turner, 'Investor behaviour', p. 197).
[146] Rait, *The History of the Union Bank of Scotland*, p. 310.
[147] Clapham, *Bank of England*, vol. 2, p. 309.
[148] Fleming, 'On the theory and practice of banking'.
[149] *The Bankers' Magazine*, November 1878, p. 921.
[150] French, *Unlimited Liability*, p. 12.

reserve of £161,000 having been dissipated.[151] Similar to the CGB case, loans had been concentrated, accounts had been falsified and attempts had been made to conceal the real financial position of the bank from its shareholders.[152] Five of the bank's directors went through a criminal trial; however, at that trial, the jury found that the directors had not knowingly defrauded the shareholders.[153]

Similar to the CGB failure, other banks in the region were willing to help the customers of the West of England Bank. *The Manchester Guardian* remarked that 'this prompt and timely action will no doubt do much to abate any disquietude that may have arisen in that district'.[154] Another similarity with the CGB failure was that a relief fund was established to help distressed and destitute shareholders: several banks contributed £100 to the fund and Sir Stafford Northcote, the Chancellor of the Exchequer, contributed £20.[155]

In addition to the West of England and South Wales District Bank, four other English joint-stock banks failed during the 1878–9 crisis, but all of them were small and three were relatively new concerns. The Commercial Bank of Manchester Ltd. (established in 1875) failed in November 1878.[156] The Chesterfield and North Derbyshire Bank (established in 1834), which had advanced £35,000 (i.e., 100 per cent of its paid-up capital) to one brewery that had failed, also collapsed in late 1878.[157] The bank's general manager, George Holland (who was declared insane after the bank's failure), had kept two sets of books – a fact to which directors had been oblivious.[158] Criminal charges against the directors for knowingly issuing false financial statements subsequently were dropped.[159]

The Metropolitan Bank (established 1867), which had closed in 1866 and been revived, was voluntarily taken by its directors into winding-up court in early 1879 and was again resurrected, this time as the Royal Exchange Bank.[160] The Western District Bank Ltd. (established in 1875) failed in July 1879, and it appears that at its closure, the bank's assets covered its liabilities to the public.[161]

---

[151] *The Manchester Guardian*, 7 January 1880, p. 5.
[152] *The Manchester Guardian*, 28 April 1880, p. 6.   [153] *The Times*, 6 May 1880, p. 13.
[154] *The Manchester Guardian*, 11 December 1878, p. 6.
[155] *The Times*, 4 January 1879, p. 6.
[156] *The Manchester Guardian*, 30 November 1878, p. 7.
[157] The bank was taken over by the Crompton and Evans' Union Bank in June 1879 (Gregory, *The Westminster Bank*, vol. 2, p. 83).
[158] *The Manchester Guardian*, 14 March 1879, p. 6.
[159] *The Manchester Guardian*, 14 March 1879, p. 6.
[160] *The Manchester Guardian*, 28 January 1879, p. 6; Orbell and Turton, *British Banking*, p. 460.
[161] *The Manchester Guardian*, 24 July 1879, p. 4; 29 July 1879, p. 4; 4 August 1879, p. 8.

Collins argues that the 1878 crisis was a severe liquidity crisis across England as well as Scotland, featuring a sharp contraction in deposits, an increased holding of reserves and an increase in the cash-to-deposit ratio, which began weeks before the failure of the CGB.[162] Some banks experienced significant withdrawals after the CGB collapse, but they subsided quickly. For example, the North and South Wales Bank experienced a drain of £1 million of its deposits (i.e., one fifth of its total) in the few days after the CGB collapse; however, the drain was more in response to false rumours that the bank had been manipulating its share price.[163] Notably, however, Scottish banks did not experience severe bank-wide panic withdrawals after the CGB collapse.[164]

In addition to the CGB and the West of England Bank, other banks that failed were all small and typically young concerns; despite liquidity pressures, there was never any threat of a systemic collapse in 1878–9. This may have been purely serendipitous: the absence of an external drain and a stagnant economy before the crisis may have contributed to preventing a system-wide collapse. However, the economy had been in the doldrums for several years before the 1878–9 crisis and the banking system was exposed to the decline of certain key industries. In addition, the collapse of the largest bank to ever fail in the United Kingdom before 2008 must have been a substantial test of the systemic stability of the UK banking system.

1974

The long period of banking stability that Britain enjoyed after 1879 lasted for almost a century, without even a hint of banking instability during the Great Depression of the 1930s. However, this century of banking tranquillity ended in 1974 with a crisis centred on finance companies that had sprung up in the 1960s and that had originally focused on hire purchase and consumer lending or some form of stock-market activity.[165] These companies provided an intermediary function in that they raised most of their funds on the expanding wholesale money markets and used them to make equity investments and to lend large sums to institutions and individuals to whom conventional banks were reluctant to lend (i.e., mainly property developers and second mortgages).[166] These finance companies were referred to as wholesale, secondary or fringe banks because

---

[162] Collins, 'The banking crisis of 1878'.
[163] Crick and Wadsworth, *A Hundred Years of Joint Stock Banking*, p. 190.
[164] Crick and Wadsworth, *A Hundred Years of Joint Stock Banking*, p. 190; Rait, *The History of the Union Bank of Scotland*, p. 313.
[165] Reid, *Secondary Banking Crisis*, p. 35.   [166] *The Banker*, February 1974, p. 88.

they obtained funds on the wholesale and secondary money markets and they operated on the fringes of the banking system. Secondary banks 'came in a variety of breeds, but the formula was basically the same: borrow short and cheaply and lend long and expensively'.[167]

The growth of the secondary-banking sector in the 1960s was stimulated by two developments. First, the money market – which the secondary banks tapped for funds – had expanded rapidly in the 1960s with the development of the interbank market and the market for certificates of deposit (CDs).[168] The second development was the passing of the 1967 Companies Act, of which Section 123 allowed the Board of Trade to certify that particular finance companies were operating as banks.[169]

The clearing banks were frustrated in their ability to compete with these banks because their own lending was constrained by government, whereas secondary banks were not subject to constraints; therefore, they could lend to borrowers that conventional banks turned away. In addition, the deposit rates of the clearing banks were lower than secondary banks due to the interest-rate cartel. To level the competitive playing field as well as to stimulate the economy, in September 1971, the Conservative Government launched Competition and Credit Control, which removed constraints on bank lending. This resulted in a money boom during the next two and a half years, as well as a massive expansion of the secondary-banking system. As shown in Table 4.4, the major secondary banks experienced substantial growth in the late 1960s and their assets grew phenomenally between 1971 and 1973.

The rapid growth in lending from late 1971 onwards is illustrated in Table 4.5, which shows a particularly rapid expansion of M4 lending in 1972 and 1973. Between October 1971 and December 1973, sterling advances to UK resident borrowers by the clearing banks grew from £5,367 million to £11,379 million; however, throughout the same period, advances made by the secondary banks grew from £395 million to £3,366 million.[170] This growth in lending was mirrored in the wholesale money markets in the same period, with the CD market growing from £1,860 million to £6,000 million and the interbank market growing from £2,000 million to £7,700 million.[171]

Controls on property development were relaxed at the beginning of the 1970s, resulting in a surge in the demand for finance among property developers. Consequently, a large proportion of the huge increase in lending was channelled to the property sector; bank advances increased

---

[167] *The Guardian*, 17 May 1974, p. 16.   [168] Reid, *Secondary Banking Crisis*, pp. 24–6.
[169] Reid, *Secondary Banking Crisis*, p. 49.   [170] Reid, *Secondary Banking Crisis*, p. 60.
[171] Reid, *Secondary Banking Crisis*, p. 62.

Table 4.4 *Profile and crisis experience of major secondary banks*

Name	Established	Gross assets 1965 (£m)	Gross assets 1971 (£m)	Gross assets 1973 (£m)	Pre-tax profit/loss 1975 (£m)	Peak share price in 1972 (£)	Share price at end 1974 (£)	Lifeboat loans (£m)	Post-crisis experience
Burston Group	1955	n/a	70	100		2.24	0.16	25.5	Receiver appointed in February 1975
Cannon Street Investments	1968	0.4	3	122	0.70	1.19	0.06	40.0	Receiver appointed in September 1974
Cedar Holdings	1958	8.0	18	128	−2.70	0.99	0.13	50.0	Capital reconstruction in 1975 and Lifeboat loans repaid
Edward Bates and Sons	1967	n/a	24	74	−16.3	3.37	0.20	2.5#	Reconstructed
First National Finance Corporation	1963	20.0	182	543	−83.2	1.39	0.04	350.0	Capital reconstruction in 1975 and still had £250 million of Lifeboat loans in 1980
J. H. Vavasseur	1968	n/a	12	52	−3.90	4.00	0.03	10.2	Capital reconstructed twice and Lifeboat loans repaid in 1979
Keyser Ullmann Holdings	1962	n/a	13	161	−59.20	3.85	0.36	65.0	Loans repaid in 1976
London and County Securities Group	1961	3.6	15	129	n/a	3.58	0.40	39.8	Receiver appointed in March 1975
Mercantile Credit	1934	12.0	243	377	−10.80	1.47	0.11	167.0	Loans repaid and taken over by Barclays in 1975
Slater Walker Securities	1964	20.0	280	588	−39.90	3.09	0.35	0.0	Received £54.8 million loan from Bank of England and SWS bank taken over by the Bank in 1977
Triumph Investment Trust	1964	n/a	61	203	−19.40	1.50	0.05	30.2	Receiver appointed in November 1974
United Dominions Trust	1922	265.0	466	896	−53.50	1.59	0.13	430.0	Remaining support loans repaid in 1980; taken over by TSBs in 1981

Source: Reid, *Secondary Banking Crisis*, pp. 40–1; 153–69; Capie, *The Bank of England*, pp. 573–5.
Notes: n/a = not available; # = plus DM7.1 million and $67.3 million.

Table 4.5 *Quarterly house-price inflation, RPI, M4 lending and GDP,*
1971–1975

		ONS annual house-price change (%)	Nationwide annual house-price change (%)	Real GDP growth quarter on quarter (%)	RPI (annualised) (%)	M4 lending growth rate (annualised) (%)
1971	Q1	8.8	8.3	−1.40	8.8	11.0
	Q2	10.2	10.3	1.20	10.3	9.6
	Q3	11.7	16.3	1.44	9.9	12.9
	Q4	16.6	20.7	0.33	9.0	17.5
1972	Q1	21.0	26.7	−0.39	7.6	24.1
	Q2	28.7	33.6	2.27	6.1	31.9
	Q3	39.7	41.0	0.65	7.0	32.7
	Q4	43.5	42.4	1.88	7.7	35.2
1973	Q1	50.4	39.8	5.23	8.2	32.4
	Q2	44.2	34.7	0.71	9.3	26.9
	Q3	33.8	24.2	−1.01	9.3	27.6
	Q4	26.2	24.0	−0.17	10.6	26.7
1974	Q1	14.9	18.2	−2.34	13.5	22.9
	Q2	9.7	13.5	1.98	16.5	21.6
	Q3	3.7	10.5	1.45	17.1	18.6
	Q4	3.9	4.5	−1.39	19.1	13.0
1975	Q1	3.0	4.6	0.25	21.2	10.8
	Q2	5.5	7.0	−1.49	26.1	8.3
	Q3	7.7	8.2	−0.39	26.6	5.6
	Q4	7.3	10.6	1.62	24.9	5.7

Sources: Data for Retail Prices Index, ONS annual house-price change and real GDP are from *Office for National Statistics*. Nationwide annual house-price change data are from the *Nationwide Building Society*. M4 lending data are from the Bank of England.
Notes: The house-price-change data are in nominal terms and based on samples of all houses. The M4 lending data are not seasonally adjusted.

by 614 per cent between February 1971 and February 1974.[172] By the end of 1973, secondary banks had overtaken clearing banks as the main lenders for property development.[173] As shown in Table 4.5, this major increase in lending to the property sector was accompanied by substantial increases in house prices from the last quarter of 1971 until the last quarter of 1973. Thereafter, house prices declined significantly in real terms.

[172] Capie, *The Bank of England*, p. 527.   [173] Reid, *Secondary Banking Crisis*, p. 61.

In the summer of 1973, the Bank of England became concerned about the position of London and County Securities, one of the larger secondary banks.[174] London and County offered full banking services (including risky second mortgages) through its network of twenty-two branches operating in retail stores throughout the United Kingdom.[175] It also had £11.2 million (i.e., 12.7 per cent of its deposits) invested in equity stakes in several industrial and commercial companies. In addition, through one of its wholly owned subsidiaries, it had £7.4 million in development property. All of these risks would have been acceptable if they had been financed by shareholder capital, but London and County's deposit-to-capital ratio was only 10 per cent. To compound this risky profile, London and County had made loans of £2.7 million on the security of its own shares and had made substantial loans to directors; for example, Robert Potel, the deputy chairman, had a £1 million loan.[176] As the money markets tightened following the monetary squeeze, London and County Securities needed assistance from the Bank of England by the end of November 1973; this triggered a run on other secondary banks, with small depositors queuing up outside the branches.[177]

The first public sign that there was a wider problem with the secondary-banking system came when it was announced on 20 December 1973 that trade in the shares of Cedar Holdings, a leading secondary bank that specialised in second mortgages, had been suspended following a £72-million support package arranged by the Bank of England in a nineteen-hour meeting fuelled by ham sandwiches and whiskey. Following this announcement, the shares of many secondary banks fell as panic set in on the stock market. Consequently, on 21 December, the Bank of England convened a secret meeting with the heads of the Big Four clearing banks to arrange an emergency liquidity-support scheme to aid the secondary banks and to prevent any spillovers into the commercial-banking system. Because deposits were being withdrawn from the secondary banks and deposited in the clearing banks, the plan – which was referred to as the 'Lifeboat operation' – was to recycle these deposits back to the secondary banks.

The secondary-banking crisis occurred because institutions on the fringe of the banking system engaged in risk shifting by lending their deposits – which had been garnered mostly from the money markets – to the historically risky property sector. The risk taken by secondary banks was compounded by the facts that at times they took equity stakes in

---

[174] Capie, *The Bank of England*, p. 531; *The Observer*, 12 May 1974, p. 15.
[175] *The Banker*, January 1974, p. 14.   [176] *The Banker*, January 1974, p. 15.
[177] *The Guardian*, 17 May 1974, p. 16.

property developments and that they typically had loan-to-value ratios to the property sector ranging from 90 to 100 per cent, leaving them extremely vulnerable to the decline in property values in 1974.[178] During the entire episode, however, there was never any doubt about the stability of the clearing banks, other than a rumour at the end of 1974 that the National Westminster Bank was receiving support from the Bank of England. This rumour was vigorously denied by the bank and proved to be unfounded.

2007–2008

The common view is that the 2007–8 crisis can be traced back to global macro imbalances that emerged from *c.* 2000 onwards, where the high savings rates in China, Japan and oil-exporting economies resulted in these economies accumulating claims on other advanced economies, such as the United Kingdom and the United States.[179] One result of these imbalances was that real-interest rates and the real rate on Treasury bills in the United Kingdom fell from 2000 onwards and reached historically low levels (Table 4.6).

The low real-interest rates had two proximate effects. First, they stimulated the demand for credit, particularly for residential mortgages. As shown in Table 4.6, the private debt-to-GDP ratio increased substantially from 2000 to 2008; most of this increase came from households rather than firms.[180] The last column in Table 4.6 shows that relative to incomes, household debt in the United Kingdom grew substantially during the 2000s. Table 4.7 shows that between 2000 and 2007, the average size of residential-mortgage advances doubled, the total gross mortgage advances made by all financial intermediaries and the total gross mortgage advances made by banks trebled in the same period, and the outstanding number of buy-to-let mortgages mushroomed.

The second proximate effect of low real-interest rates was that they stimulated the demand for yield uplift among investors who preferred to invest in fixed-rate instruments.[181] This demand was met by financial innovation in the form of complex securitised credit products, which were AAA-rated securities that paid a higher yield than conventional first-class fixed-income securities. To meet this demand, banks and shadow banking

---

[178] Reid, *Secondary Banking Crisis*, pp. 64–5.
[179] *Turner Review*, pp. 11–12.   [180] *Turner Review*, p. 13.
[181] *Turner Review*, p. 14; House of Commons Treasury Committee, *Banking Crisis: Dealing with the Failure of the UK Banks* (London: Stationery Office, 2009), p. 12.

Table 4.6 *UK household indebtedness and interest rates, 2000–2010*

	Bank of England base rate (%)	Real-interest rate (%)	Real rate on Treasury bills (%)	Private-debt-to-GDP ratio (%)	Household-gross-debt-to-income ratio (%)
2000	6.00	2.98	3.0	148.2	100.40
2001	4.00	3.28	4.4	157.3	104.53
2002	4.00	1.03	1.0	167.5	114.07
2003	3.75	0.92	0.8	173.0	122.90
2004	4.75	1.22	0.9	182.9	135.32
2005	4.50	2.24	2.5	194.4	137.48
2006	5.00	0.55	0.3	206.3	146.39
2007	5.50	1.39	1.6	205.7	151.77
2008	2.00	1.04	4.1	221.2	153.61
2009	0.50	−1.86	−1.7	219.7	148.56
2010	0.50	−4.08	−4.1	209.2	143.07

Sources: Private-debt-to-GDP and household-gross-debt-to-income ratio data are from Eurostat. The Bank of England base rate is from the Bank. The inflation data used to calculate the real-interest rate, as well as the real rate on Treasury bills, are from Dimson, Marsh and Staunton, *Credit Suisse Global Investment Returns Sourcebook 2011*, p. 165.
Notes: Based on year-end data. The Bank of England base rate is the repo rate until 2006 and the official bank rate thereafter. The real-interest rate is based on the Bank of England base rate adjusted for inflation.

Table 4.7 *UK mortgage market, 2000–2009*

	Average size of mortgage advance made by banks and building societies (£ million)	Gross mortgage advances (£ million)	Gross mortgage advances made by banks (£ million)	Outstanding number of buy-to-let mortgages
2000	70,606	119,794	83,335	120,300
2001	76,258	160,123	119,765	185,000
2002	84,489	220,737	162,423	275,000
2003	98,254	277,342	194,959	417,500
2004	109,920	291,249	202,756	576,000
2005	122,049	288,280	201,833	699,400
2006	138,407	345,355	234,390	835,900
2007	150,405	362,758	247,147	1,026,000
2008	145,666	254,022	192,940	1,156,000
2009	137,028	143,276	118,458	n/a

Source: Mortgage data are from the Department for Communities and Local Government, available at http://www.communities.gov.uk/housing/housingresearch.
Notes: Based on year-end data. n/a = not available.

institutions (e.g., broker dealers and investment banks) pooled residential mortgages and other debts (e.g., credit-card debt and car loans) into a portfolio and packaged them into fixed-income securities that were sold to investors. The resultant securities were known as collateralised debt obligations (CDOs) or, if the portfolio of assets consisted of mortgages, mortgage-backed securities (MBSs). Subprime mortgages, which are mortgages to individuals with low credit scores, were also pooled and mixed in with small amounts of other mortgages and debts. Because it was assumed – wrongly, with the benefit of hindsight – that the risks of default on individual subprime mortgages were uncorrelated, the rating agencies gave high investment-grade ratings to those pools of subprime mortgages. The risk of the MBSs could be reduced and AAA ratings could be gained by mixing credit default swaps (CDS) – which, in effect, are insurance contracts against the risk of default by an MBS – into the pool of mortgage assets.

Securitisation experienced an unprecedented period of growth between 2000 and 2007, particularly in the United States. Such was the growth that by 2007, banks held only about 30 per cent of US home mortgages in terms of value, with the other approximate 70 per cent of outstanding mortgage debt being securitised.[182] In the United Kingdom, securitisation issuance increased from around £20 billion in 2000 to £180 billion in 2007, when 18 per cent of UK mortgage credit was funded through securitisation.[183]

The combined effect of increases in securitisation and in regular mortgage lending resulted in a boom in the UK housing market. As shown in Table 4.8, real average UK house prices increased twofold between 2000 and 2007, with the price-to-earnings ratio increasing from 3.22 to 5.68 in the same period. Concurrently, commercial property prices in the United Kingdom increased by 50 per cent.

From early March 2007 onwards, it became apparent that there were problems in the US subprime market, with lenders announcing losses, higher-than-anticipated delinquencies on subprime mortgages, and failures of large subprime lenders. As a result, the market for securitised credit effectively came to a halt in the summer of 2007. In addition, because no one was certain of who held subprime MBSs or CDSs on subprime MBSs, the LIBOR (i.e., the rate on the interbank market) increased and the market for interbank deposits effectively froze on 9 August 2007.[184] This created a problem for UK banks, which during

---

[182] Adrian and Shin, 'The changing nature of financial intermediation', fig. 4.
[183] *Turner Review*, p. 14.
[184] House of Commons Treasury Committee, *The Run on the Rock*, p. 35.

Table 4.8 *UK housing market, 2000–2010*

	Real average UK house prices (£)	Price-to-earnings ratio	Real change in house prices (%)	House sales in England and Wales (millions)
2000	85,579	3.22	1.34	1.139
2001	98,162	3.58	14.70	1.236
2002	116,874	4.30	19.06	1.327
2003	133,414	4.81	14.15	1.211
2004	147,831	5.22	10.81	1.227
2005	152,989	5.32	3.49	1.021
2006	158,930	5.49	3.88	1.281
2007	163,386	5.68	2.80	1.247
2008	131,671	4.47	−19.41	0.640
2009	135,668	4.67	3.04	0.615
2010	127,139	4.50	−6.29	0.656

Sources: Real average UK house prices, price-to-earnings ratio and real changes on house prices are from the Halifax. House sales in England and Wales are based on Land Registry data and are from the Department for Communities and Local Government, available at http://www.communities.gov.uk/housing/housingresearch.
Notes: Based on year-end data. Real house prices are based on 2000.

the 2000s had become increasingly reliant on wholesale funding markets and which required mortgages to be securitised.

The continued bad news about subprime mortgages and the decline in the UK residential- and commercial-property markets resulted in Northern Rock's nationalisation on 17 February 2008. Then, on 7 September 2008, Fannie Mae and Freddie Mac were taken into conservatorship by US federal authorities. One week later, Lehman Brothers collapsed and financial markets panicked.

Table 4.9 lists both the share-price depreciation of the major UK banks during the financial crisis and their crisis experience. Two of the major banks listed in Table 4.9 (i.e., Northern Rock and Bradford and Bingley) were in such trouble that they were wholly nationalised by the government. As shown in Table 4.9, the Royal Bank of Scotland, HBOS and Lloyds-TSB – banks that were ranked second, third and fifth, respectively, in the UK in terms of 2006 assets – all required a major injection of capital from the government and would have failed otherwise. The Alliance and Leicester was ultimately saved through its takeover by Santander; otherwise, it too would have required a substantial injection of capital from the government.

	Total assets in 2006 (£ million)	Asset growth 2000–2007 (%)	Loans/ deposits in 2000	Loans/ deposits in 2007	Share-price depreciation (February 2007–February 2009) (%)	Crisis experience
Abbey	191,805	2.0	0.92	1.49	–	No direct government support required.
Alliance and Leicester	67,401	130.0	0.87	1.12[a]	74.0[b]	16 September 2008: Shareholders agree to takeover by Santander.
Barclays Bank	996,787	288.0	0.95	1.00	87.0	31 October 2008: Bank announced an injection of capital of £7.3 billion from Middle Eastern sovereign wealth funds. Existing shareholders were not given preemption rights.
Bradford and Bingley	45,354	111.0	1.10	1.63	100.0	29 September 2008: Business taken into public ownership, with retail branches and deposits transferred to Abbey.
HBOS	591,029	114.0	1.25	1.54	93.4[c]	18 September 2008: Lloyds–TSB takeover of bank was announced and completed in January 2009.
HSBC	440,760	231.00	0.45	0.46	44.9	No direct government support required.
Lloyds–TSB	345,664	62.0	0.96	1.25	89.8	13 October 2008: Announced a £17 billion capital-raising programme. Shares were not taken up so the government took up the remaining shares and acquired a 43% stake in the bank.
Northern Rock	101,010	348.0	1.01	3.18	100.0	17 September 2007: Government guarantee of deposits. 17 February 2008: Nationalised by the government.
Royal Bank of Scotland	871,432	494.0	0.94	1.05	95.6	13 October 2008: £20 billion capital-raising programme underwritten by the Treasury announced. Only 0.24 per cent of shares taken up by the public; government had to take up the remaining shares and acquired a 57.9 per cent stake in the bank.

Sources: Total assets for 2006 are from bank annual reports. Share-price depreciation is based on data from Thomson Reuters Datastream and OSIRIS BvD. Crisis experience is from the House of Commons Treasury Committee, *Banking Crisis*. Abbey profits for 2008 and 2009 are from its 2009 Annual Report.

Notes: [a] If deposits from other banks are omitted, this becomes 1.73. [b] Alliance and Leicester was taken over by Santander in September 2008. [c] HBOS was taken over by Lloyds–TSB in January 2009.

Why did five of the nine major UK banks fail in the 2007–8 crisis? As shown in Table 4.9, almost all banks grew rapidly in the 2000–7 period; however, growth is not necessarily a good predictor of the fate of banks during a crisis. What is clear from Table 4.9 is that several banks funded their loans through volatile wholesale markets rather than deposits. This resulted in a doubling of the median leverage in the UK banking system and its growth from about 300 per cent of GDP in 2000 to about 500 per cent in 2007.[185] In particular, Northern Rock, Bradford and Bingley, Alliance and Leicester, and HBOS were increasingly dependent on the 'permanent availability of a large-scale interbank funding and/or their continuous ability to securitise and sell down rapidly accumulating credit assets, particularly in the mortgage market'.[186] The collapse of Northern Rock well before the worst of the crisis is not surprising, given its high loan-to-deposits ratio (see Table 4.9) and its total dependency on the wholesale markets and securitisation of mortgages.[187] The Royal Bank of Scotland had a weak liquidity position relative to its peers in that much of its funding was very short term and from the overnight money market.[188]

Ultimately, however, the liquidity problems at these banks were simply the first manifestation of deeper problems on the asset side of their balance sheets. Most of the problems faced by UK banks came not from holding US subprime MBSs but rather from lending to the residential- and commercial-property sectors in the United Kingdom and Ireland.

Bradford and Bingley was heavily exposed to the risky buy-to-let and self-certified mortgage markets, with 60 per cent of its mortgage portfolio in the former and 20 per cent in the latter.[189] This bank, the smallest of the major banks, had an astonishing 20 per cent of the UK buy-to-let market.

Northern Rock also loaned to riskier parts of the mortgage market and on loan-to-value ratios close to or more than 100 per cent. The bank's infamous 'Together' mortgages, wherein individuals borrowed up to 125 per cent of the value of their home, attracted subprime borrowers and resulted in high levels of arrears in the subsequent downturn.[190] When the wholesale money markets and the securitisation system froze,

---

[185] 'Evolution of the UK banking system', *Bank of England Quarterly Bulletin* (2010), pp. 325, 329.
[186] *Turner Review*, p. 35.
[187] *The Run on the Rock*, p. 19; Shin, 'Reflections on Northern Rock'.
[188] *The Failure of the Royal Bank of Scotland*, p. 46.
[189] House of Commons Treasury Committee, *Banking Crisis*, p. 17.
[190] *The Daily Telegraph*, 5 August 2009.

Northern Rock was left holding many of these mortgages, which it had hoped to securitise and remove from its books.[191]

HBOS's problems derived from three of its major divisions. The impairments in its corporate division between 2008 and 2011 were estimated to be £25 billion.[192] Preliminary results for 2008 revealed that HBOS's corporate division lost £6.793 billion in that year alone, mainly on commercial-property loans. These huge losses occurred because the commercial-property market collapsed even further than the residential-property market in the eighteen months after June 2007: retail property had fallen to 2002 levels and the office market had fallen to 1998 levels.[193]

HBOS's corporate division had as its objective becoming the United Kingdom's best real-estate bank. To this end, it adopted three reckless strategies: (1) as well as providing traditional loans to the property sector, it offered mezzanine debt and equity financing; (2) it sought out subinvestment-grade lending; and (3) it had large individual credit exposures. (In 2008, one borrower had a £2.9-billion loan and nine had more than £1-billion loans; the contrast with 2002, when no single loan exceeded £1 million, is staggering.)[194]

HBOS's international division expanded rapidly and aggressively in Ireland and Australia; as a result, it became heavily exposed to the real-estate sector in both countries. Loan impairments in these two jurisdictions between 2008 and 2011 totalled £14.5 billion, and HBOS was the second-worst-performing bank in Ireland relative to the proportion of its loan book that was impaired.[195]

HBOS's treasury division invested heavily in asset-backed securities and credit derivatives in the years before the crisis. Losses on its structured-investment portfolio totalled £7.2 billion between 2008 and 2011, which alone would have required the recapitalisation of HBOS.[196]

Like HBOS, the Royal Bank of Scotland was heavily exposed to the commercial-property sector. This bank suffered cumulative impairment losses on loans and advances of £30.396 billion in the period 2008–10. Of these losses, 8 per cent came directly from residential mortgages and 34 per cent came directly from commercial-property lending.[197] Unlike

[191] Buckley, *Financial Crisis*, p. 202.
[192] Parliamentary Commission on Banking Standards, '*An Accident Waiting to Happen*': *The Failure of HBOS*, p. 12.
[193] *The Daily Telegraph*, 2 February 2009.
[194] Parliamentary Commission on Banking Standards, '*An Accident Waiting to Happen*': *The Failure of HBOS*, pp. 10–11.
[195] Parliamentary Commission on Banking Standards, '*An Accident Waiting to Happen*': *The Failure of HBOS*, pp. 14–15.
[196] Parliamentary Commission on Banking Standards, '*An Accident Waiting to Happen*': *The Failure of HBOS*, p. 16.
[197] *The Failure of the Royal Bank of Scotland*, p. 50.

other UK banks, the Royal Bank of Scotland also suffered substantial losses on its holdings of structured-credit products, which were composed primarily of US subprime mortgages. In 2008, the bank posted a loss of £34.3 billion, of which £12.2 billion came from its structured-credit products.[198]

According to its directors and insiders, Lloyds-TSB entered the crisis in a strong position because it had avoided the riskier parts of the lending market; the only reason that it needed an injection of capital from the government was its misjudged takeover of HBOS.[199] However, even if the merger had not happened, Lloyds-TSB still would have needed to raise capital of £7 billion, which most likely would have had to come from the government.[200]

The United Kingdom was not alone in experiencing a banking crisis in 2007–8. In addition to the United States, there was a severe banking crisis in at least fifteen European economies.[201] There were several noteworthy commonalities between these crises and the crisis in the United Kingdom. First, there was a rapid rise in property prices in many of these economies, fuelled by bank credit. Notably, this was also a common feature of the five largest advanced-economy crises of the recent era (i.e., Finland, 1991; Japan, 1992; Norway, 1987; Sweden, 1991; and Spain, 1977).[202] The second commonality was that there was a major expansion of credit, particularly to households, from 2000 onwards, with the result that households became more leveraged, particularly in Ireland and Spain. The third commonality was the subprime lending that was taking place, particularly in the United States, the United Kingdom and Ireland. Similar to the United States, Ireland, and Spain, the collapse of domestic property was a proximate cause of the banking crisis in the United Kingdom; whereas for other economies – most notably Belgium, France, Germany and the Netherlands – the proximate cause was exposure to the US mortgage market, primarily via structured-credit products.[203]

Conclusions

The purpose of this chapter was to develop narrative accounts of the major systemic crises of 1825–6 and 2007–8, as well as narrative accounts of the minor crises between these two major crises. The narrative account

---

[198] *The Failure of the Royal Bank of Scotland*, pp. 48–50.
[199] House of Commons Treasury Committee, *Banking Crisis*, p. 52.
[200] House of Commons Treasury Committee, *Banking Crisis*, pp. 52–3.
[201] Laeven and Valencia, 'Resolution of banking crises', p. 9.
[202] Claessens, Dell'Ariccia, Igan and Laeven, 'Lessons and policy implications', p. 5.
[203] Claessens, Dell'Ariccia, Igan and Laeven, 'Lessons and policy implications'; Hüfner, 'The German banking system'; Xiao, 'French banks'.

clearly demonstrates that the Great Crash of 2007–8 was unprecedented in the history of British banking; it also suggests that the categorisation of the 1825–6 and 2007–8 crises as major and the remainder as minor appears to be accurate. Indeed, the crisis narrative reveals that some of the minor banking crises should be viewed more as 'commercial crises' or 'money-market crises'.

In terms of precursors to crises, monetary or credit expansion in varying degrees seems to have taken place before six of the eight crises, and asset speculation is associated with five of the eight. However, in only three episodes is there evidence of the crisis being endogenous – that is, the asset-price bubble was attributable to the expansion of bank credit. Notably, two of the crises were the major ones: 1825–6 and 2007–8 and the other was the 1974 crisis. This is consistent with the argument in Chapter 2 that endogenously produced crises will be more severe than those generated by exogenous shocks. Bank lending before the 1974 crisis was mainly to property developers, with the majority of advances being made by the fringe or secondary banks rather than the clearing banks, which explains why this was a minor rather than major crisis. Chapter 7 explores how government regulation meant that the clearing banks avoided this crisis.

As the narrative accounts were developed, we analysed the banks that collapsed (or were bailed out by the authorities) during the various crises to determine whether they engaged in risk shifting before their collapse. Because risk shifting cannot be directly observed as such, we use the indirect means to determine whether failed banks had taken excessive or unusual risks as a way to assess whether risk shifting had occurred before their collapse. Notably, in almost every case of bank collapse, we found that managers (and shareholders) had taken excessive risks; that the risks taken were at the extremes of the prevailing risk-taking distribution; and that, in many cases, they were fraudulent or almost fraudulent. We also observed that the difference between the major and minor crises is that risk shifting prior to a crisis is systemic in the case of the former in that the majority of banks are, to some degree, risk shifting; whereas in the case of the latter, risk shifting is limited to a small number of institutions.

5   Banking stability, shareholder liability and bank capital

> A substantial banquier is to bee hanged hear today for making bankerupt; I know not whether that bee ye best way of preventing others from ye like practices....[1]
>
> Henry Savile (Envoy at Paris) in a letter from Paris, 31 January 1682

Introduction

Chapters 3 and 4 discuss the two major or systemic banking crises that the UK banking system has had since 1800. The first major crisis occurred in 1825–6, when almost one fifth of the English banking system collapsed; the second major crisis was the Great Crash of 2007–8. In the period between these two crises, there were episodes of stress in the banking system and occasionally banks failed, but the banking system proved robust to the shocks that it experienced. Ultimately, we might ask why the British banking system was free of major banking crises between 1826 and 2006 and why it experienced major crises at the beginning and end of this period. This chapter describes how both major crises occurred in an environment of poorly capitalised banking institutions.

The stability of the banking system in the long hiatus between these two major crises was not due to the absence of shocks to the banking system, as discussed in the previous chapter. Rather, as argued in this chapter, the stability of the system appears to be associated with banks having adequate capital until the interwar period and the fact that, after this period, substitutes for adequate capital were available. In particular, it was of central importance to the stability of the British banking system in the period before the 1930s that contingent capital (i.e., capital that could be called up in case of bank failure) was available in the form of unlimited shareholder liability, uncalled capital and reserve liability. The latter two types of contingent capital were similar to the double-liability rules that existed in the United States until the 1930s, except

---

[1] Quoted in Pressnell, *Country Banking*, p. 501.

that the liability faced by shareholders was decided on by individual banks rather than imposed by legislation. This chapter argues that the presence of bank shareholders and managers incentivised by contingent capital ameliorated risk shifting, with the result that most banks could weather the shocks that periodically affected the banking system and, more important, there were no endogenously created banking crises. This is consistent with the theory outlined in Chapter 2, in which it is argued that having extended liability for bank shareholders restrains managers and shareholders from risk shifting at the expense of depositors.

The second section of this chapter explains how the characteristics of English partnership law meant that English banks had inadequate capital prior to the formation of joint-stock banks. The third section explains how the unlimited liability of joint-stock banks underpinned the stability of the banking system in the half-century after 1826. The fourth section documents the rapid demise of unlimited liability following the failure of the CGB in 1878. The fifth section traces the diminution of paid-up and contingent capital in British banking in the era of limited liability. The sixth section explains the fall in bank capital during the post-1914 period.

Partnership banks

As discussed in Chapter 3, before the mid 1820s – when legislation was passed to allow greater freedom to incorporate – bank organisation across the United Kingdom was formally restricted to the partnership model. However, partnership law in Scotland differed from that in England, with the main legal difference being that Scottish partnerships could have facets of a separate legal personality similar to the partnership law found in Continental Europe at the time.[2] In effect, this meant that Scottish partnership banks could have managers or directors who entered contracts on behalf of all other partners and non-managing partners who were not allowed to enter binding contracts on behalf of the bank or interfere in any way with its day-to-day operations. In addition, this meant that partners in Scottish partnership banks could transfer their ownership in the bank without the partnership needing to be dissolved, thereby creating a market for bank shares.[3] Even after the Act of Union in 1707, when English common law began to exert more influence on Scottish commercial law, partnerships in Scotland maintained these facets

---

[2] Acheson et al., 'Organisational flexibility'.
[3] Acheson et al., 'Organisational flexibility'.

of a separate legal personality.[4] Thus, in Scotland, a distinction could be drawn between a bank and its owners, which enabled ownership to separate from control.

In contrast, English partnerships were held to be a 'mere aggregation of individuals indistinguishable from the individuals themselves'.[5] Although English partnership banks had partners who did not actively participate in the bank's day-to-day operation, unlike in Scotland, no partners could be legally excluded from participating in the bank's usual business contracting and managerial decisions. In other words, under English partnership law, ownership could not be separated from control.

This inability to separate ownership from control meant that English partnership banks were subject to potential hold-up costs and untimely dissolution costs, both of which would have increased proportionately with the number of partners. This alone would have meant that English partnership banks would have been small. However, English note-issuing banks, unlike their Scottish equivalents, were restricted to six partners at most. Still, this six-partner rule may not have been a major binding constraint. For example, in 1822, the average English note-issuing banks had only three partners, with less than 5 per cent of the 522 banks actually having six partners.[6] In contrast, as shown in Table 5.1, Scottish partnership banks (usually referred to as provincial banks) had an average of 43.1 partners; 11 banks had more than 50 partners and one bank had 424.

The small size of English partnership banks meant that they had two inherent weaknesses. First, the low number of homogeneous partners left English banks vulnerable to shocks to partners' wealth. If their wealth were to decrease for some reason, the result would be that the partners would have had incentives to risk shift with depositors' funds. As owners, they faced a much-reduced downside in the event of bank failure and stood to gain if the risks they took with depositors' funds available. In addition, banks with many partners would have been better able to absorb losses arising from nonperforming assets, which increased during monetary or real shocks, because they typically had a larger equity cushion. Furthermore, because partners had unlimited liability, the more partners there were, the greater were the funds available to cover losses in the event of bankruptcy. Indeed, note-holders and depositors may have preferred bank ownership to be dispersed among many partners because

[4] Campbell, 'Law and joint-stock company', p. 141; Clark, *Treatise*, p. 3.
[5] Brown, *Early Scottish Joint-Stock Companies*, p. 6.
[6] Pressnell, *Country Banking*, p. 226.

Table 5.1 *Size and failures of Scottish provincial banks, 1747–1864*

	Population of banks	Banks that did not fail	Banks that failed with no losses to customers	Banks that failed with losses to customers
Year of formation (median)	1788	1787	1779	1802
Average lifespan	32.3	34.4	26.5	29.0
Average number of partners at formation of partnership	34.1	37.3	54.3	7.1
Average number of partners at end of partnership	43.1	48.7	67.7	3.5
Number of banks <10 partners	24	14	2	8
Number of banks >50 partners	11	9	2	0
Number of banks	44	30	6	8

Sources: Munn, *The Scottish Provincial Banking Companies*, pp. 16, 222–4; Acheson, Hickson and Turner, 'Organisational flexibility', p. 508.

a small number of owners would have been at greater risk of losing their entire wealth.

The second inherent weakness was that a small number of partners acted as a constraint on the size of a bank so that it functioned in only one narrow geographical location. This would have limited a partnership bank's ability to diversify its asset portfolio, making it more difficult for the bank to survive shocks. Such a constraint on asset diversification, however, may have been alleviated by the wide-ranging and close relationships between English partnership banks and London correspondents, who invested funds on their behalf. In 1824, for example, 59 per cent of the country banks with London correspondents had at least one partner who was also a partner of the London correspondent.[7] However, these interlocking partnerships also created vulnerabilities in the banking system because partners in a bank could face several calls on their personal wealth unbeknownst to the depositors and note-holders of their various banks.

These inherent weaknesses within the English banking system left it prone to instability. As shown in Table 5.2, in the period 1792–1826, the average failure rate for the English country-banking system was 1.85 per cent. During periods of economic stress, however, the failure rate was

[7] Pressnell, *Country Banking*, p. 116.

Table 5.2 *Bank failure rates for England and Scotland, 1792–1826*

	Number of Scottish provincial-bank failures	Annual failure rate of Scottish provincial banks (%)	Alternative annual failure rate of Scottish provincial banks (%)	Number of English country-bank failures	Annual failure rate of English country banks (%)
1810	0	0.00	0.00	13	1.66
1815–17	1	3.85	0.80	50	7.15
1825	1	3.85	4.62	60	11.03
1826	1	4.17	0.71	43	7.76
1792–1826 (mean)	0.26	1.16	0.86	9.80	1.85

Sources: Author's calculations based on Munn, *The Scottish Provincial Banking Companies*, pp. 222–4; Pressnell, *Country Banking*, pp. 11, 538; and Acheson, Hickson and Turner, 'Organisational flexibility', p. 521.

Notes: The alternative failure rate for the Scottish provincial banks scales the Scottish failures in terms of size. The annual failure rate is calculated as the number of partners in failed banks divided by the total number of partners in Scottish banks.

even higher, with 7.15 per cent of banks failing in 1815–17 and 11.03 and 7.76 per cent failing in 1825 and 1826, respectively.

In contrast, with its larger banks, Scottish banking had a lower average failure rate (which is not statistically significant) than English banking throughout the entire 1792–1826 period; more important, however, the Scottish banking system was more robust during times of economic difficulties. For example, the alternative failure rate listed in Table 5.2, which considers the varying sizes of Scottish banks, was only 0.80 per cent in 1815–17 and was 4.64 and 0.71 per cent in 1825 and 1826, respectively.

Even within Scottish banking, it is clear that size mattered. As Table 5.1 shows, the eight banks that failed and produced losses for depositors and note-holders were all small partnership banks, with an average of 3.5 partners when they failed and with none having more than seven.

The historiography of Scottish banking has largely attributed its relative success to the absence of the six-partner rule.[8] However, as argued previously, this rule was not a binding constraint on English partnership banks because they would have been small even without it, due to

[8] Kerr, *History of Banking*, pp. 69–70; Cameron, *Banking in the Early Stages of Industrialization*, pp. 97–8; Munn, *The Scottish Provincial Banking Companies*, p. 236; White, *Free Banking in Britain*, pp. 47–8.

inherent and substantial hold-up problems stemming from the characteristics of English partnership law.

The previous failure-rate data perhaps do not adequately reflect the greater strain on the English country-banking system than on the Scottish system during financial crises. Even J. R. McCulloch, who was not well disposed towards Scottish banking structure, acknowledged that Scotland's financial system and economy were more robust during periods of commercial distress.[9] Indeed, the relative stability of the Scottish banking system, according to petitioners to Parliament, was the reason that Scottish bank notes circulated widely in the border counties of England.[10]

The relative stability of the Scottish system resulted in it being eulogised and held up as an exemplar by contemporary pamphleteers including Joplin, Parnell and Watt.[11] It is noteworthy that one of the pamphleteers, Thomas Joplin, argued that the relative stability of the Scottish banking system vis-à-vis the English system was not the six-partner rule but rather the differences in partnership law (discussed previously), which permitted Scottish banks to operate with numerous partners.[12]

In this matter of the six-partner rule, the situation in Ireland at this time proves instructive. Following the numerous bank failures in the Irish depression of 1819–20, the Bank of Ireland Restriction Act (1821) was passed. Whereas the situation had resembled that in England in that note-issuing banks could have no more than six partners, this Act permitted banks with any number of partners to issue notes provided that they were located 50 Irish miles (i.e., 65 statutory miles) outside of Dublin.[13] Notably, no banks took advantage of this legislation and no large-scale partnership banks were formed, implying that the problems experienced by English and Irish banking were related more to problems inherent in the partnership organisational form than to the six-partner rule.[14] Only when banks were allowed to adopt the corporate form in Ireland, as a result of an Act passed in 1825, is there evidence of the emergence of large multi-owner banks.

The greater stability and robustness of the Scottish system was appreciated by leading Parliamentarians, including Lord Liverpool (the

---

[9] White, *Free Banking in Britain*, p. 40.   [10] White, *Free Banking in Britain*, p. 38.

[11] Joplin, *An Essay on the General Principles*; Parnell, *Observations on Paper Money*; Watt, *The Practice of Banking in Scotland and England*.

[12] Joplin, *An Essay on the General Principles*, p. 6.   [13] 1 & 2 Geo. IV, c.72.

[14] As a quid pro quo for relaxing its monopoly at this time, the Bank of Ireland was allowed to increase its capital by £500,000, which it loaned to the government, perhaps suggesting that the ultimate purpose of the 1821 Act was relief for the Exchequer rather than banking reform (Barrow, *The Emergence of the Irish Banking System*, p. 64).

Prime Minister) and Sir Robert Peel.[15] Lord Liverpool argued that the small size of English partnership banks made them vulnerable to failure.[16] When introducing a bill to reform English banking in the House of Lords on 17 February 1826, Lord Liverpool described the existing banking system as 'the most absurd and the most inefficient, with not one recommendation to stand upon, it was one of the fullest liberty as to what is rotten and bad, but one of the most complete restriction as to all that is good'.[17]

As a result of England's banking crisis of 1825–6, a majority of Parliamentarians resolved to support Lord Liverpool's bill and change the structure of banking by introducing joint-stock principles.[18] Thus, Parliament passed an act that permitted English banks to form freely as co-partnerships or joint-stock companies with the same institutional characteristics as the Scottish provincial banks: separation of ownership and control, managerial hierarchies, transferable shares and unlimited liability.[19] As the first step in the United Kingdom's liberalisation of incorporation law, this was an historic piece of legislation.

The available evidence on English partnership banks makes it difficult to determine whether their smallness due to legal restrictions contributed to ex-ante or ex-post problems relative to equity capital. In other words, we do not know whether partners' wealth was first substantially reduced, which then resulted in their risk shifting and the bank failing because of this, or whether partners' wealth was simply inadequate and poorly diversified, leaving them with insufficient capital to meet exogenous shocks to their bank's balance sheet. It is possible that both ex-ante and ex-post factors were involved in the 1825–6 crisis.

The era of unlimited-liability joint-stock banking

The legislation of the mid 1820s, which enabled banks to become joint-stock companies, required shareholders to have joint and several unlimited liability. In other words, banks could have all of the typical features of a corporation other than limited liability. As argued in Chapter 2, the unlimited-liability commitment is more credible for joint-stock companies than for partnerships because ownership is diversified among many heterogeneous owners, and multiple ownership means that the bank has a larger pool of resources backing its deposits and notes. The main economic function of unlimited liability in these banks was to prevent them

---

[15] Thomas, *Rise and Growth*, pp. 65–6.
[16] Hansard, House of Commons Debates, 1825–6, vol. XIV, Cols. 7–11.
[17] Thomas, *Rise and Growth*, p. 79.   [18] Harris, *Industrializing English Law*, p. 214.
[19] Banking Copartnerships Act (1826), 7 Geo. IV, c.46.

from engaging in risk shifting. Because shareholders stood to lose all of their wealth in the event of a bank collapse, they had a powerful incentive to ensure that their bank and its managers did not take excessive risks.

However, joint-stock companies with joint and several unlimited liability faced three potential problems in assuring creditors and shareholders of the credibility of the unlimited-liability commitment – that is, that shareholders are sufficiently wealthy to meet potential calls on their wealth. First, because shares in joint-stock companies are tradable, the equilibrium of wealthy bank owners might become unstable because shares could be sold to low-wealth individuals. Second, given that the calls that each shareholder might face in the event of bank failure would be a function of the wealth of the co-owners, how could shareholders ensure that the co-owners had adequate wealth? Third, given that being a joint-stock company implies a separation of ownership and control as well as a managerial hierarchy, shareholders in banks with unlimited liability – whose entire wealth might be in jeopardy – need to ensure that managers operate the bank prudently.

British banks with unlimited liability ensured the stability of the wealthy-owners equilibrium by having bank directors vet potential new owners at the formation of the bank as well as during its continued existence. Rather like a club, a bank had directors who controlled entry to its shareholding membership, thereby ensuring that the aggregate wealth of the shareholding constituency was not diluted. Section 22 of the Irish Banking Copartnership Regulation Act (1825) specified that 'no share transfer shall take place without the consent of the directors; nor is any transfer valid unless signed by one or more of such directors'.[20] However, it appears that this section was somewhat redundant in that Irish banks would have voluntarily implemented such a scheme. Notably, the English Banking Copartnership Act (1826) did not contain this provision, but English bank promoters chose to insert it into their banks' constitutions.[21] All of the banks listed in Table 5.3 – which is based on a large representative sample of banking constitutions including their deeds of settlement or contracts of copartnership – required share transfers to be vetted by bank directors.

How did directors obtain information about applicant shareholders? Evidence on these unlimited-liability banks indicates that many shareholders were also bank customers.[22] In addition, it appears that shareholders typically lived close to one of the bank's branches, which

---

[20] 6 Geo. IV, c.42, s.22.   [21] Plumptre, *Grant's Treatise on the Law*, p. 444.
[22] Newton, 'Assessment of information'; Newton, 'Birth of joint-stock banking', pp. 43–4; Acheson and Turner, 'Investor behaviour'.

Table 5.3 *Director vetting of share transfers and ownership limits*

Bank	Establishment	Director vetting of share transfers	Upper limit on proportion of shares owned by an individual (%)
London banks			
City Bank	1855	yes	6.66
London Joint Stock Bank	1836	yes	none
London and Westminster	1834	yes	none
Union Bank of London	1839	yes	none
London and provincial banks			
London and County	1836	yes	0.75
National Provincial Bank	1833	yes	none
English provincial banks			
Ashton, Stalybridge, Hyde and Glossop	1836	yes	none
Bank of Liverpool	1831	yes	none
Bank of Whitehaven	1837	yes	none
Bilston District Banking Company	1836	yes	1.00
Birmingham and Midland	1836	yes	1.00
Birmingham Town and District	1836	yes	none
Bradford Banking Company	1827	yes	2.86
Burton, Uttoxeter and Staffordshire	1840	yes	none
Carlisle and Cumberland	1837	yes	1.00
Carlisle City and District	1837	yes	2.00
County of Gloucester Bank	1836	yes	2.50
Hampshire Banking Company	1834	yes	3.33
Herefordshire Banking Company	1836	yes	2.50
Huddersfield Banking Company	1827	yes	4.00
Hull Banking Company	1834	yes	1.25
Lancaster Banking Company	1826	yes	3.33
Leeds and West Riding	1836	yes	0.50
Leicestershire Banking Company	1829	yes	2.00
Manchester and Liverpool District	1829	yes	none
North and South Wales Bank	1836	yes	none
Royal Bank of Liverpool	1836	yes	1.00
Sheffield and Hallamshire Bank	1836	yes	1.00
Sheffield and Rotherham	1836	yes	none
Sheffield Banking Company	1831	yes	2.66
Stamford and Spalding Banking Company	1832	yes	2.00
Stourbridge and Kidderminster	1834	yes	1.00
Wilts and Dorset	1835	yes	none
York Union Banking Company	1833	yes	1.66
Yorkshire Banking Company	1843	yes	none
Yorkshire District Bank	1834	yes	none

Table 5.3 *(cont.)*

Bank	Establishment	Director vetting of share transfers	Upper limit on proportion of shares owned by an individual (%)
Scottish banks			
Central Bank of Scotland	1834	yes	2.00
City of Glasgow Bank	1839	yes	none
Commercial Banking Company	1810	yes	none
National Bank of Scotland	1825	yes	none
Union Bank of Scotland	1830	yes	none
Irish banks			
Belfast Banking Company	1827	yes	2.00
Northern Banking Company	1825	yes	2.00
National Bank of Ireland	1835	yes	none
Ulster Banking Company	1836	yes	2.00

Sources: Contracts of Copartnership and deeds of settlement of various banks. See Bibliography for archival locations of these records.

implies that bank directors could have used their branch networks to gain information on prospective shareholders.[23]

Minimal archival records of share transfers have survived and, even where they are available, banks did not often record those cases when a transfer was refused by directors. One bank that did so is the Sheffield and Rotherham Bank, whose directors' minutes record ten refusals of transfer between 1848 and 1877. One of the refusals has a reason appended, which states that the transfer was refused due to 'the purchaser's circumstances not being satisfactory'.[24]

The nature of joint and several unlimited liability means that wealthy shareholders stood to lose all of their wealth if too many of their co-owners lacked funds. Consequently, such individuals had the greatest incentives to act as directors and oversee the shareholder-vetting process. Evidence based on the detailed ownership records of the Ulster Banking Company, a large Irish bank, reveals that the directors of the bank and members of its supervisory committee were its largest and wealthiest

[23] Newton, 'Assessment of information'; Newton, 'Birth of joint-stock banking', p. 37; Hickson and Turner, 'Trading in the shares', pp. 954–5; Acheson and Turner, 'Investor behaviour', pp. 205–7.

[24] Royal Bank of Scotland Archives, SR/1/2, Sheffield and Rotherham Directors' Minute Book, February 1851.

shareholders.[25] In addition, one consequence of this bank's limiting its liability in 1883 was that its directors were no longer among its wealthiest shareholders; rather, they were selected for their professional expertise.[26]

Director vetting normally may have prevented the dilution of aggregate shareholder wealth; however, when the probability of financial distress increased, directors and shareholders could have opportunistically exited banks en masse. Preventing such opportunistic dumping was the fact that owners were still liable for their bank's debts for some time after they sold or transferred their ownership stake. Both the Irish Banking Copartnerships Act (1825) and the English Banking Copartnerships Act (1826) placed a post-sale extended liability on the shareholders of unlimited-liability joint-stock banks, which made shareholders liable for the bank's debts for three years after they sold their shares.[27] In Scotland, previous owners of unlimited-liability joint-stock shares were held liable for debts incurred during their tenure if the incumbent owners were unable to cover these losses from their own personal assets.[28]

Several wealthier shareholders of the Agricultural and Commercial Bank of Ireland, which collapsed in 1836, attempted to avoid calls on their wealth arising from the bank's failure by assigning their shares to a pauper in an attempt to be released from their responsibility.[29] However, they were not able to evade their obligations using this strategy because the post-sale extended-liability requirement held them liable for three years.

Was the existence of the director-vetting mechanism and the post-sale extended-liability requirement enough to ensure that bank shares were owned by individuals with adequate wealth and that shares were not transferred to low-wealth individuals? There are two pieces of evidence that this mechanism and this requirement worked.

First, there is evidence on shareholder wealth for four unlimited banks derived from probate and bequest records. Fortuitously, several bank records that survived contain the probated wealth of shareholders who died whilst they were holding the bank's shares. In addition, the shareholder records of the Ulster Banking Company were so detailed that it was possible to match shareholders who died between 1858 and 1879 with probate records.

---

[25] Hickson and Turner, 'Trading in the shares'.
[26] Acheson and Turner, 'Impact of limited liability', pp. 342–3.
[27] Established English, Irish and Scottish banks that registered as unlimited-liability companies under the Companies Act (1862) were able to reduce their post-sale extended-liability requirement to one year.
[28] Bell, *Commentaries on the Laws of Scotland*, p. 224.
[29] *Select Committee Report on Joint-Stock Banks*, P.P. 1837, LXXVIII, q. 3838.

Table 5.4 *Probated wealth of individuals who died whilst owning bank shares*

	Bradford Banking Company (1851–83)	Hampshire Banking Company (1834–79)	Sheffield and Hallamshire Banking Company (1836–88)	Ulster Banking Company (1858–79)
Average (£)	27,298	10,445	12,962	6,623
Median (£)	9,000	5,500	4,000	3,000
Largest (£)	400,000	70,000	656,450	120,000
Total wealth of 10 richest shareholders (£)	1,610,000	445,000	2,035,593	570,000
Average wealth of females (£)	13,621	8,367	4,066	3,756
Deposits and notes in 1874 (£)	2,120,000	2,116,000	571,000	3,710,000
Number of shareholders in 1874	211	286	326	1,020
Aggregate shareholder wealth (£) in 1874 (est.)	5,759,878	2,987,270	4,225,612	6,755,460
Sample size	152	136	413	272

Sources: The probated values of shareholder wealth are from HSBC Archives, 236/4, Bradford Banking Company Registry of Wills; Lloyds-TSB Archives, 1085, Hampshire Banking Company Shareholders' Register; and HSBC Archives, 598/1–2, Sheffield and Hallamshire Share Registers. Biographical details of the Ulster Banking Company's deceased shareholders between 1858 and 1879 were obtained from Public Record Office of Northern Ireland (PRONI), D/3499/CC/2–3, Ulster Banking Company's Share Transfer Journals. The probated value of their wills was obtained from the appropriate Will Calendar Books at PRONI. Deposits and notes in 1874 are from Dun, 'The banking institutions', pp. 46–59, and shareholder numbers are from the *Banking Almanac and Yearbook*, 1875.
Notes: Monetary values have not been adjusted to account for inflation. The estimate of shareholder wealth in 1874 is calculated by taking the average wealth of shareholders who died and multiplying by the number of shareholders in 1874.

Table 5.4 lists statistics on shareholder wealth for the four banks the records of which are available. However, caveats must be placed on these data. First, *inter vivos* gifts may mean that the bequeathed wealth underestimates the actual wealth.[30] Second, the wealth of some shareholders who died may not reflect the wealth of the overall shareholding constituency.

According to Lindert's estimates, the average wealth of various occupational categories in 1875 was as follows: gentlemen (£9,855), merchants (£11,804), professionals (£1,201), farmers (£800), retailers (£606), female household heads (£405), and labourers (£143). This suggests that bank shareholders in Table 5.4 came from the wealthier sections of

[30] Green and Owens, 'Gentlewomanly capitalism?'; Hickson and Turner, 'Trading in the shares', p. 944.

society.[31] In addition, the Bradford Banking Company and Sheffield and Hallamshire Banking Company had several extremely wealthy shareholders by contemporary standards.[32] It is important that there is no evidence from the bequeathed wealth of the shareholders of these banks to suggest that shareholder wealth diminished over time.

To provide further perspective on the wealth of the Ulster Banking Company shareholders, we can compare their wealth with the average wealth of the top 10 per cent of all decedents in the six north-easterly counties of Ireland (where the majority of Ulster Banking Company shareholders lived) in 1871.[33] The average wealth of the top 10 per cent of decedents was £1,596 and the median was only £300, which suggests that Ulster Banking Company shareholders were easily among the wealthiest percentiles of society, given that the average and median wealth of its shareholders was £6,623 and £3,000, respectively. Between 1858 and 1879, only six decedents in the six northeasterly counties were wealthier than the wealthiest shareholder in the Ulster Banking Company who died during this period.

Bank shareholders had more than enough wealth to cover their total liabilities to depositors and note-holders. As shown in Table 5.4, if we assume that the average wealth of living shareholders was similar to that of those who had died, the aggregate wealth of all shareholders greatly exceeded banks' public liabilities. Notably, the aggregate bequeathed wealth of the 156 shareholders of the Sheffield and Hallamshire Banking Company who left wills and were owners in 1874 was £2,135,771, which is approximately four times the size of its public liabilities.

The second indication that shareholders of unlimited-liability banks were wealthy is evidence on the socio-occupational composition of the shareholder constituencies of a representative sample of banks. In essence, we are assuming that there is a close correlation between wealth and socio-occupational status, which – based on Lindert's estimates (discussed previously) – seems to be a reasonable assumption for Victorian Britain. As Table 5.5 indicates, surviving bank-ownership records imply that most shareholders and most of the share capital came from the wealthiest sections of Victorian society: gentry, merchants and professionals. In addition, few shareholders came from the working classes or white-collar professions; in all probability, those who did were relatively wealthy. The other major category of shareholder, which is not listed in Table 5.5, was women, who became an increasingly important part of

---

[31] Lindert, 'Unequal English wealth'.
[32] See, for example, Rubenstein, 'The Victorian middle classes'.
[33] Turner, 'Wealth concentration'.

Table 5.5 *Socio-occupational status of bank shareholders*

Bank (year established)	Year	Gentry, professional and mercantile classes		White-collar professions		Working class	
		(% of owners)	(% of capital)	(% of owners)	(% of capital)	(% of owners)	(% of capital)
London-based banks							
London and County Bank (1836)	1878	52.9	–	3.9	–	0.6	–
National Provincial Bank of England (1833)	1878	41.8	–	4.9	–	0.7	–
Union Bank of London (1839)	1878	58.8	–	4.7	–	0.2	–
English provincial banks							
Sheffield and Hallamshire Bank (1836)	1836	63.0	76.7	8.2	4.53	0.5	0.1
Wilts and Dorset (1836)	1836	61.9	–	10.5	–	0.0	–
Wilts and Dorset (1836)	1853	61.4	–	8.6	–	0.0	–
Wilts and Dorset (1836)	1860	46.8	–	3.0	–	0.0	–
Manchester and Liverpool District (1829)	1856	59.4	–	5.7	–	0.2	–
Birmingham Town and District (1836)	1866	65.5	–	3.1	–	0.0	–
North and South Wales Bank (1836)	1874	47.7	66.6	9.0	4.80	0.1	0.1
North and South Wales Bank (1836)	1878	47.8	66.6	9.0	4.80	0.0	0.1
Bank of Liverpool (1831)	1879	56.1	78.5	5.5	3.90	0.0	0.0
Scottish and Irish joint-stock banks							
Aberdeen Town and Country Bank (1825)	1846	55.0	–	4.4	–	0.0	–

(*cont.*)

Table 5.5 *(cont.)*

Bank (year established)	Year	Gentry, professional and mercantile classes		White-collar professions		Working class	
		(% of owners)	(% of capital)	(% of owners)	(% of capital)	(% of owners)	(% of capital)
Caledonian Banking Company (1838)	1846	39.4	–	8.4	–	2.7	–
Caledonian Banking Company (1838)	1878	34.8	46.5	2.9	3.10	1.1	0.6
Central Bank of Scotland (1834)	1846	43.8	–	6.0	–	1.5	–
Central Bank of Scotland (1834)	1863	28.9	–	3.5	–	3.3	–
City of Glasgow Bank (1839)	1846	55.5	–	5.9	–	0.7	–
City of Glasgow Bank (1839)	1878	37.6	53.3	2.5	2.00	0.3	0.3
Clydesdale Bank (1838)	1846	55.9	–	5.9	–	0.6	–
Clydesdale Bank (1838)	1878	43.6	–	2.7	–	0.2	–
Commercial Bank of Scotland (1810)	1846	46.2	–	3.2	–	0.4	–
Eastern Bank (1838)	1846	45.4	–	7.8	–	1.2	–
Edinburgh and Glasgow Bank (1844)	1846	50.7	–	5.5	–	1.2	–
National Bank of Scotland (1825)	1846	53.4	–	3.6	–	0.5	–
National Bank of Scotland (1825)	1878	36.4	–	1.5	–	0.3	–
North British Bank (1845)	1846	77.5	–	6.0	–	0.2	–

Table 5.5 (cont.)

Bank (year established)	Year	Gentry, professional and mercantile classes		White-collar professions		Working class	
		(% of owners)	(% of capital)	(% of owners)	(% of capital)	(% of owners)	(% of capital)
North of Scotland Bank (1836)	1846	59.2	–	5.4	–	0.5	–
Union Bank of Scotland (1830)	1846	53.4	–	5.0	–	0.5	–
Western Bank of Scotland (1832)	1846	55.8	–	6.4	–	0.5	–
Western Bank of Scotland (1832)	1857	43.9	–	4.5	–	0.9	–
Ulster Banking Company (1836)	1878	41.8	58.0	6.6	3.90	0.0	0.0

Sources: Acheson and Turner, 'The death blow to unlimited liability', tables 1 and 2; Acheson and Turner, 'Investor behaviour', tables 2, 4 and 5; Acheson and Turner, 'Impact of limited liability', table 4; Turner, 'Wider share ownership', tables 3, 4 and 5; HSBC Archives, 598/1, Sheffield and Hallamshire Share Registers.

Notes: Gentry, professional and mercantile classes include clergy, military officers, doctors, lawyers, bankers, sharebrokers, architects, accountants and auctioneers, merchants, manufacturers, retailers and members of the gentry. White-collar professions include teachers, bank managers, bank clerks, salesmen, agents, managers and clerks. Working class includes skilled and unskilled members. Because tradesmen could be businessmen or artisans, they are not considered part of the mercantile classes. Farmers could well be included as members of the gentry or as businessmen, but they are excluded from these figures.

bank-shareholder constituencies as the nineteenth century progressed.[34] The women typically came from well-to-do middle-class backgrounds and had their own wealth. For example, Table 5.4 shows that the average female bank shareholder was relatively prosperous.[35]

The presence of unlimited liability means that the wealthiest owners would want to own large stakes in banks because they had the most wealth to lose if the bank fails and their wealth makes them the major target for

[34] Newton and Cottrell, 'Female investors'; Acheson and Turner, 'Shareholder liability'.
[35] For example, when the Royal Bank of Liverpool collapsed in 1867, one of its shareholders was an eighty-year-old woman who faced calls of £23,000; to help meet those calls, she sold her house for the sum of £5,000 (*The Manchester Guardian*, 7 August 1868, p. 4).

creditors.[36] Notably, however, many smaller banks limited the proportion of shares that any one individual could own (see Table 5.3). One reason for such ownership restrictions may have been that bank depositors and note-holders preferred to see the shares of the bank dispersed among many owners because there was less risk of many rather than a few owners becoming bankrupt. This was recognised by contemporaries; for example, the chairman of the Union Bank of Scotland, when interviewed by a Parliamentary committee in the aftermath of the Western Bank collapse in 1857, stated that 'so long as unlimited liability exists, the greater the number of partners of a respectable class, the more is the security to the public undoubtedly'.[37] Several of the larger banks listed in Table 5.3 did not have such provisions because they either discouraged the holding of a large block of stock by placing a low upper limit on the number of votes attached to share ownership, or because they were large metropolitan banks that required numerous shareholders to raise capital.[38]

The role of unlimited liability in these joint-stock banks was to prevent risk shifting and, in most cases, this seemed to work. There were, however, some notable failures of unlimited-liability banks, which may raise doubts about the ability of unlimited liability to constrain risk shifting. However, these failures actually illustrate the effectiveness of unlimited liability in underpinning the stability of the banking system. First, given the size of the population of banks, failures of unlimited-liability joint-stock banks were rare events (Table 5.6). Second, as discussed in Chapter 4, the failures that occurred were due to poor management or fraudulent behaviour, wherein managers had limited stakes in the bank or had borrowed heavily from it and were effectively bankrupt. Third, the failures of unlimited-liability banks did not result in widespread runs on other banks because their depositors knew that their deposits were safe and would be repaid even if another bank failed. In a sense, unlimited liability helped to make banks run-proof. Fourth, and perhaps most important, when unlimited-liability banks collapsed, depositors were paid in full (see Table 5.6), which indicates that shareholders of unlimited-liability banks had more than adequate wealth to cover the deficits between assets and liabilities. Table 5.6 reveals the calls made on the average shareholder (i.e., those holding an average number of shares) as a result of bank collapses. Calls were made on a per-share basis;

[36] Hickson and Turner, 'Trading in the shares'.   [37] Anon., *Western Bank Failure*, p. 42.
[38] For example, the upper limits on votes for the largest English banks were as follows: Union Bank of London (twenty); National Provincial Bank of England (four); London and Westminster Bank (four); London Joint Stock Bank (twenty); and Wilts and Dorset (five). These figures were obtained from contracts of copartnership.

Table 5.6 *Banks with unlimited shareholder liability that failed during crises,*
1836–1878

Bank	Year of failure	Deficit between assets and liabilities (£)'000s	Number of shareholders	Call on average shareholder (£)	Depositors and note-holders paid in full
Agricultural and Commercial Bank of Ireland	1836	n/a	n/a	n/a	yes
Northern and Central Bank of England	1836	n/a	1,204	n/a	yes
North of England Joint Stock Banking Company	1847	433	420	1,000	yes
Liverpool Borough Bank	1857	395	317	1,000	yes
Western Bank of Scotland	1857	1,089	1,280	851	yes
Northumberland and Durham District Bank	1857	1,947	407	4,785	yes
Birmingham Banking Company	1866	235	618	400	yes
Royal Bank of Liverpool	1867	650	200	3,250	yes
City of Glasgow Bank	1878	5,190	1,819	2,310 (1st) 10,395 (2nd)	yes
West of England and South Wales District Bank	1878	749	1,800	416	yes
Chesterfield and North Derbyshire Bank	1878	24	90	277	yes

Sources: Shareholder numbers are from *The Banking Almanac and Yearbook* (various issues). Data on deficit and calls are from Philips, *A History of Banks*, pp. 333–4, 344; *Select Committee on the Bank Acts*, P.P. 1858, LXXVIII, Evidence of J. Dixon, q. 4323; Anon., *How to Mismanage a Bank*, p. 25; Holmes and Green, *Midland*, p. 47; *The Times*, 24 October 1867, p. 7; Acheson and Turner, 'The death blow to unlimited liability', p. 243; *The Manchester Guardian*, 12 November 1867, p. 5; 7 January 1880, p. 5; 14 March 1879, p. 6; and 27 September 1880, p. 8.

hence, wealthier shareholders had to pay substantially more than others. The fact that shareholders were able to meet such large calls is further evidence – if it were needed – that shareholders in unlimited banks were wealthy.

Such were the stability-inducing properties of unlimited liability that when one bank failed, the payments system was largely unaffected because other banks were willing to receive the notes and deposits of banks that had failed. This happened when the Western Bank of Scotland failed in 1857. The deputy governor explained that the reason for its doing so was that it was 'known that a great number of the shareholders of the Western Bank were men of undoubted and very large capital and there never was, at any time, any doubt entertained as to the ultimate payment of the notes and of other claims upon that bank'.[39] Another contemporary observed that the confidence in the Scottish banking system was preserved by the fact that the Western Bank and others had unlimited liability and if the Western Bank had had limited liability, 'the panic and distress . . . would be infinitely greater than what is caused by the present system'.[40]

As perceived by many contemporaries, unlimited liability was a major factor that created confidence in the banking system and ultimately assured its stability,[41] whereas limited liability transferred risk to those who had no means or power to regulate a bank's risk taking (i.e., depositors).[42] As a result, they argued that limited liability would result in substantial bank failures.[43] However, it was almost 150 years before this prophecy came true.

The sudden death of unlimited-liability banking

In the decades following the liberalisation of incorporation law in 1826, vocal opposition had been expressed in Parliament to unlimited liability in banking (e.g., William Clay and Thomas Headlem), from the banking profession (e.g., George Rae) and from the press (e.g., Walter Bagehot).[44] The basic tenet of this opposition was that if shares of unlimited-liability banks were not already owned by low-wealth investors, the inevitable dynamic was that they soon would be, rendering unlimited liability useless.

The proponents of limited liability in banking were given abundant ammunition following the failure of the City of Glasgow Bank (CGB) in October 1878. As shown in Table 5.6, this was by far the largest unlimited-liability bank ever to fail, and the consequences for its shareholders were severe. The deficit between the CGB's assets and liabilities

---

[39] Anon., *Western Bank Failure*, p. 13.
[40] Callender, *The Commercial Crisis of 1857*, p. 35.
[41] Anon., *Western Bank Failure*, p. 42.   [42] Anon., *How to Mismanage a Bank*, p. 40.
[43] Anon., *How to Mismanage a Bank*, p. 41.   [44] See Turner, 'Last acre and sixpence'.

meant that at the bank's liquidation, calls were made on the wealth of its 1,819 shareholders. The CGB had ten thousand shares with a paid-up value of £100. However, before its closure – and was the case with several failed banks during the 1866 panic – the manager and directors were deceptively supporting its share price by buying its stock using bank funds, with the result that by 1 October 1878, the bank was holding 1,535 of its own shares.[45] As a result, the shortfall between the bank's assets and liabilities was £613 per share instead of £519. The first call was £500 per share and was made at the beginning of December 1878, with installments payable on 22 December and 24 February. This call resulted in the bankruptcy of 599 of the bank's shareholders. A final call of £2,250 per share was made in April 1878 that resulted in the deficit being met in full. However, only 254 shareholders remained solvent after these calls, and many families suffered financial hardship as a consequence of losing all or most of their worldly possessions.[46] Such was the penury in which many previously well-to-do middle-class families found themselves that a relief fund was set up, which raised £400,000 in donations to aid them.[47]

The Scottish and UK press exaggerated the suffering of shareholders as a result of the crisis.[48] For example, *The Economist* gave an exaggerated picture of the misery suffered by many shareholders as a consequence of the CGB collapse: 'in hundreds and thousands of cases homes have been broken up, health and life destroyed, dismay and ruin spread over towns and parishes, sons and daughters left penniless – by the wickedness and folly which perverted a public trust in so infamous a manner'.[49]

The press also resurrected the arguments made by Clay and Bagehot by arguing that the CGB collapse clearly revealed that the shareholding constituencies of large banks consisted mainly of investors of modest means.[50] This was not surprising, claimed *The Scotsman*, because unlimited liability 'only drives away really wealthy men and substitutes for them those who do not have much to lose'.[51] However, the previous evidence on shareholder wealth and occupations indicates that this was far from being the case.

There was also a fear that bank-shareholding constituencies would soon deteriorate as wealthy shareholders of unlimited-liability banks rapidly exited in the aftermath of the CGB failure. For example, George Rae, the banker and banking expert, stated that after the failure, shareholders asked themselves 'whether it was not an act of insanity, to

---

[45] French, *Unlimited Liability*, p. 9.   [46] Checkland, *Scottish Banking*, p. 471.
[47] Checkland, *Scottish Banking*, p. 477.   [48] Lee, 'A helpless class of shareholder'.
[49] *The Economist*, 27 December 1879, p. 1480.
[50] *The Economist*, 27 December 1879, p. 1480.   [51] *The Scotsman*, 2 October 1880.

Table 5.7 *Average returns (per cent) on British bank-share prices in the months after the City of Glasgow Bank failure*

	1 month	2 months	3 months	10 months
All British banks				
Limited (N = 34)	−3.51	−6.16	−9.69	−14.22
Unlimited (N = 56)	−2.45	−4.10	−6.53	−14.92
P > |t|	0.53	0.32	0.19	0.45
Scottish banks				
Limited (N = 3)	−0.21	−14.27	−18.49	−13.54
Unlimited (N = 6)	0.08	−22.53	−27.50	−24.80
P > |t|	0.37	0.12	0.13	0.01
Returns on industrial shares	−3.59	−5.28	−8.24	−13.31

Sources: Bank returns are from Acheson and Turner, 'The death blow to unlimited liability', table 5; the return on industrial shares is from Smith and Horne, *An Index Number of Securities, 1867–1914.*

Notes: Caledonian Bank is excluded from these figures because it was suspended during this period. P > \|t\| is the significance level of a two-sided test of differences in means between limited- and unlimited-liability banks.

continue owners of a description of property, the holding of which had brought even wealthy men to the ground and hundreds of the well-to-do to privation or beggary, with as little warning as an earthquake gives'.[52] As a result, according to Rae, 'unlimited liability . . . might thus become in time the mere shadow of itself – a husk without a kernel' and thus would provide no security to depositors.[53]

Acheson and Turner provided several pieces of evidence that suggest that wealthy shareholders were in fact not exiting in the aftermath of the CGB collapse.[54] First, they examined the shareholder constituencies of seven major English and Scottish banks before and after the CGB failure and found that they did not deteriorate. Second, using banks' archival records, they examined the trading of bank shares in the months after the CGB failure and found that trading activity did not increase in any except three Scottish banks. The reason for the increased activity in these three banks is that CGB shareholders owned shares in other banks and they were forced to sell those shares to meet calls from the CGB liquidator.[55]

As shown in Table 5.7, the average return on British unlimited-liability bank shares after the CGB collapse did not differ much from the return

[52] Rae, *The Country Banker*, p. 257.   [53] Rae, *The Country Banker*, p. 258.
[54] Acheson and Turner, 'The death blow to unlimited liability'.
[55] Acheson and Turner, 'The death blow to unlimited liability', table 4.

on industrial shares. In addition, there was – statistically or economically speaking – no difference in returns between limited- and unlimited-liability British banks. The main reason for the great difference between Scottish limited- and unlimited-liability banks is that many CGB shareholders were forced to sell their shares in other unlimited-liability banks to meet calls from the liquidator. Specifically, those two Glasgow banks, Clydesdale Bank and Union Bank of Scotland, had many shareholders who were also CGB shareholders. As a result, the two banks experienced the largest declines in share price of any Scottish bank (i.e., 40.3 and 35.7 per cent, respectively, after three months).[56]

The hysteria surrounding the CGB failure and pressure from shareholders resulted in Parliamentary intervention in the form of the 1879 Companies Act.[57] The primary purpose of this legislation apparently was 'to pacify bank shareholders and to prevent the transfer of shares into weak hands'.[58] The 1879 Companies Act included Rae's idea of reserve liability, which enabled banks to limit their liability and simultaneously provide protection for depositors.[59] Reserve liability was a form of extended liability wherein banks set aside a fixed portion of their capital as an inalienable fund, with the sole purpose of protecting depositors.[60] Although some established banks hesitated at first, nearly all of them limited their liability after the enactment of the Companies Act in August 1879; by 1884, only nine small English banks still had unlimited liability. This led Rae to observe that the CGB failure 'brought unlimited liability in banking to a violent end'.[61]

Limited-liability banking

Pressure for company-law reform resulted in the passing of the Limited Liability Act in 1855, but this Act was repealed soon after and then subsequently reenacted in 1856 as the Joint Stock Companies Act.[62] Banks

---

[56] Acheson and Turner, 'The death blow to unlimited liability', pp. 248–9.
[57] 42 & 43 Vict., c.76.   [58] Gregory, *The Westminster Bank*, vol. I, p. 206.
[59] Crick and Wadsworth, *A Hundred Years of Joint Stock Banking*, pp. 33–4.
[60] Rae, *The Country Banker*, p. 252.   [61] Rae, *The Country Banker*, p. 257.
[62] 18 & 19 Vict., c.133; 19 & 20 Vict., c.47. The two main forces opposed to the introduction of general limited liability were conservative common-law lawyers (Cottrell, *Industrial Finance*, p. 45) and prominent political economists, who were concerned about share speculation, monopoly power and agency problems (Amsler, Bartlett and Bolton, 'Thoughts of some British economists'). The pressure for reform came from several quarters. First, it is suggested that pressure for reform came partly from the rising class of traders who were averse to raising debt finance from banks, most of all because of interest-rate risk (Alborn, *Conceiving Companies*, pp. 127–8). Second, some argue that the main instigators of reform were the rising ranks of middle-class investors (Bryer, 'The Mercantile Laws Commission'; Jefferys, *Business Organisation*). Third,

were initially excluded from the provisions of this legislation primarily due to concerns about depositor safety.[63] The Joint Stock Bank Companies Act (1857) removed the exclusion of banks from the Joint Stock Companies Act (1856), but there was still an explicit prohibition on the limitation of liability.[64] Essentially, other than the continuing requirement of unlimited liability, the 1857 Act meant that banking companies faced the same company laws as other joint-stock companies with respect to constitution, management and winding up.[65] Within a year of the passing of the 1857 Act, another piece of legislation was enacted that permitted banks to adopt limited liability.[66] Banks, however, appeared reluctant to constitute on a limited-liability basis until the minimum-share denomination of £100, required under the Joint Stock Banking Companies Act of 1857,[67] was eliminated by the Companies Act of 1862.[68]

Only seven established English banks, and no Irish or Scottish established banks, took advantage of this liberalisation. By the late 1870s, the majority of established joint-stock banks had not adopted limited liability. A possible reason for this was that it was not attractive for note-issuing banks to convert to limited status because liability was still unlimited with respect to note issue. Notably, this argument was made with respect to Scottish banks, which at that time were also permitted to move to limited liability.[69] However, by the mid 1870s, seven unlimited English banks, four of which issued notes, had converted to limited liability. Furthermore, London banks and a considerable number of provincial banks (in particular, those in the Liverpool and Manchester districts) did not issue notes, and the note issue was so small for other provincial banks that the unlimited-liability requirement effectively was of no concern to English banks.[70]

A contemporary banking expert argued that established joint-stock banks were reluctant to limit their liability because unlimited liability was 'thought by the shareholders more conducive to profit and by the depositors, more likely to give safety'.[71] He went on to argue that

---

further pressure for reform may have stemmed from the fact that some firms were evading the law by incorporating under American and French laws (Cottrell, *Industrial Finance*, p. 51).

[63] Alborn, *Conceiving Companies*, p. 129.   [64] 20 & 21 Vict., c.49.

[65] Cooke, *Corporation, Trust and Company*, p. 166.

[66] 21 & 22 Vict., c.91.   [67] 20 & 21 Vict., c.49, s.13.

[68] 25 & 26 Vict., c.89. See Crick and Wadsworth, *A Hundred Years of Joint Stock Banking*, p. 36.

[69] Carr, Glied and Mathewson, 'Unlimited liability and free banking in Scotland'.

[70] Cooke, *Corporation*, p. 166.   [71] Wilson, *Banking Reform*, p. 69.

... unlimited banks had an enormous advantage over their competitors in the struggle for deposits. A depositor would be much more likely to trust his money with a bank whose shareholders he knew must yield up to him the uttermost farthing that they possessed, in making good losses should the bank fail, than with a bank whose shareholders were liable only to the amount uncalled on their shares.[72]

Indeed, the reluctance of the established banks to adopt limited liability would have been confirmed by the collapse in May 1866 of Overend, Gurney and Co., which had recently limited its liability. The collapse of this discount house greatly undermined several of the newly established limited-liability banks and fostered greater depositor scepticism, which encouraged a more conservative approach by bank owners to the adoption of limited liability.[73]

This raises another question: How were the limited-liability banks that established at this time able to assure depositors of the security of their deposits? Indeed, the only possible way in which the limited-liability banks could compete with the larger and longer established unlimited-liability banks was to provide an alternative form of commitment. As shown in Table 5.8, limited-liability banks had much higher levels of paid-up capital and shareholder reserves than their unlimited-liability counterparts. In addition, limited-liability banks had much higher levels of uncalled capital – that is, a fixed amount of capital that could be called from shareholders in the event of bank failure or by directors at any time.[74] Table 5.8 shows that the average limited-liability bank had enough uncalled capital to cover 64.8 per cent of deposits. In 1875, the average and median multiples of paid-up capital per share that was uncalled were 3.7 and 3.3, respectively.[75] In other words, for every £1 that shareholders in the average limited-liability bank had paid on their shares, they were liable for another £2.74. From the depositors' point of view, this uncalled margin made the limited banks 'practically as safe as an unlimited bank'.[76] Indeed, the liabilities to the public of the average

---

[72] Wilson, *Banking Reform*, p. 71. A similar view is given in Crick and Wadsworth, *A Hundred Years of Joint Stock Banking*, p. 31.

[73] Clapham, *Bank of England*, vol. II, p. 406. See also Anderson and Cottrell, *Money and Banking in England*, p. 249.

[74] Why did banks with unlimited liability have uncalled capital? The most likely explanation is that directors could tap uncalled capital if they needed funds to expand the bank, whereas calls on shareholder wealth for unlimited liability could be made only in the event of bank failure (Acheson, Turner and Ye, 'The character and denomination', pp. 865–6).

[75] Based on data for forty banks obtained from *Investor's Monthly Manual*, July 1875.

[76] Dun, 'The banking institutions', p. 28.

Table 5.8 *Capital of English limited- and unlimited-liability banks, 1874*

	Unlimited-liability banks	Limited-liability banks
Uncalled capital/liabilities to public (%)		
Mean	24.8	64.8
Median	13.9	50.6
Standard deviation	31.4	37.6
Paid-up capital/liabilities to public (%)		
Mean	13.4	29.6
Median	10.1	25.2
Standard deviation	8.5	22.3
Paid-up capital + shareholder reserves/liabilities to public (%)		
Mean	20.3	37.2
Median	15.8	30.5
Standard deviation	12.4	24.5
Total shareholder resources/liabilities to public (%)		
Mean	45.0	100.1
Median	31.9	88.4
Standard deviation	39.7	53.3
N	30	33

Source: Author's calculations based on data in Dun, 'The banking institutions'.
Notes: Only sixty-three English banks issued financial reports. Of these, only fifty-five reported the breakdown of their assets. All of the major banks issued reports; therefore, only small banks are omitted from these ratios. Total shareholder resources include uncalled capital, paid-up capital and shareholder reserves. The difference in means for each variable is statistically significant, with p-values close to zero in each case.

limited-liability bank in 1874 were totally covered by shareholder capital (Table 5.8).

The collapse of the CGB in 1878 may have changed investor perceptions about the risk of unlimited liability, and the Companies Act of 1879 facilitated the limitation of liability by enabling banks to create reserve liability, which was a halfway house between unlimited and pure limited liability. Reserve liability was exactly like uncalled capital except that it was not callable at the discretion of directors. In other words, it could be called on only in the event of a bank collapsing with inadequate funds to pay its depositors. The system of reserve liability and uncalled capital was almost a direct replacement for unlimited liability except that

Table 5.9 *Reserve liability and uncalled capital of British banks, 1885*

	Reserve liability/ paid-up capital		Reserve liability + uncalled capital/ paid-up capital		Number of banks with callable capital	Number of banks
	mean	median	mean	median		
England	1.64	1.38	3.12	3.00	111	116
Ireland	3.18	3.56	3.67	4.00	8	9
Scotland	2.64	3.00	2.85	4.00	8	10
United Kingdom	1.76	1.83	3.13	3.00	127	135

Source: Calculations based on data obtained from *Banking Almanac and Yearbook*, 1885.

shareholders now knew their maximum liability in the event of bank failure.[77] It also played a role in ameliorating bank risk taking.[78]

Similar to unlimited shareholder liability, one possible risk was that shares with reserve liability and uncalled capital could end up with individuals who had insufficient resources to cover the additional liability. Liability remained joint and several, which meant that shareholders were still concerned about the wealth of their co-owners but to a lesser degree. Similar to the case of unlimited liability, bank directors were able to prevent individuals with insufficient wealth from acquiring shares.[79] There is no evidence on the wealth of bank shareholders from a failed bank with reserve liability because, unlike the era in which unlimited liability was the norm, there were no major collapses. However, evidence presented before the National Monetary Commission in the United States suggested that directors of English banks were careful in admitting individuals to ownership and they frequently rejected transfers to those deemed unsuitable.[80] In addition, under the 1862 Companies Act, former shareholders of banks were liable for all unpaid capital for up to one year after they ceased to hold shares.[81]

Table 5.9 shows that the mean and median reserve liability for UK banks in 1885 was 1.76 and 1.83, respectively; however, taking callable capital into account, the average UK bank had a mean and median ratio

[77] Evans and Quigley, in 'Shareholder liability regimes', argued that the move away from unlimited liability was facilitated by the requirement placed on banks to have their accounts audited. However, it is difficult to explain how this would have assured depositors that their bank was not risk shifting.

[78] See Grossman and Imai, 'Contingent capital and bank risk-taking'.

[79] Rae, *The Country Banker*, p. 233.

[80] Withers and Palgrave, *The English Banking System*, p. 93.

[81] Plumptre, *Grant's Treatise on the Law*, p. 507.

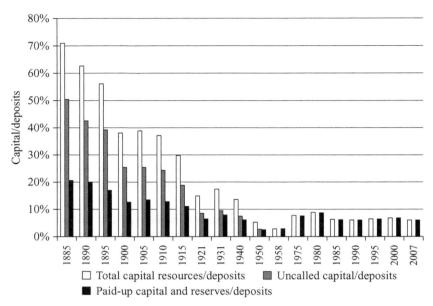

Figure 5.1 Aggregate capital-to-deposits ratio for the British banking system, 1885–2007

Sources: Banking Almanac and Yearbook (1900 and 1910), *Bankers' Almanac and Yearbook* (1921 and 1931) and *Stock Exchange Official Yearbook* (1940, 1950); Bank of England Archives, C40/102, Memo on bank capital (September 1958); *Annual Abstract of Banking Statistics* (1985, 1991, 1995); bank annual reports (2000 and 2007).

Notes: All major UK banks are included in these figures, but southern Irish banks are excluded from 1921 onwards. From 1975 onwards, only the major clearing banks are included. Total capital resources are the sum of uncalled capital, paid-up capital and shareholder reserves.

of reserve liability and callable capital to paid-up capital of 3.13 and 3.00, respectively. This implies that for the average bank in 1885, shareholders were liable for another £2.13 for every £1 that they had invested in the bank. As shown in Table 5.9, 127 of 135 UK banks had either reserve liability or callable capital. In essence, from the perspective of depositors, the limitation of liability had little immediate effect on the security of their deposits because banks were still constrained from risk shifting by the presence of reserve liability and uncalled capital.

Figure 5.1 shows that, on aggregate, slightly more than 70 per cent of deposits in 1885 were covered by shareholder capital, defined as uncalled

Table 5.10 *British bank capital, 1900–1958*

	1900	1910	1921	1931	1940	1950	1958
All Banks							
Total capital/deposits							
Mean	51.9	45.8	17.4	21.0	17.5	7.6	4.2
Median	44.3	40.3	16.2	20.4	17.4	7.4	3.5
Standard deviation	25.2	22.0	8.8	7.9	7.1	3.1	1.7
Maximum	126.4	101.8	46.2	38.9	36.2	13.6	9.4
Minimum	15.8	15.6	6.7	7.6	5.8	1.6	2.2
Number	90	57	25	22	16	16	17
Callable capital/deposits							
Mean	33.9	29.3	10.3	11.3	9.4	3.7	–
Median	28.6	24.4	10.5	11.9	10.1	4.2	–
Standard deviation	20.9	19.1	6.7	7.2	7.4	2.8	–
Maximum	93.6	84.7	23.7	25.9	27.7	10.1	–
Minimum	0.0	0.0	0.0	0.0	0.0	0.0	–
Number	90	57	25	22	16	16	–
Five Largest Banks							
Top five banks' share of deposits	28.1	37.8	73.1	76.8	80.6	83.4	76.6
Mean total capital/deposits	30.4	29.0	15.1	15.6	12.6	5.1	3.0
Median total capital/deposits	36.1	31.1	13.2	14.7	11.0	4.7	3.0
Mean callable capital/deposits	20.6	19.2	8.7	8.5	7.1	2.8	–
Median callable capital/deposits	25.8	20.8	7.3	7.3	5.8	2.5	–
Mean number of shareholders	10,104.0	16,827.0	48,674.7	64,717.4	n/a	n/a	n/a

Sources: Author's calculations based on data from *Banking Almanac and Yearbook* (1900 and 1910), *Bankers' Almanac and Yearbook* (1921 and 1931) and *Stock Exchange Official Yearbook* (1940, 1950); and Bank of England Archives, C40/102, Memo on Bank Capital (September 1958).

Notes: The Bank of England is excluded from these figures. From 1921 onwards, the figures exclude southern Irish banks, whereas the 1900 and 1910 figures include them. Total capital consists of reserve liability, uncalled capital, paid-up capital and shareholder reserves, whereas callable capital consists of reserve liability plus uncalled capital.

capital, reserve liability, paid-up capital and reserves. However, as shown in Figure 5.1, this ratio fell until 1900, where it stabilised at slightly less than 40 per cent. It fell again during World War I, reaching 15 per cent by 1921.

Table 5.10 shows that the average and median capital-to-deposits ratio between 1900 and 1921 also fell. Between 1921 and 1940, the average and median capital of all British banks did not change significantly, although the average and median capital-to-deposits ratio of the largest

Table 5.11 *The capital position of the top six London clearing banks, 1958*

	Loans (£ million)	British government securities (£ million)	Deposits (£ million)	Published capital and reserves (£ million)	Published capital and reserves/ deposits (%)	'True' capital estimate (£ million)	'True' capital/ deposits (%)	Provisions for 5% drop in government securities and 1% bad debts (£ million)	'True' ratio after deduction of provisions (%)
Barclays	377.7	476.8	1,511.7	43.9	2.9	92.2	6.1	27.6	4.3
Lloyds	341.5	326.3	1,259.6	37.4	3.0	68.4	5.4	19.7	3.9
Martin's	91.9	88.1	334.3	11.3	3.4	26.8	8.0	5.3	6.4
Midland	398.2	451.5	1,507.1	33.2	2.2	83.0	5.5	26.5	3.7
National Provincial	240.1	215.2	831.6	24.3	2.9	50.3	6.0	13.1	4.5
Westminster	248.4	249.3	889.1	28.7	3.2	60.0	6.7	14.9	5.1

Sources: Bank of England Archives, C40/102, Memo on bank capital (September 1958). The 'true' capital estimate is from Billings and Capie, 'Capital in British banks', p. 150.

Notes: Because the 'true' capital estimate for the National Provincial is not available for 1958, the average ratio of 'true' capital to published capital for other banks is used.

five banks fell slightly. By 1950, however, the ratio had fallen to a very low level and, by 1958, it had fallen even farther.

Until 1970, British banks were not required to disclose all of their reserves. Banks accumulated earnings in hidden reserves and, consequently, their true capital ratios were much higher than was implied by the capital published in their financial accounts.[82] According to estimates calculated by Billings and Capie, the average ratios of true capital to published capital in 1920, 1930, 1940, 1950 and 1960 were 1.25, 1.34, 1.57, 1.97 and 1.92, respectively.[83] In 1958, the average bank's true-capital position was 2.07 times that of its published figure. Nevertheless, making this adjustment means that the Big Five banks in 1958 had an average total capital-to-deposits ratio of only 6.0 per cent. However, as shown in Table 5.11, using Bank of England figures for loss provisions suggests that the average 'true' capital-to-deposit ratio of the Big Five banks in 1958 was actually closer to 4.3 per cent.

Notwithstanding the existence of hidden reserves, there is a significant decline in capital relative to deposits from the early 1880s to 1958. Why did this happen? The major contributory factor before World War I was that when banks amalgamated, they typically reduced the combined total of the two banks' reserve liability and uncalled capital, which came at the 'expense of some of the security of the depositors'.[84] The fall in the capital-to-deposits ratio during World War I was due to high wartime inflation. During the period 1915–18, inflation averaged 18.5 per cent, enough to erode a substantial part of the real value of capital. Indeed, the Colwyn Committee, reporting in 1918, was concerned about the 'unusual aggregation of deposits without fully adequate capital and reserves'.[85] The capital-to-deposits ratio fell again due to inflation during and after World War II: the average annual inflation rate between 1940 and 1950 was 5.5 per cent.

In 1921, Barclays Bank was the first bank to extinguish its uncalled capital. In 1937, the Bank of Scotland extinguished the uncalled capital on its shares in an attempt to increase the popularity of its shares and boost its dwindling number of shareholders.[86] The other major banks

---

[82] Goodhart, *Business of Banking*, pp. 23–5; Wilcox, 'Capital in banking', p. 211. Hidden reserves consisted mainly of the differences between the market and book values of a bank's investments. See Bank of England Archives, C44/304, Discount Office (Banking Supervision) Files, Memo, 7 December 1960; and Balogh, *Studies in Financial Organisation*, p. 102.

[83] Billings and Capie, 'Capital in British banks', p. 150.

[84] *Report of the Treasury Committee on Bank Amalgamations*, pp. 5–6.

[85] *Report of the Treasury Committee on Bank Amalgamations*, p. 7.

[86] Bank of England Archives, G14/75, Confidential internal memo (3 November 1937).

(i.e., Lloyds, Midland, Williams Deacon's, Martin's, National Provincial and Westminster) only extinguished their uncalled capital between 1956 and 1958 in a reorganisation that was supported and ultimately coordinated by the Bank of England.[87] However, even before its extirpation, there were doubts about the usefulness of uncalled capital in terms of constraining risk-shifting behaviour, as well as the wisdom of making calls on shareholders in the middle of a crisis. For example, in 1937, a deputy governor of the Bank of England was sceptical about the value of reserve liability, arguing that it was 'a survival from the time when banks were smaller and numerous; to-day a bank could not in a crisis make a call on shareholders without aggravating the crisis'.[88]

As highlighted in this quotation from the Bank's deputy governor, it may have been an issue of whether it would be easy to call up uncalled capital in the event of a crisis. As shown in Table 5.10, the average number of shareholders in the five largest banks grew dramatically between 1900 and 1940. One consequence of increasing shareholder numbers is that it may have become costly for directors to vet share transfers, and these costs may have led to the dwindling of directors' vetting of share transfers into a rubber-stamping exercise. Indeed, Sykes speculated at the time that most of the shareholders in the 1920s were individuals of modest means;[89] however, he produced no evidence to support his claim. Another consequence may have been the dramatically increased administrative costs associated with the collection of uncalled and reserve capital from shareholders in the event of bankruptcy. However, even if this were the case, the directors of these banks were required to invest significant amounts of capital to qualify as directors, and this investment meant that they were liable for significant amounts of uncalled capital in the event of bank failure. For example, four of the Big Five banks with uncalled capital in 1940 had an average of 28.5 directors whose average liability in 1940 could have been at least £3,762.50 – not a trivial sum.[90]

As shown in Figures 5.1 and 5.2, the capital position of British banking had improved by 1975. However, much of this improvement is illusory because reserves that were hidden in 1958 were shown in the published accounts in 1975. It is interesting that, as shown in Figure 5.2, from 1980 onwards, the aggregate capital-to-total-assets ratio falls as does the

---

[87] Bank of England Archives, C40/102, Confidential internal memo (30 April 1958).
[88] Bank of England Archives, C48/61, Capital of the Bank of Scotland secret memo (27 October 1937).
[89] Sykes, *The Present Position of English Joint Stock Banking*, p. 141.
[90] Calculated from *Stock Exchange Yearbook*, 1940.

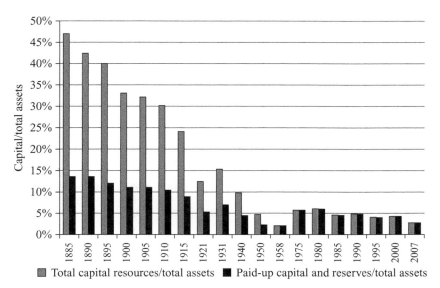

Figure 5.2 Aggregate capital-to-total-assets ratio for the British banking system, 1885–2007
Sources: Banking Almanac and Yearbook (1900 and 1910), *Bankers' Almanac and Yearbook* (1921 and 1931) and *Stock Exchange Official Yearbook* (1940, 1950); Bank of England Archives, C40/102, Memo on bank capital (September 1958); *Annual Abstract of Banking Statistics* (1985, 1991, 1995); bank annual reports (2000 and 2007); Sheppard, *The Growth and Role of UK Financial Institutions*, pp. 126–7.
Notes: All the major UK banks are included in these figures, but southern Irish banks are excluded from 1921 onwards. From 1975 onwards, only the major clearing banks are included. Total capital resources are the sum of uncalled capital, paid-up capital and shareholder reserves.

average capital-to-total deposits ratio (Table 5.12). The deterioration in this ratio between 2000 and 2007 is remarkable. Notably, the aggregate capital-to-deposits ratio does not fall after 1985 because banks increasingly borrowed on the money markets to fund their asset expansion.

Not only did the relative amount of total capital fall in the twentieth century; the quality of capital also fell. Paid-up capital is recognised by modern-day regulators as the highest quality capital because it is the money that shareholders actually pay into the bank. In 1900, the average paid-up capital-to-deposits ratio was 11.08 per cent; by 1950, this average had fallen to 1.70 per cent and, by 2007, it was a paltry 0.47 per cent.

Table 5.12 *Total shareholder funds/total assets (per cent) of major banks, 1975–2007*

	1975	1980	1985	1990	1995	2000	2007
Abbey National/Abbey	–	–	3.87	5.81	3.82	2.57	1.68
Bank of Scotland (HBOS from 2001)	7.03	7.32	5.55	4.90	4.43	5.59[1]	3.67
Barclays Bank	5.30	6.47	5.03	4.88	4.37	4.17	1.90
Bradford and Bingley	–	–	–	–	–	4.53	2.33
Lloyds (Lloyds-TSB from 1995)	6.06	7.02	5.29	4.94	3.27	4.47	3.52
Midland Bank	5.85	5.39	3.59	4.33	3.65	–	–
HSBC	–	–	–	–	–	4.76	4.55
National Westminster	5.95	5.41	4.18	4.99	4.39	–	–
Northern Rock	–	–	–	–	–	4.10	2.15[2]
Royal Bank of Scotland	6.91	8.07	5.89	5.04	4.28	5.96	2.79
Average	*6*	*6*	*4*	*4*	*4*	*4*	*2*

Sources: Annual Abstract of Banking Statistics 1985, 1991, 1995; bank annual reports 2000 and 2007.

Notes: [1] 2001 figure; [2] 2007 figure. Total shareholder funds include paid-up capital, retained profits, other reserves and share premium account.

Why did bank capital fall?

Bankers and banking theorists in the late nineteenth century were of the opinion that the proportion of capital to liabilities was the best measure of a bank's stability.[91] However, by the middle of the twentieth century, this was not the view of the Bank of England. During the 1940s and 1950s, several discussions were held between the banks and the Bank of England about strengthening the capital-to-deposit ratio. Indeed, most of the leading banks were eager to strengthen their capital position, with fourteen separate approaches made to the Bank of England by various clearing banks between 1943 and 1958.[92] The Bank and the Treasury were always reluctant to allow one bank to strengthen its capital position because this meant that other banks would have to follow suit, which would potentially divert capital away from productive industry.[93] In addition, the Bank realised that if the banks issued capital, it would reduce the funds available to support the government's large borrowing

---

[91] Rae, *The Country Banker*, p. 264.

[92] Bank of England Archives, C40/102, Confidential internal memo, 8 October 1958; Confidential internal memo, 6 February 1959.

[93] Bank of England Archives, C44/304, Discount Office (Banking Supervision) Files, Memo, 7 December 1960.

Table 5.13 *Published capital and reserves of the London clearing banks in 1958 and 1959*

	Published capital and reserves in 1958 (£ million)	Published capital and reserves/ deposits in 1958 (%)	Published capital and reserves in 1959 (£ million)	Published capital and reserves/ deposits in 1959 (%)	Increase in capital from 1958 to 1959 (%)
Barclays	43.9	2.9	60.8	3.7	38.5
Lloyds	37.4	3.0	58.8	4.5	57.2
Martin's	11.3	3.4	12.1	3.3	7.1
Midland	33.2	2.2	42.3	2.7	27.4
National Provincial	24.3	2.9	34.2	4.1	40.7
Westminster	28.7	3.2	37.0	4.0	28.9

Sources: Bank of England Archives, C40/102, Memo on bank capital, September 1958; and Memo on capital increases by clearing banks, 5 November 1959.

programme.[94] In the latter half of 1958 and into 1959, banks were permitted to issue new capital because the severe postwar credit squeeze was over.[95] As shown in Table 5.13, after this capital injection, the capital-to-deposits ratio increases by only a small order of magnitude.

The Bank of England's view in the 1940s and 1950s was that 'banks were not suffering in prestige from the low ratio of capital to deposits' and that the banks' capital had 'long ceased to bear any serious relation either to their liabilities or functions'.[96] Indeed, there was no indication that the banking public was concerned that low capital would materially affect banking stability; depositors were more concerned with a bank's liquidity than its capital.[97] This raises two questions: (1) Why did UK banks remain stable despite the fall in the capital-to-deposits ratio that occurred between 1914 and 1958? and (2) Why had the important relationship between capital and deposits deteriorated by the middle of the twentieth century?

One possibility is that banking became intrinsically more stable in this period and this improvement meant that banks needed substantially

---

[94] Bank of England Archives, C40/102, Confidential internal memo on bank capital, 30 September 1958.

[95] Bank of England Archives, C40/102, Memo on capital increases by clearing banks, 5 November 1959.

[96] Bank of England Archives, C40/102, Confidential internal memo on bank capital, 30 September 1958.

[97] Bank of England Archives, C40/102, Confidential internal memo, 10 April 1958; Jones, 'The business of banking'.

less capital.[98] Well-known directors of leading banks, including Edward
Holden (Midland) and F. C. Goodenough (Barclays), argued that the
intrinsic stability of the banking system had improved as a consequence
of banks growing stronger due to the amalgamation process.[99] As a consequence of the growth of large nationally branched banks, it is believed
that banks' assets and liabilities became more diversified and therefore
they were better able to absorb regional shocks.[100] For example, Holmes
and Green suggested that scale and geographical diversification meant
that 'emergencies which would have once threatened the life of dozens
of country banks were now absorbed quickly and without panic'.[101] Furthermore, it is suggested that the growth of banks with national-branch
networks led to reduced discretion for branch managers and the rise of a
mechanistic and more scientific approach to lending, which restricted it
to borrowers with adequate security.[102]

However, there are at least three pieces of evidence that cast doubt
on the explanation that capital fell due to a change in intrinsic stability.
First, the timing in some of the declines in capital does not correlate
with the changes in the structure of British banking. For example, the
basic structure of British banking did not change significantly between
1921 and 1958, yet capital ratios fell substantially. Second, from the perspective of the theory outlined in Chapter 2, an increase in scale does not
rule out risk-shifting behaviour. Indeed, increased scale may result in a
greater incentive to risk shift because the potential profit from so doing
is greater. In addition, there may be a perception, justified or not, that
large banks are too large to let fail, which creates a moral hazard. Third,
it is notable that although the basic structure of the Scottish banking
system remained relatively unchanged in the period 1900–58 in that the
dominant banks did not grow in scale or diversify geographically, bank
capital fell by a similar degree to that in England. This suggests that
diversification and growth in bank size may not have been a major contributing factor to the decline in the capital-to-deposits ratio. Similarly,
other advanced nations experienced a similar trend of decreasing capital
in this era without any radical change in their banking structures.[103]

[98] Sayers, *The Bank of England*, vol. I, p. 11.
[99] Sykes, *Amalgamation Movement*, p. 162. Bank of England Archives, G1/10, Extract
from an address delivered by F. C. Goodenough in Sweden, 9 May 1927.
[100] Bank of England Archives, G1/9, Draft of an article in *Bankers' Magazine*, May 1924,
'Bank Amalgamations – the Last Phase'.
[101] Holmes and Green, *Midland*, p. 119.
[102] Sykes, *The Present Position*, p. 120; Holmes and Green, *Midland*, p. 113.
[103] Grossman, *Unsettled Account*, pp. 148–9; Berger, Herring and Szegö, 'The role of
capital', p. 402.

Another possibility (developed in Chapter 7) is that there were substitutes for bank capital that constrained banks' ability to risk shift. In particular, the informal system of constraints and controls prevalent from the 1930s until the 1970s, in which the Bank of England acted as a Janus-like intermediary between banks and the Treasury, may have been a substitute for bank capital.

A global perspective

From 1826 onwards, banking in the United Kingdom was dominated by large joint-stock banks with shareholders having unlimited liability. Unlimited liability acted as a constraint on risk shifting, which meant that banks were able to weather frequent political, economic and monetary shocks. Unlimited liability also had an important role in underpinning the stability of other banking systems during their formative years in the nineteenth century (e.g., France, Germany, Holland, Japan and Sweden).[104] Although the then-newly emerging economies of Australia, Canada, and the United States eschewed unlimited liability early in the history of their banking systems, bank shareholders faced double liability, other than state banks in several US states where shareholders had full limited liability.[105]

The move away from unlimited liability in Britain occurred after the hysteria surrounding the CGB failure. The arguments for moving away from unlimited liability were fallacious, but the proponents of limited liability seized opportunistically on the CGB collapse to push through reforms that enabled banks to drop unlimited liability. Because depositors still required assurance that banks would not engage in risk shifting, the banks adopted reserve liability and had uncalled capital. This was a compromise between unlimited liability and pure limited liability. These systems, as discussed previously, existed in Australia, Canada and the United States.

In the case of the United States, double liability applied to all national banks, but different states imposed different liability regimes on state-chartered banks, with most states imposing double liability by the beginning of the twentieth century and some imposed even stricter regimes (e.g., California had pro rata unlimited liability). Several studies have found that double liability in the United States reduced bank risk

---

[104] Hickson and Turner, 'Free banking and the stability', p. 912.
[105] Hickson and Turner, 'Free banking and the stability', pp. 905–6.

taking.[106] Nevertheless, as observed by Grossman, double liability did not prevent the banking crises in the United States in the early 1930s.[107] Why not? The UK experience may prove instructive in this regard.

First, the security provided to depositors by extended liability can be substantially weakened by inflation: under unlimited liability, a shareholder is fully liable to their last penny, whereas the maximum liability under the reserve-liability and uncalled-capital system was a fixed amount denominated in pounds sterling. This weakness was demonstrated during World War I, when wartime inflation substantially eroded the real value of paid-up and uncalled capital. Like the United Kingdom, the United States experienced high inflation at that time.

Second, unlike British banks in the 1930s, US banks were small unitary institutions as a result of branch-banking restrictions. This meant that US banks were small companies with concentrated stock ownership and an undiversified pool of owners.[108] In one sense, a parallel could be drawn between the United States at that time and the situation in England before the liberalisation of joint-stock banking in 1826, when it had small unitary banks. The case of Canada is also informative because its large commercial banks had double liability, yet it did not experience a banking crisis during the Great Depression.

It is interesting that the United States, Canada and Great Britain terminated extended liability for banks at roughly the same time. In the United States, the Banking Act of 1935 permitted national banks to eliminate double liability and the states gradually followed, with most having completed the process by 1940.[109] However, extended liability was only formally abolished in the United States in 1953. Canada phased out double liability for banks between 1936 and 1950.[110] In the United Kingdom, the extirpation of the remnants of uncalled capital occurred between 1956 and 1958 in an operation coordinated by the Bank of England.

At the same time that double and extended liability was disappearing, capital-to-asset and capital-to-deposit ratios were also falling in these three economies and elsewhere.[111] The low ebb reached in the 1940s did not improve much in the remainder of the twentieth century; indeed,

---

[106] Esty, 'The impact of contingent liability'; Grossman, 'Double liability'; Macey and Miller, 'Double liability'; Mitchener and Richardson, 'Does skin in the game reduce risk taking'.
[107] Grossman 'Double liability'.
[108] Mitchener and Richardson, 'Does skin in the game reduce risk taking'.
[109] Mitchener and Richardson, 'Does skin in the game reduce risk taking'.
[110] Wagster, 'Wealth and risk effects', p. 1653.
[111] Berger, Herring and Szegö, 'The role of capital', p. 402; Grossman, *Unsettled Account*, pp. 148–9; Saunders and Wilson, 'The impact of consolidation'.

from the 1990s onwards, the capital position of British and other banks deteriorated further, if anything. It was in these conditions, when (to use modern parlance) bank shareholders 'had hardly any skin in the game' that the United Kingdom and many other developed economies experienced the worst banking collapse ever.

6 Averting or creating banking crises? The lender of last resort and bank rescues

Any propping up of shaky positions postpones liquidation and aggravates unsound conditions.[1]

Murray Rothbard

In ordinary times the Bank [of England] is only one of many lenders, whereas in a panic it is the sole lender...[2]

Walter Bagehot

The Bank of England financed merely the crisis: the private bankers of London and the provinces financed the boom.[3]

Arthur D. Gayer, W. W. Rostow and Anna Jacobson Schwartz

Thus far in this book, we discovered that the UK banking system experienced two major crises: one in 1825–6 and the other in 2007–8. We also discovered that the stability of the system for a significant part of the interim period (at least until the 1920s and possibly beyond) is closely connected to the incentives provided first by unlimited liability and then by reserve liability and uncalled capital. The aim of this chapter is to understand how the Bank of England and the Treasury may have contributed (or otherwise) to the stability of the UK banking system in the past two centuries. In particular, the chapter analyses the evolution of the Bank's (and the Treasury's) fire-fighting role during crises. The chapter argues that the Bank's role as a classical lender of last resort (LLR) was key to ending stress in the banking system during episodic pressure in the money market. However, the evolution of its role as a bailout coordinator or facilitator, backed by the Treasury, ultimately undermined the stability of the banking system.

Bagehot and Thornton on the theory of the lender of last resort

According to Kindleberger, the LLR 'stands ready to halt a run out of real and illiquid financial assets into money by making more money

---

[1] Rothbard, *America's Great Depression*, p. 167. [2] Bagehot, *Lombard Street*.
[3] Gayer, Rostow and Schwartz, *Growth and Fluctuation*, p. 205.

available'.[4] However, when we ask more questions, the LLR becomes a complex notion that means different things to different economists and that has changed over time.[5] For example, who should be the LLR? How much should be loaned and on what terms? Should its availability be unambiguously signalled ex-ante? Should last-resort loans be made to the market or to individual institutions? If last-resort loans are to be made to individual institutions, should it be only to illiquid institutions or also to insolvent institutions? Can last-resort lending be structured so as to prevent moral hazard?

In terms of the origins of the concept, the classical LLR position was first articulated by Francis Baring and Henry Thornton during the Restriction period at the end of the eighteenth century.[6] It was further developed by Thomas Joplin.[7] Walter Bagehot is most closely associated with the idea of the LLR but, in many ways, through his influential writings he merely popularised and articulated concepts that had already been developed by Thornton and Joplin.

For Bagehot, the rationale for an LLR simply arose from the Bank of England's privileged monopoly, acquired over time, which resulted in its holding the nation's monetary reserve. For Thornton, however, the rationale for an LLR existed even if the banking and monetary systems had not evolved in this manner.[8] Bagehot argued that the single reserve system that had evolved in the United Kingdom was not the natural order.[9] However, Bagehot was a pragmatist.[10] He argued that the Bank – because it held the ultimate banking reserve of the country (i.e., gold) and because its notes were de facto legal tender – had two main duties to the public: (1) defending reserves from an external drain by raising the bank rate to attract gold into and prevent it from flowing out of the country; and (2) lending freely in times of an internal drain, whatever the reason for the panic.[11]

Both Bagehot and Thornton recognised that the Bank of England, which was a profit-making company at the time, had a public responsibility during times of panic to keep lending even as other bankers contracted theirs.[12] For both Thornton and Bagehot, one aim of the LLR

---

[4] Kindleberger, *Manias, Panics and Crashes*, p. 146.
[5] For an overview of the literature, see Bordo, 'The lender of last resort'; and Freixas, Giannini, Hoggarth and Soussa, 'Lender of last resort'.
[6] Thornton, *An Enquiry into the Nature and Effects of the Paper Credit*; Baring, *Observations on the Establishment of the Bank of England.*
[7] O'Brien, 'The lender-of-last-resort concept'.
[8] Laidler, 'Two views of the lender of last resort', p. 13.
[9] Bagehot, *Lombard Street*, pp. 67, 94.   [10] Bagehot, *Lombard Street*, p. 69.
[11] Bagehot, *Lombard Street*, pp. 46–8.
[12] Humphrey and Keleher, 'The lender of last resort', p. 284.

function was to prevent a collapse in general liquidity. Bagehot ultimately was concerned about the effect of illiquidity on the supply of credit and potential fire-sale losses for banks.[13] For his part, Thornton was more concerned about the effect of illiquidity on bank liabilities in the form of a contraction of and instability in the money supply, as well as the velocity of its circulation.[14]

When asked who should receive last-resort loans, some economists infer that Bagehot and Thornton would have supported the idea of using open-market operations (i.e., wherein a central bank buys government securities on the open market, thereby pumping reserves into the banking system) rather than the discount window (i.e., the discount office wherein a central bank discounts securities of banks) to address systemic liquidity crises.[15] However, in the context about which Bagehot and Thornton were writing, LLR loans were made to specific institutions that had liquidity problems in the middle of a panic; they were not made to bolster a vague concept such as the market or system.

Thomson Hankey, an experienced director of the Bank of England, was critical of Bagehot's views on the LLR, describing them as 'the most mischievous doctrine ever broached in the monetary or banking world'; he believed that this doctrine would undermine prudent banking behaviour.[16] Hankey recognised the potential moral hazard associated with the provision of last-resort lending: the ex-ante behaviour of banks changes, making it more likely that last-resort lending will be required. However, both Bagehot and Thornton were aware of this problem and, for this reason, they were opposed to lending to institutions that clearly were insolvent and that had been reckless.[17] In other words, the classical LLR concept as developed by Bagehot and Thornton was not a matter of lending to or bailing out banks that had taken excessive risks. In addition, the moral hazard that arises from the LLR could be ameliorated by charging a penalty rate for LLR loans, providing LLR loans on the basis of high-quality security or collateral, or being constructively

---

[13] Bagehot, *Lombard Street*, pp. 51–2, 58 and 61.

[14] Laidler, 'Two views of the lender of last resort', p. 13.

[15] O'Brien, 'The lender-of-last-resort concept', p. 4; Humphrey and Keleher, 'The lender of last resort', p. 287.

[16] Bagehot, *Lombard Street*, p. 169. According to Clapham, 'in this clash the chief antagonists were unequally matched, Bagehot with as good a head and as good a pen as any in England, Hankey with – well – neither' (Clapham, *Bank of England*, vol. II, p. 283).

[17] For example, Thornton suggested that 'it is by no means intended to imply, that it would become the Bank of England to relieve every distress which the rashness of country banks may bring upon them. The bank, by doing this, might encourage their improvidence' (Thornton, *An Enquiry into the Nature and Effects of the Paper Credit*, p. 188).

ambiguous about whether LLR loans would be provided and on what terms.[18]

Bagehot is generally believed to have advocated the dictum that last-resort lending should be at a penalty rate.[19] However, although he suggested that last-resort loans be 'made at a very high rate of interest', he did not mean a penalty rate.[20] Bagehot simply meant that to protect the banking reserve, the LLR should not lend at a rate below the prevailing market rate in order to discourage institutions that did not need reserves from seeking them.[21] For Bagehot, internal drains were typically accompanied by external drains, and the latter usually required high interest rates to stymie them.[22] Consequently, last-resort lending was typically at a high interest rate but was offered at the prevailing market rate, not a penalty rate.

Bagehot advocated that last-resort loans should be collateralised by being 'made on all good banking securities'.[23] What Bagehot meant by a good security was one that in ordinary circumstances was reckoned to be a good security.[24] Bagehot's rule does not necessarily mean that the Bank of England should not lend to insolvent banks; it is generally impossible to distinguish between insolvency and illiquidity when a bank approaches the LLR.[25] However, if a bank is close to insolvency because it has been risk shifting, we would expect that it would have few good bills or securities to pledge as collateral for last-resort loans.

Bagehot recognised that 'the Bank, more or less, does its duty' as an LLR but that it 'did not distinctly acknowledge that it was its duty'. The lack of ex-ante commitment by the Bank troubled Bagehot; he knew that when a panic occurred, the public was uncertain whether the Bank was going to act as an LLR, with the result that the scramble for cash at the beginning of a panic was exacerbated.[26] Therefore, Bagehot argued that the availability of last-resort lending in a panic should be a preannounced policy. In this, Bagehot was anticipated by Joplin.[27] However, despite Bagehot's dictum, the Bank of England – like many other central banks – has never explicitly acknowledged its LLR function. A possible reason for this is that it curbs moral hazard by means of constructive ambiguity.[28] In

---

[18] For a survey, see Moore, 'Solutions to the moral hazard problem'.
[19] Humphrey and Keleher, 'The lender of last resort', p. 287.
[20] There is no reference to a penalty rate in either Bagehot or Thornton (Goodhart, 'Myths about the lender of last resort', p. 4).
[21] Bagehot, *Lombard Street*, p. 197.   [22] Bagehot, *Lombard Street*, pp. 56–7.
[23] Bagehot, *Lombard Street*, p. 197.   [24] Bagehot, *Lombard Street*, p. 198.
[25] Goodhart, 'Myths about the lender of last resort'.
[26] Bagehot, *Lombard Street*, pp. 173, 206–7.
[27] O'Brien, The lender-of-last-resort concept', p. 11.
[28] Giannini, 'Enemy of none but a common friend of all?', p. 14.

other words, it is not certain that last-resort lending will be made available or on what terms and conditions. However, such a policy suffers from a time-inconsistency problem, which raises doubt about its ability to alleviate the moral hazard associated with the LLR.

The practice of last-resort lending in the United Kingdom

Having reviewed the theory of the LLR, we turn now to what the Bank of England actually did during crises.[29] James argues that the Bank was acting occasionally and inconsistently as a de facto LLR before 1825.[30] Similarly, according to Lovell, the Bank was acting as an LLR during episodes of instability that occurred in the last four decades of the eighteenth century, in that it expanded its discount operations during those episodes.[31] During the crisis that peaked in December 1825, demand for specie by country-bank depositors and note-holders increased sharply and suddenly, and 'the want of confidence became so general, that there was an immediate application to the Bank for assistance upon commercial discounts and every other species of security; the market rate of interest immediately rose to the Bank's rate, and the Bank was the only resource'.[32] At first, however, the Bank was averse to lending freely and was reluctant to lend even on the security of government debt.[33] As a result, something of a standoff ensued between the Bank of England and the government, with the former wanting the latter to suspend convertibility and issue exchequer bills as it had in 1793. However, the government held firm and the Bank had to back down. On 14 December 1825, it started to lend freely but was unable to raise the bank rate because the usury laws limited it to 5 per cent.[34] According to Jeremiah Harman, a Bank of England director from 1794 to 1827, it would seem that the Treasury pressured the Bank to increase its note issue by discounting freely.[35] Subsequently, according to Harman, the Bank lent freely

---

[29] The Bank of Ireland may have been a quasi-LLR to Irish banks; see Ó Gráda, 'Moral hazard and quasi-central banking' and 'The last major Irish bank failure'; and Munn, 'The emergence of central banking in Ireland'.

[30] James, 'Panics'.   [31] Lovell, 'The role of the Bank of England as lender of last resort'.

[32] *Committee of Secrecy on the Bank of England Charter*, P.P. 1831–32 VI, Evidence of J. Palmer, q. 608.

[33] *Committee of Secrecy on the Bank of England Charter*, P.P. 1831–32 VI, Evidence of N. M. Rothschild, qq. 4895–6.

[34] *Committee of Secrecy on the Bank of England Charter*, P.P. 1831–32 VI, Evidence of Jeremiah Harman, qq. 2216–25; John Richards, qq. 5031–35.

[35] *Committee of Secrecy on the Bank of England Charter*, P.P. 1831–32 VI, Evidence of Jeremiah Harman, qq. 2218–20.

... by every possible means, and in modes that we never had adopted before; we took in stock as security, we purchased exchequer bills, we made advances on exchequer bills, we not only discounted outright, but we made advances on deposit of bills of exchange to an immense amount; in short, by every possible means consistent with the safety of the Bank; and we were not upon some occasions over nice; seeing the dreadful state in which the public were, we rendered every assistance in our power.[36]

The Bank of England was further pressured in February 1826 when the British government urged it to lend up to £3 million against goods repayable within three months in order to help the mercantile community. It appears from the Bank's minutes that they reluctantly agreed to this 'request'; ultimately, only £3,000 to £4,000 pounds was advanced.[37] The government put immense pressure on the Bank in February 1826 and was even willing to resign if Parliament did not support its policy vis-à-vis the Bank.[38] Clapham stated that 'the Bank was never so inert in the hands of ministers, so much ordered about, as in 1826'.[39]

As shown in Figure 6.1, the volume of bills and notes under discount by the Bank of England reached extremely high and unusual levels from December 1825 to February 1826. However, when the crisis had abated, discounting by the Bank fell back to its normal pre-crisis level. This clearly indicates that the Bank started to lend freely and substantially in December 1825. Table 6.1 provides details of the Bank's half-yearly balance sheets, which indicate that its position changed radically by February 1826 but returned to normal after the crisis had ended. Between August 1825 and February 1826, the Bank's holdings of securities increased by 31 per cent and private securities increased by 60 per cent. These increases are reflected in the 31 per cent increase in the Bank's note circulation. It is clear from this evidence that the Bank was lending freely in this period.

The directors of the Bank of England were commended for their actions in 1825–6 by N. M. Rothschild, for they 'did all in their power to relieve the distress, and they discounted as liberally as any body of men could do, and they deserve the greatest credit from the country for what they did'.[40] The Bank's liberality was not without risk to itself.[41]

---

[36] *Committee of Secrecy on the Bank of England Charter*, P.P. 1831–32 VI, Evidence of Jeremiah Harman, q. 2217.

[37] *Committee of Secrecy on the Bank of England Charter*, P.P. 1831–32 VI, Evidence of J. Palmer, q. 581; Clapham, *Bank of England*, vol. II, p. 108.

[38] Fetter, 'A Historical Confusion in Bagehot's *Lombard Street*'.

[39] Clapham, *Bank of England*, vol. II, p. 107.

[40] *Committee of Secrecy on the Bank of England Charter*, P.P. 1831–32 VI, Evidence of N. M. Rothschild, q. 4897.

[41] *Committee of Secrecy on the Bank of England Charter*, P.P. 1831–32 VI, Evidence of J. Palmer, q. 596.

Table 6.1 *Bank of England's half-yearly balance sheets, 1824–1828*

	Public securities (£ million)	Private securities (£ million)	Bullion (£ million)	Deposits (£ million)	Circulation (£ million)
February 1824	14.341	4.530	13.810	10.097	19.736
August 1824	14.649	6.255	11.787	9.679	20.132
February 1825	19.447	5.503	8.779	10.168	20.753
August 1825	17.414	7.691	3.634	6.410	19.398
February 1826	20.573	12.345	2.459	6.935	25.467
August 1826	17.713	7.369	6.754	6.754	21.563
February 1827	18.685	4.844	10.159	8.801	21.890
August 1827	19.809	3.389	10.463	8.052	22.747
February 1828	19.818	3.762	10.347	9.198	21.980
August 1828	20.682	3.222	10.498	10.201	21.357

Source: Committee of Secrecy on the Bank of England Charter, P.P. 1831–32 VI, Appendix 5.

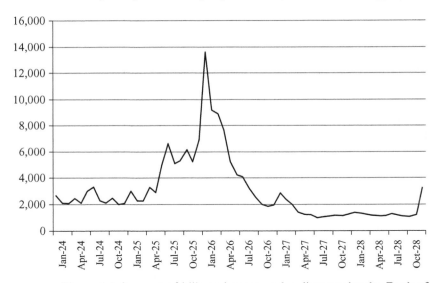

Figure 6.1 Amount of bills and notes under discount by the Bank of England (£'000), 1824–1828
Source: Committee of Secrecy on the Bank of England Charter, P.P. 1831–32 VI, Appendix 5.

For example, George Grote, a City banker, stated that the Bank 'did actually take a great risk upon itself... the Directors ran the matter very close to a suspension, and fortunately escaped it, the event might have been otherwise. Their conduct at the crisis of 1825 is of course to have been considered as having been liberal and daring... they certainly did very great good by the assistance they rendered to the commercial world'.[42] Thomas Tooke, however, was slightly sceptical about the good done by the Bank's liberal lending policy.[43] Bagehot commended the Bank for lending freely in 1825–6 but criticised it for being slow to implement this policy and doing so only under compulsion from the government.[44]

According to Bagehot, the crisis of 1836–7 did not result in a panic demand for cash and therefore did not affect the Bank.[45] However, at the end of 1836, the Bank was approached by two of the large banks that would subsequently fail. In mid November 1836, the Bank of Ireland refused to discount the bills of the Agricultural and Commercial Bank of Ireland, which then approached the Bank of England for assistance but was refused.[46] At the end of November, the Northern and Central Bank of England (NCBoE) approached the Bank of England for assistance, looking for £100,000 immediately and access to an additional £400,000 as and when required.[47] The Bank of England gave assistance but on strict terms: the NCBoE had to close most of its branches and only the Bank could discount its bills. However, the subsequent exposure of the NCBoE's abysmal financial position in mid December 1836 – as well as the fact that its officials had been less than forthright about the bank's state of affairs when they originally requested assistance – resulted in the refusal by the Bank of England to provide further assistance and the establishment of a committee of shareholders to assist with the bank's liquidation.[48] Clearly, the Bank of England was not prepared to bail out this large insolvent bank, but the official position of the Bank's Court in 1836 was that it recognised its responsibility to be an LLR.[49]

The Bank Charter Act of 1844 was an attempt to make the currency behave like a pure metallic monetary system by restricting the Bank of England from issuing more currency above its fiduciary limit unless it was 100 per cent backed by bullion, which obliged the Bank to maintain a reserve against its currency in circulation.[50] In terms of the LLR role that it had assumed since 1825 (or earlier), the Bank Charter Act complicated the matter because it was 'interpreted to mean that if the reserve fell to zero, the Bank would refuse to lend at all. There would be no lender of

---

[42] *Committee of Secrecy on the Bank of England Charter*, P.P. 1831–32 VI, Evidence of George Grote, q. 4648.

[43] *Committee of Secrecy on the Bank of England Charter*, P.P. 1831–32 VI, Evidence of Thomas Tooke, q. 3864.

[44] Bagehot, *Lombard Street*, pp. 202–3.   [45] Bagehot, *Lombard Street*, p. 203.

[46] Ó Gráda, *Ireland: A New Economic History*, p. 143.

[47] *Select Committee on Joint Stock Banks*, P.P. 1837 XIV, Evidence of Thomas Evans, q. 1171.

[48] *Select Committee on Joint Stock Banks*, P.P. 1837 XIV, Appendix IV.

[49] See Horsefield, 'The Bank of England as mentor'.   [50] 7 & 8 Vict., c.32, s.2.

last resort, and the discount market would dry up altogether'.[51] In effect, the Bank was restrained by the Bank Charter Act and the stage was set for trouble.[52]

When the accelerated rate of mercantile failures hit the money markets in September 1847, the Bank of England could not meet the panic demand for cash. Indeed, under the terms of the Bank Charter Act, the Bank's sole objective during the crisis was to ensure that its reserve was adequate, with the consequence that – unlike in previous crises – it was unable to lend freely.[53] Indeed, such were the constraints of the Bank Charter Act that the Bank did the opposite of what it typically had done during a money-market panic: it sold Consols (government-issued bonds) and contracted its discount lending.[54] Such were the strains on the money market by mid October that a relaxatory letter was sent from the Prime Minister and Chancellor of the Exchequer to the Bank of England recommending that the Bank 'enlarge the amount of their discounts and advances upon approved security'. In turn, the Bank would be indemnified against infringing the Bank Charter Act; that is, the Bank could exceed its fiduciary issue without the need for additional bullion.[55] This gave the Bank freedom to discount without the need to be concerned about the size of its reserve.

The relaxatory letter was enough to ease concerns in the money markets.[56] The Bank of England did not even have to increase its issue beyond the limit stipulated in the Bank Charter Act because the letter quelled the panic: it held out to 'persons the certainty that they might get accommodation whereas before they feared that they should not'. This released the notes hoarded by bankers and merchants, a sum estimated to be £4 million.[57] At the same time, following the relaxatory letter, the Bank also appears to have discounted freely.[58]

Three banks that benefitted greatly from the Bank's LLR assistance in 1847 were the Liverpool Borough Bank, the Northumberland and

---

[51] Hawtrey, *A Century of Bank Rate*, p. 21.

[52] Clapham, *Bank of England*, vol. II, p. 283; O'Brien, The lender-of-last-resort concept', p. 13.

[53] *Secret Committee of the House of Lords on Causes of Commercial Distress*, P.P. 1847–8 I, Evidence of C. Turner, qq. 716–7.

[54] Dornbusch and Frankel, 'The Gold Standard'.

[55] *Secret Committee of the House of Lords on Causes of Commercial Distress*, P.P. 1847–8 I, Committee Report, p. x.

[56] Evans, *The Commercial Crisis*, p. 83; *Secret Committee of the House of Lords on Causes of Commercial Distress*, P.P. 1847–8 I, Evidence of James Morris and H. J. Prescott, q. 2671.

[57] *Secret Committee of the House of Lords on Causes of Commercial Distress*, P.P. 1847–8 I, Committee Report, p. x.

[58] *Secret Committee of the House of Lords on Causes of Commercial Distress*, P.P. 1847–8 I, Evidence of James Morris and H. J. Prescott, q. 2671.

Durham District Bank, and the Western Bank of Scotland.[59] However, the subsequent collapse of these three institutions in 1857, in circumstances 'more injurious both to their own proprietors and to the public', contributed greatly to the 'commercial disaster and discredit of 1857'.[60] The three banks never fully recovered after 1847 and they carried over accumulating bad and doubtful debts from year to year. The Bank, acting as an LLR, may have postponed liquidation and facilitated the continuing existence of unsound banks, which ultimately shifted risk in their attempt to recover. Nevertheless, the Bank appears to have taken a stricter stance with problem banks in subsequent periods of commercial stress. Although it is mere speculation, it is possible that the pressure on the money market had grown so intense before the 1847 relaxatory letter that the Bank was not sufficiently discriminating once the letter was published.

As the panic in the money markets worsened during the autumn of 1857, banks limited their discounts and hoarded liquidity by building up their cash reserves. According to the Bank's Governor, 'discounts almost entirely ceased in London, except at the Bank of England'.[61] Such was the pressure that, as in 1847, a relaxatory letter was issued by the government on 12 November 1857 that indemnified the Bank if it exceeded the statutory limit on its note issue. However, the issuance of the letter did not immediately becalm the market as in 1847; the Bank continued to meet the huge demand for discounts and advances, as shown in Figure 6.2. As a consequence of this increase, by the end of November, the Bank had exceeded its statutory note issue by £2 million.[62]

According to its Governor, Sheffield Neave, the Bank of England had been lending freely before the relaxatory letter was published and had done so on public grounds and not for profit.[63] Indeed, according to Neave, the Bank was acting as liberally as it had ever done in a crisis and was not hindered in its liberality by the Bank Charter Act.[64] As shown in Figure 6.2, by the time of the government's letter, the Bank's discounting had increased from £7 million in September to £13 million in November. The consensus view from the witnesses before the Select Committee on the Bank Acts was that the Bank of England appears

---

[59] Bank of England Archives G16/1, Secretary's Index Book, 29 October and 5 November 1847.

[60] *Select Committee on the Bank Acts*, P.P. 1858, LXXVIII, Committee Report, p. xxi.

[61] *Select Committee on the Bank Acts*, P.P. 1858, LXXVIII, Committee Report, p. viii.

[62] *Select Committee on the Bank Acts*, P.P. 1858, LXXVIII, Committee Report, p. x.

[63] *Select Committee on the Bank Acts*, P.P. 1858, LXXVIII, Evidence of Sheffield Neave, qq. 456–6, 870–2.

[64] *Select Committee on the Bank Acts*, P.P. 1858, LXXVIII, Evidence of Sheffield Neave, qq. 600–3.

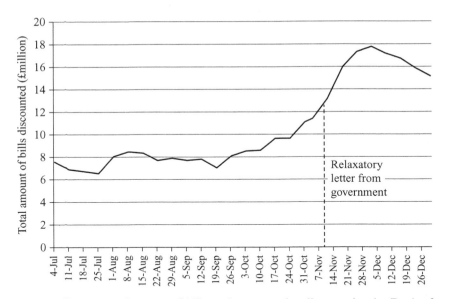

Figure 6.2 Amount of bills and notes under discount by the Bank of England, 1857
Source: Select Committee on the Bank Acts, P.P. 1858, LXXVIII, Appendix 6.

to have lent freely during the 1857 crisis, in that every institution that applied for and that warranted help from the Bank promptly received it.[65] However, one banker testifying before this committee argued that the Bank of England acting as an LLR created a moral-hazard problem in that banks expanded credit to an excessive degree in the knowledge that they could always obtain liquidity from the Bank.[66]

It seems that by the crisis of 1866, the Bank of England and the government had both learned how to respond to a panic in the money markets. On 11 May 1866, the day after the failure of Overend, Gurney and Co., there was great pressure on the Bank. On 11 May, it freely loaned about £4 million on the security of government stock and did not refuse any legitimate application for assistance.[67] On the following

[65] *Select Committee on the Bank Acts*, P.P. 1858, LXXVIII, Committee Report, p. viii; Evidence of J. E. Coleman (qq. 1957–60), George Foster (q. 2133) and John Torr (q. 4980).

[66] *Select Committee on the Bank Acts*, P.P. 1858, LXXVIII, Evidence of Joshua Dixon, qq. 4266–7.

[67] Bank of England Archives G4/89, Minutes of Court of Directors, 11 May 1866.

day, the usual relaxatory letter was issued by the government. However, the Bank did not exceed its statutory note issue as it had done in 1857.

In the 1866 crisis, unlike those of 1847 and 1857, lending by the Bank of England increased substantially and quickly at the onset: the sum of Bank discounts and advances increased from £10 million in April 1866 to close to £24 million in May.[68] Furthermore, unlike in the two previous panics, the Bank does not appear this time to have rationed credit. In other words, there is evidence to suggest that over time, the Bank was becoming more liberal during crises.[69] An alternative interpretation is that at the time of the earlier crises, they were difficult to identify as such; whereas in 1866, it was easier to identify, being somewhat more straightforward.[70]

Capie argued that the failure of the CGB in October 1878 was not accompanied by an immediate rush to cash as had happened in previous crises; therefore, there was no great need for an LLR.[71] However, Collins found that there was as much pressure on commercial banks as there had been in previous crises.[72] Lloyds, for example, experienced a persistent cash drain in the half-year after the CGB collapse, with a 20 per cent decrease in deposits.[73] Collins provided evidence that suggests that this cash drain suffered by banks was met by the Bank of England.[74] He suggested that the Bank's cash position going into the crisis was much healthier than in previous crises so that it was never under any serious pressure. Notably, Bagehot recommended that the Bank should always maintain a large banking reserve due to the 'inevitable vicissitudes of Lombard Street'.[75]

Another reason that there was no money-market panic was that, unlike the previous crises of the nineteenth century, the 1878–9 crisis was not accompanied by the bursting of a speculative mania and had not been preceded by an expansion of credit; the result was that the system was not as vulnerable as in previous crises. In addition, after 1866, banks held a greater proportion of their total assets, on average, in cash and near-cash liquid assets.[76]

---

[68] Collins, 'The Bank of England', p. 151.
[69] Bignon, Flandreau and Ugolini, 'Bagehot for beginners'.
[70] Rockoff, 'Walter Bagehot', p. 172.   [71] Capie, 'Banking in Europe', p. 126.
[72] Collins, 'The Bank of England'.
[73] Sayers, *Lloyds Bank*, p. 211; Ogden, 'An analysis of Bank of England discount and advance behaviour', p. 322.
[74] For example, the Yorkshire Banking Company received discounts of £102,000 and the Clydesdale Bank received discounts of £315,000 in November 1878 (see Ogden, 'An analysis of Bank of England discount and advance behaviour', p. 322).
[75] Bagehot, *Lombard Street*, pp. 158–9.
[76] Collins and Baker, *Commercial Banks and Industrial Finance*, p. 88.

At the end of July 1914, the breakdown of European-capital markets and a foreign-exchange crisis – with foreign borrowers unable to remit due to the start of the war – resulted in severe liquidity pressures on UK banks and an increase in the demand for gold. This pressure may have been aggravated by the aggressive liquidity hoarding of commercial banks in anticipation of gold hoarding by depositors.[77] Initially, the Bank of England could not deal with this crisis due to the need to maintain gold convertibility. However, rather than the typical policy of suspending the Bank Charter Act, the liquidity crisis was averted this time by a three-day extension of the usual Bank Holiday (3 August) and an issue of £1 and 10 shillings Treasury notes redeemable in gold at the Bank of England.[78] When the banks reopened on 7 August, there was no rush for gold by depositors even though Britain was officially at war. The 'crisis' was over. In subsequent weeks, the Bank, underwritten by the Treasury, played an important role in rehabilitating the bill market and London money markets.[79]

By 1873, the year in which *Lombard Street* was published, the Bank of England and the government had developed a coordinated response to crises in the money market: the Bank lent freely on good collateral and the government temporarily suspended the Bank Charter Act. Despite a lack of public acknowledgement of its duty, after *Lombard Street*, 'every student of the subject was brought up on the doctrine that the Bank had an inescapable duty as lender of last resort irrespective of anything said in the Bank Charter Act'.[80] Consistent with this statement is that in the period 1870–1914, when the market as a whole was short of liquidity, the Bank was prepared to lend freely.[81]

However, the ultimate question is: To what extent did the Bank's LLR role contribute to banking stability both before and after Bagehot? During the crises of the nineteenth century, the demand for cash from banks and the money market increased. The Bank of England, as the ultimate reserve of the entire system, was the institution that could meet this increased demand for currency. A major part of the increased demand for cash came from banks concerned that liquidity was going

---

[77] Seabourne, 'The summer of 1914', p. 90–2.
[78] Sayers, *Bank of England*, vol. I, 1976, pp. 74–6. The decision to issue Treasury notes rather than suspend the Bank Charter Act was taken because there was a question of whether Bank of England notes would be accepted as legal tender in Scotland and Ireland.
[79] Seabourne, 'The summer of 1914', pp. 105–6.
[80] Sayers, *Bank of England*, vol. I, p. 3. However, it is claimed that until 1914, bankers faced uncertainty as to 'whether and when and how the Bank might so act to check a crisis' (Pressnell, 'Cartels and competition', p. 379).
[81] Ogden, 'An analysis of Bank of England discount and advance behaviour'.

to evaporate because the Bank was restrained by the need to maintain convertibility and later by the Bank Charter Act. When the government and Bank intervened, the panic in the money markets rapidly subsided. It is entirely possible that if the Bank had not acted as an LLR, the major crises of 1825 and subsequent minor crises would have been more severe.[82]

The stability of the British banking system after 1878 may have been due to the Bank's willingness to act as an LLR.[83] For example, Hartley Withers, giving evidence before the National Monetary Commission, stated that 'there is an impression that the Government is always behind the Bank, and that the Bank is always behind the other banks, and this feeling has certainly done much to foster the confidence of the British public in its banking system'.[84] But how did the Bagehotian LLR reduce moral hazard? Moreover, did the existence of a classical LLR constrain banks from risk shifting?

To address the first question, the Bagehotian LLR did not provide implicit deposit insurance; rather, it provided liquidity support to banks with suitable collateral. For example, the Bank did not lend to (or bail out) the CGB in 1878. This being so, the moral hazard associated with providing last-resort lending was minimal.[85] Indeed, rather than reduce the proportion of cash and near-cash assets in their balance sheets after the 1866 and 1878 crises, banks went on to substantially increase their holdings of liquid assets precisely because the Bank would provide loans only in the last resort.[86]

To answer the second question, we could hypothesize that the Bank of England, empowered by its position as an LLR, could use moral suasion to ensure that banks did not engage in risk shifting or risky behaviour. There is no evidence that it ever did so before 1914.[87] Indeed, such was the spirit of rivalry between joint-stock banks and the Bank immediately before World War I that several major joint-stock banks questioned the Bank's privileged position within the monetary system and demanded a Royal Commission to investigate it.

After World War I, however, there is evidence that the Bank's role as an LLR may have given it leverage over other banks because it could always

---

[82] Collins, 'The Bank of England', p. 152.
[83] Capie, 'Banking in Europe', p. 126. See Wood, 'Bagehot's lender of last resort', for a contrary view.
[84] Withers and Palgrave, *English Banking System*, p. 4.
[85] See Bignon, Flandreau and Ugolini, 'Bagehot for beginners', who provided evidence that no moral hazard was associated with the Bank's LLR function.
[86] Collins and Baker, *Commercial Banks and Industrial Finance*, p. 88.
[87] Ogden, 'An analysis of Bank of England discount and advance behaviour', p. 333.

threaten implicitly that noncompliant banks would not have access to its discount window.[88] For example, from the 1920s onwards, it was Bank policy that large banks that merged with other banks would not be entitled 'to support from the Bank nor to recognition of its paper as prime for the purpose of discount, security or otherwise'.[89] The role of moral suasion in curbing bank risk taking is explored further in the next chapter.

Beyond Bagehot: Bailouts and reorganisations

Beginning with the Barings crisis of 1890, the Bank of England – supported and encouraged by the government – did much more than lend freely on good collateral during times of financial distress or crisis: it nursed ailing banks, bailed them out, organised private-sector support schemes and facilitated the takeover of failing banks. In this section, we examine how this role evolved and whether the Bank's and the Treasury's intervention prevented crises from occurring or mitigated the deleterious effects of stress on the banking system. Ultimately, however, it is shown that although such intervention may have prevented short-term deterioration of stability, the assisting or bailing out of errant banks had the long-term effect of creating an environment in which there was a greatly reduced downside risk for banks, for those who deposited with them, or for those who lent to them.

In the nineteenth century, Messrs Baring Brothers and Co. was one of the most powerful merchant banks in Europe and its bills were regarded as among the highest quality in England.[90] During the 1880s, in the search for yield, Barings invested heavily in the emerging economies of Argentina and Uruguay, lending to infrastructure and railway projects. By 1890, Barings had about 75 per cent of its portfolio in these two economies.[91] In addition, it held *cedulas*, which were bonds issued by Argentine banks against their mortgage portfolio.[92] As well as making risky investments, Barings was highly leveraged compared to its merchant-banking peers; for example, the Barings' ratio of capital to liabilities was only 14 per cent in 1890 compared to 39 per cent at N. M. Rothschilds.[93]

---

[88] Bank of England Archives G12/1 Committee on the Working of the Monetary System, memoranda of evidence, June 1957, p. 5. See also Hirsch, 'The Bagehot problem', p. 243.

[89] Bank of England G8/56, Committee of Treasury Minutes, 8 April 1925.

[90] Batchelor, 'The avoidance of catastrophe', p. 51.

[91] Bank of England Archives C5/183, Baring Brothers and Co. crisis papers.

[92] See Ziegler, *The Sixth Great Power*, pp. 237–43, for further details.

[93] Ferguson, *The House of Rothschild*, p. 341.

In late 1889, inflation in Argentina was 94 per cent, which resulted in a substantial increase in its foreign-debt-servicing costs. Subsequently, the property boom in Argentina came to an end, with prices falling by 50 per cent in 1890. This resulted in a run on Argentine banks and an attempted revolution at the end of July.[94] As a consequence, there was an attempt to reconstruct the finances of the River Plate region. These circumstances reduced the value of Barings' assets by approximately a third, which resulted in its borrowing heavily from its London bankers.

By 8 November 1890, Barings had realised that the firm was in a perilous condition and, using Hambros as an intermediary, requested a meeting with the Governor of the Bank of England (William Lidderdale) on Monday, 10 November. At the meeting, Francis Baring and Edward Baring, a director of the Bank of England from 1879 to 1891, laid before Lidderdale a preliminary statement that raised doubt about whether the firm could cover its liabilities.[95] Immediately after this meeting, Lidderdale met with G. J. Goschen, the Chancellor of the Exchequer, who expressed 'great concern, and a strong desire that the Bank should support Messrs Baring and Co. if solvent, but [declared] that if the House were not solvent, the Government could not interfere'.[96] At Lidderdale's request, the Chancellor enlisted the assistance of Messrs Rothschild 'towards any necessary measures of relief'.[97]

The report on Barings' financial position concluded that its assets of £24.7 million exceeded its liabilities by about £3.8 million but that the cash advance necessary to meet the firm's liabilities as they matured was £8 million to £9 million.[98] On the same day, immediately after the Bank of England had received this report, Lidderdale met with W. H. Smith (the First Lord of the Treasury) and Lord Salisbury (the Prime Minister). The government agreed to the Bank of England's request that it should increase its balance with the Bank to give it any assistance required but not exceeding £9 million. The government also agreed to bear half the loss of any Barings bills taken in by the Bank of England in the next 24 hours. The purpose in doing so was to buy time for the Bank of England to put together a guarantee fund from banks and

---

[94] Körnert, 'The Barings crises of 1890 and 1995', p. 190.
[95] Bank of England Archives G4/113, Minutes of Court of Directors 20 November 1890, p. 138.
[96] Bank of England Archives G4/113, Minutes of Court of Directors 20 November 1890, p. 138.
[97] Bank of England Archives G4/113, Minutes of Court of Directors 20 November 1890, p. 138.
[98] Bank of England Archives G4/113, Minutes of Court of Directors 20 November 1890, p. 140.

merchants.[99] The Bank declined the offer of the usual relaxatory letter regarding the Bank Charter Act.

By 15 November, the Bank had created a guarantee fund wherein joint-stock banks and City firms agreed to 'make good to the Bank of England any loss which may appear whenever the Bank of England shall determine that the final liquidation of liabilities of Messrs Baring Brothers and Co. has been completed'.[100] Each contributor to the guarantee fund was to contribute rateably up to the maximum that they had pledged. The maximum period for which the liquidation, and therefore the guarantee fund, could extend was three years. Of the £6.5 million pledged by 15 November, £1 million was from the Bank of England and £3.25 million was from the five largest London joint-stock banks. The final size of the fund was £17.105 million (equivalent to 1.2 per cent of 1890 GDP, or 24.0 per cent of the Bank's total assets), with joint-stock banks contributing 65 per cent. Because the public announcements regarding Barings' difficulties and the guarantee fund were simultaneous, there was no panic in the money markets.[101] According to Goschen, if Barings had not been assisted, it would have made the 1866 crisis look like 'child's play'.[102]

Towards the end of November 1890, Barings Brothers and Co. entered liquidation and a new bank, Barings Brothers and Co. Ltd., was established. The liquidation and guarantee fund had to be extended beyond the original November 1893 deadline, and it was not until January 1895 that the Barings' liquidation was completed. However, at the end of the liquidation process, none of the guarantee fund was called on and Barings paid off all of its liabilities at maturity.[103]

The ultimate success of the Barings' liquidation was far from obvious and, in one sense, the Bank of England and members of the guarantee were simply fortunate that after a long period of assistance, Barings' assets were sufficient to cover its liabilities. For example, in 1891, guarantors were bracing for losses on their guarantees that N. M. Rothschild thought might be as high as 25 per cent.[104]

---

[99] Bank of England Archives G4/113, Minutes of Court of Directors 20 November 1890, pp. 140–1.

[100] Bank of England Archives G4/113, Minutes of Court of Directors 20 November 1890, p. 140.

[101] Before receiving a complete report of Barings' position on 12 November, the Bank bolstered its gold reserves in anticipation of an increase in demand for gold once Barings' position became public. The Bank purchased £1.5 million from the Russian government and borrowed £3 million from the Bank of France, the latter transaction being facilitated by N. M. Rothschild.

[102] Pressnell, 'Gold reserves', p. 200.   [103] Clapham, *Bank of England*, vol. II, p. 107.

[104] Pressnell, 'Gold reserves', p. 217.

Why was Barings Brothers and Co. supported in this way by the government, the Bank of England and other banking and finance houses?
The standard explanation is that the purpose was to prevent a panic
in the money markets and a subsequent run on Britain's gold reserves.
However, Barings was not a commercial bank and was not involved in
the payments system; it was a merchant bank that had overinvested in
the newly emerging and unstable economies of the River Plate. An alternative and more likely explanation is that the country's political and
financial elite wanted to protect the institutions that were engaged in
Britain's empire building. Another possible explanation is that this was
the Bank and the City looking after one of their own: the 'establishment
had closed ranks and saved its own'.[105] Regardless of the reasons, there
was a significant cost to the bailout of Barings. *The Economist* raised the
question of whether banks that provided guarantee funds were receiving an appropriate risk-adjusted return with which their shareholders
would be satisfied.[106] More fundamentally, as recognised at the time,
the bailout of Barings created a dangerous precedent.[107] As discussed
previously, a Bagehotian LLR did not present a significant moral-hazard
problem. However, guarantees and the long-term nursing of assets in the
hope that they will recover their value create all types of malincentives
that, unless checked, can fundamentally weaken banking systems.

The next occasion when the Bank of England coordinated a bailout was
in 1911, when it helped to rescue the Yorkshire Penny Bank (YPB). In
October 1910, the Charing Cross Bank – a major loan company – failed,
causing a run on the Birkbeck, which was a building society in name but a
bank in reality.[108] As it had done when facing a run in 1892, the Birkbeck
looked to the Bank of England for funds, borrowing £1.5 million using
repossessions. Subsequently, in June 1911, the Birkbeck was declared
insolvent.[109] As a result of its closure, the YPB – a savings bank limited
by guarantee with £18.5 million in deposits and 700,000 depositors –
was facing rumours about its solvency. Like the Birkbeck, it had among
its assets large holdings of fixed-interest securities, which had depreciated
by nearly £1 million from their book value during the previous decade or
longer.[110] Sir Edward Holden, chairman of the London City and Midland Bank, made initial contact with the YPB's board. After ascertaining
the perilous condition of the bank, he contacted the chairmen of other

---

[105] Ziegler, *The Sixth Great Power*, p. 266.   [106] *The Economist*, 22 November 1890.
[107] *The Times*, 25 November 1890.   [108] Cleary, *The Building Society Movement*, p. 156.
[109] Cleary, *The Building Society Movement*, pp. 144, 156–7. Depositors and shareholders of
   the building society were eventually paid 16 shillings and 9 ½ pence on the £ (equivalent
   to a haircut of 16 per cent).
[110] Bank of England Archives C5/111, Yorkshire Penny Bank papers.

Table 6.2 *Subscribers and guarantors of the Yorkshire Penny Bank Ltd.*

	Share capital subscribed (£'000)	Guarantee (£)
London City and Midland Bank	500	
London Joint Stock Bank	250	
Barclays Bank	250	
Lloyds Bank	250	
Union of London and Smiths Bank	250	
Beckett and Company	100	
Bank of Liverpool	100	
Manchester and Liverpool District Banking Company	100	
Williams Deacon's Bank	100	
Lancashire and Yorkshire Bank	50	
Manchester and County Bank	50	
Total	2,000	
Bank of England		223,214
London County and Westminster Bank		223,214
Parr's Bank		89,286
Capital and Counties Bank		89,286
Glyn Mills Currie and Company		89,286
United Counties Bank		89,286
London and South Western Bank		44,643
Metropolitan Bank		44,643
National Bank		44,643
London and Provincial Bank		44,643
Roberts, Lubbock and Co.		8,928
Martin's Bank		8,928
Total		1,000,000

Source: Bank of England Archives G4/134, Minutes of Court of Directors 7 September 1911, pp. 107–8.

major joint-stock banks to determine whether they would be prepared to join a scheme to help the YPB. Holden subsequently contacted the Bank of England's Governor, who set about drawing up a plan to save the YPB.[111]

This scheme had two components. First, the YPB was reconstructed as YPB Ltd., with several leading joint-stock banks contributing the capital

[111] Bank of England Archives G4/134, Minutes of Court of Directors 7 September 1911, pp. 102–8.

of the new bank (Table 6.2 lists the shareholders). Second, a guarantee fund of £1 million (equivalent to 2.5 per cent of the Bank of England's total assets in 1911) was raised to cover any deficiency in the existing assets beyond what was discovered in its balance sheet in July 1911. As shown in Table 6.2, the Bank was the lead contributor to this fund, followed by several clearing and joint-stock banks. The Chancellor of the Exchequer was kept informed of these rescue efforts and may have been willing to help with the guarantee fund if the banks had not been forthcoming.[112] Indeed, by mid 1916, the fund's deficiency over the £1 million guarantee was still £374,000, and the banks that had provided capital and guarantees were unwilling to cover it. As a result, the Treasury granted an indemnity to the YPB against this and further deficiencies until after the war. As it turned out, the Treasury's indemnity was not required after the war; however, the original guarantors lost more than one third of their guarantees.

Why did the Bank of England create this rescue package for the YPB? It appears that after the collapse of the Charing Cross Bank and Birkbeck, the Bank, the Treasury and the joint-stock and clearing banks did not want depositors in other banks to panic. According to the Bank of England's Governor, the purpose of the reconstruction and guarantee scheme was to avoid 'the very serious trouble that would undoubtedly have been produced in the banking world, and the further heavy depreciation of securities which would be bound to follow any forced liquidation of the securities held by the Yorkshire Penny Bank'.[113]

The bailout of the YPB differed from the Barings bailout in terms of scale, but it was similar in that the management of both institutions was not necessarily blamed or penalised for failure.[114] However, the bailout of the YPB, in one sense, set a more dangerous precedent than that of the Barings bailout: it now appeared that not only would the Bank rescue or coordinate the rescue of large and important institutions, it also was prepared to rescue even small banks, such as the YPB.

As with its LLR role, there was never any official announcement or recognition that the Bank of England and the Treasury would rescue failed banks. However, the Bank represented by its Governor, Montagu Norman, recognised in the early 1920s that 'if any misfortune arose to any of the big Banks in this country the Chancellor would have to

---

[112] Bank of England Archives G4/134, Minutes of Court of Directors 7 September 1911, p. 106.

[113] Bank of England Archives G4/134, Minutes of Court of Directors 7 September 1911, pp. 107–8.

[114] Ogden, *The Development of the Role of the Bank of England as a Lender of Last Resort*, p. 178.

intervene'.[115] Philip Snowden, who in 1924 became the first Labour Chancellor of the Exchequer, argued in a *Financial News* article on bank amalgamations in 1926 that 'the consequences of the failure of one of these huge concerns would be so calamitous that all the financial resources of the nation would be mobilised to avert such a catastrophe'.[116]

It therefore seems that the amalgamation process had created banks that came to be regarded as being 'too big to fail'.[117] Although this was not officially acknowledged, 'at no time in the first half of the twentieth century did the Bank hesitate over its responsibility in principle for underpinning when necessary the structure of financial institutions in the London market'.[118] Indeed, in the interwar years, the Bank of England, backed by the Treasury, rescued several banks and did nothing to dispel the belief that the Treasury stood behind the Bank and that the Bank stood behind the rescued banks. Several of these rescues are worthy of comment.

Cox and Co., a private bank that acted as Army agents, was in trouble in 1918. In a meeting with the Bank of England's Governor, Hubert Cox was given 'a friendly hint that there were rumours that their bank was rather going outside their legitimate business'.[119] When the Bank reviewed details of its overdrafts and loans, it was clear that Cox and Co. had been making risky loans. As a result, the Bank suggested to Cox and Co. that it should increase its capital.[120] However, by 1923, Cox and Co. was close to collapse. The Bank and the Treasury rescued Cox and Co. by arranging for Lloyds to take it over and by providing a £900,000 guarantee (equivalent to 0.3 per cent of the Bank of England's assets in 1923), £400,000 of which was promised by the Treasury.

At the end of 1928, Williams Deacon's Bank, which had most of its branches in Lancashire and was heavily exposed to the troubled Lancashire cotton industry, reduced its published reserves by £1 million because it had to make provision for bad loans. Believing that this action could damage more banks than Williams Deacon's, the Bank of England in January 1928 gave a guarantee of £1 million against the bank's advances to forty cotton firms. The Bank then set about finding a larger bank to take over Williams Deacon's. The Royal Bank of

---

[115] Bank of England Archives G1/9, Governor's file on bank amalgamations, correspondence on 23 February 1923 between Lord Colwyn and Gaspard Farrer (writing on behalf of Norman).

[116] *Financial News*, 29 March 1926, 'Bank Amalgamations: Advantages and Disadvantages'.

[117] Sayers, 'Twentieth-century English banking', p. 7.

[118] Sayers, *Bank of England*, vol. II, p. 528.

[119] Bank of England Archives, C46/129, Cox and Co. papers.

[120] Bank of England Archives, C46/129, Cox and Co. papers.

Scotland was persuaded and, to make it feasible for its shareholders to agree to the takeover without the public's realisation of the perilous condition of Williams Deacon's, the Bank put up £1.5 million to cover the bad debts and offered its branch and business in the West End of London at well below the market rate.[121] However, a further deterioration in Williams Deacon's advances necessitated an additional contribution of £2.5 million from the Bank, which was authorised by the Committee of Treasury.[122] The Bank may have saved Williams Deacon's, but it came at great cost in terms of finance (equivalent to 1.8 per cent of the Bank of England's total assets in 1928), time and energy.[123]

Banca Italo-Britannica was a British-owned bank operating in Italy, and three of the large UK clearing banks were substantial owners and depositors. Thus, when financial irregularities in the bank's operation came to light in 1929, the Bank of England was central in co-coordinating its rescue, putting in £250,000 of the £2 million required.[124] The three clearing banks put in the remainder.

The next major intervention by the Bank of England was also in a British overseas bank: Anglo-South American Bank Ltd. (ASAB), which had extensive operations in Latin America, specifically in the Chilean nitrate trade. In September 1931, in the final days before gold convertibility was suspended, the ASAB approached the Bank of England for support. The ASAB had a substantial bad-debt problem, had exhausted its capital and reserves, and had seen its deposits fall from £11.9 million to £6.9 million since the end of June 1931.[125] It is interesting that the ASAB had uncalled capital of £4.3 million, but it appears that both the ASAB and the Bank were unsure if this could be obtained in the middle of ongoing difficulties in the financial markets.[126] To support the ASAB, the Bank put in support funds of £1.5 million, Barclays and Midland put in £0.75 million each and the National Provincial and Westminster Bank put in £0.65 million each.[127] Other smaller clearing banks put in an additional £0.9 million.[128] The total package was equal to 0.8 per cent

[121] Anon., *Williams Deacon's*, pp. 158–9; Sayers, *Bank of England*, vol. I, p. 255.

[122] Sayers, *Bank of England*, vol. I, p. 258.

[123] Bank of England Archives, G1/10, Governor's file on bank amalgamations, letter from Montagu Norman to the Duke of Buccleuch (chairman of the Royal Bank of Scotland), 21 August 1930.

[124] Sayers, *Bank of England*, vol. I, p. 258.

[125] Bank of England Archives, C48/68, Anglo-South American Bank papers.

[126] Bank of England Archives, C48/68, Anglo-South American Bank papers.

[127] Bank of England Archives, C48/68, Anglo-South American Bank papers.

[128] The smaller clearing banks that contributed to the bailout fund were Glyns, Martin's, District, Royal Bank of Scotland, Union Bank of Scotland, Commercial Bank of Scotland, and National Bank.

of the Bank of England's total assets in 1931. However, because the ASAB's condition worsened in November 1931, the Bank had to supply additional funds, which were formally guaranteed by the Treasury. When the ASAB was acquired by the Bank of London and South America in 1936, the financial losses suffered by the Bank of England totalled £2,351,000 and the clearing banks lost £2,216,000.[129]

When the Committee of Treasury was made aware of the problems with the ASAB, it decided that 'the clearing banks must recognise the imperative need in their own and the public interest of joining in the provision of the necessary assistance which cannot be furnished by the Bank of England alone'.[130] The Treasury was keen to save the ASAB at any cost.[131] The consensus of the leading clearing banks regarding the rescue of the ASAB also was that it must not be allowed to fail.[132] Why did the Bank of England, assisted by leading clearing banks, rescue a bank that clearly had taken on too much risk and become overextended in the nitrate business? The Committee of Treasury took the view that unless the ASAB were rescued, many firms in the discount market would fail.[133] Similarly, the Bank's view was that if the ASAB had been allowed to fail, it would have shaken confidence in British banking institutions, quite possibly leading to runs on smaller banks with repercussions for even the large clearing banks.[134]

Other banks in the 1930s also received assistance.[135] For example, in July 1931, following a £6 million loss in their Brussels office, Lazards received a substantial seven-year loan from the Bank of England, which was eventually repaid in full. The British Overseas Bank Ltd. – a bank formed to assist British trade in Europe after World War I and that had British banks and financial institutions as its main shareholders – experienced difficulties in the late 1930s and required an injection of deferred deposits of £1 million from the Bank.[136]

From the 1930s onwards, it is entirely possible that other banks unilaterally received assistance from the Bank of England, but this help was

---

[129] Jones, *British Multinational Banking*, p. 242.
[130] Bank of England Archives, G8/58, Committee of Treasury Minutes, 24 September 1931.
[131] Bank of England Archives, G8/58, Committee of Treasury Minutes, 24 September 1931.
[132] Bank of England Archives, G8/58, Committee of Treasury Minutes, 30 September 1931.
[133] Bank of England Archives, G8/58, Committee of Treasury Minutes, 24 September 1931.
[134] Bank of England Archives, C48/68, Anglo-South American Bank papers, memo of 10 October 1931.
[135] See Billings and Capie, 'Financial crisis', pp. 200–1.
[136] Bank of England Archives, C48/129, British Overseas Bank papers, memo November 1938.

kept secret (i.e., a policy known as 'doing good by stealth'); it remains undisclosed under the Bank's hundred-year rule regarding the disclosure of business conducted with other banks. Indeed, in evidence before the Select Committee on Nationalised Industries, the Bank revealed that it had supported twelve institutions during the 1960s; however, its losses came to only hundreds of thousands of pounds.[137]

The rescue of the secondary-banking sector in 1974 was similar to previous rescues in that the Bank of England co-opted the major clearing banks to assist with the funding of the bailout. However, the 'Lifeboat operation', as the rescue scheme became known, was larger and covered more institutions than any previous bailout. The main motivation behind the Lifeboat operation was to give secondary banks time to recover so that they did not incur fire-sale losses.[138]

The Lifeboat operation was funded by the clearing banks, including the Scottish clearing banks, and the Bank of England provided 10 per cent of the necessary funding.[139] The total loans provided by the Lifeboat operation were small at first; however, with the collapse of the property market in the summer of 1974 and the spillover effects from the collapse of Herstatt (a major German private bank), Lifeboat lending expanded dramatically. Total support loans increased from £433 million in June to £994 million in September 1974. Then, in October 1974, United Dominions Trust, the country's largest finance house, required a loan of £500 million from the Lifeboat operation. It is notable that the identity of those who were being aided through the Lifeboat operation was kept secret.[140]

Total Lifeboat-operation loans peaked at £1,285 million in March 1975, which was equivalent to 1.2 per cent of GDP or 16.3 per cent of the Bank of England's total assets. As shown in Table 4.4 in Chapter 4, all but one of the major secondary banks required support from the Lifeboat operation. At the same time, Slater Walker Securities, the only major institution that did not require support, received unilateral support of £54.8 million from the Bank of England. In total, twenty-six secondary banks received support from the Lifeboat operation, of which eight eventually went into receivership.[141] An additional five institutions were assisted unilaterally by the Bank of England outside of the Lifeboat operation, with the Bank advancing almost £300 million (equivalent to 3.8 per cent of its total assets in 1975).[142]

[137] House of Commons, *First Report from the Select Committee on Nationalised Industries: Bank of England*, p. xxxi.
[138] *The Banker*, February 1974, p. 87.   [139] Reid, *Secondary Banking Crisis*, p. 16.
[140] *The Banker*, February 1974, p. 1181.   [141] Reid, *Secondary Banking Crisis*, p. 150.
[142] Capie, *The Bank of England*, pp. 572, 581.

At the end of 1975, only eight institutions were receiving assistance from the Lifeboat operation; by 1978, this number had decreased to four. Lifeboat-operation loans were mostly repaid by the early 1980s, with losses from the scheme of £80 million to £90 million being borne by the Bank of England and approximately £50 million being borne by the clearing banks.[143] The Bank of England wrote off £54.7 million of loan-loss provisions arising from the secondary-banking crisis in 1994.[144] Ultimately, the real cost of the Lifeboat operation is difficult to assess because the loans were repaid in money terms, and inflation averaged 16 per cent per annum between 1974 and 1980.[145]

The next notable support provided by the Bank of England was in 1984 to Johnson Matthey Bankers (JMB), the banking, bullion and commodity trading subsidiary of the Johnson Matthey chemicals and precious-metals company. For most of its history, JMB was a conventional bullion dealer, but it expanded its non-bullion lending from £50 million in 1981 to £500 million in 1984.[146] However, a large proportion of its loans were risky and heavily concentrated, with many deteriorating by 1984.[147] As a result, on 1 October 1984, JMB was bought by the Bank of England for £1. The Bank also placed a £100 million deposit in JMB, which was later capitalised. In addition, the Bank of England, a group of commercial banks, and members of the London gold market provided an indemnity of £150 million (equivalent to 1.0 per cent of the Bank's total assets in 1984) for JMB's losses, with the Bank providing half of the indemnity. The private-sector pledge came reluctantly; the Bank had to coerce it into helping with the JMB bailout.[148] JMB's £248 million in bad loans was covered by its own capital (£130 million) and an injection of cash from Johnson Matthey, the parent company (£50 million); the remainder of the losses was covered by the indemnity fund.[149]

Why did the Bank of England bail out what *The Economist* called this 'wildly imprudent' bank? The reasons given were that the failure of JMB, one of London's major bullion banks, would have had serious consequences for the future of the bullion market and that JMB's failure could have threatened London as a financial centre.[150] However, the subsequent moral-hazard problem associated with bailing out this reckless

---

[143] Capie, *The Bank of England*, p. 581; Reid, *Secondary Banking Crisis*, pp. 190–1.
[144] Capie, *The Bank of England*, pp. 582–3.   [145] Ackrill and Hannah, *Barclays*, p. 208.
[146] *The Economist*, 10 October 1984, p. 86.   [147] *The Economist*, 3 August 1985, p. 75.
[148] *The Economist*, 27 July 1985, p. 69.
[149] Hansard, *House of Lords Debate 1985*, vol. 465, cc. 384–93.
[150] House of Commons, *Inquiry into the Supervision of the Bank of Credit and Commerce International*, p. 13.

bank may have been immense. An additional cost was that the coercion used by the Bank to get the commercial banks to contribute to the rescue fund was resented. This would prove to be the last time that private-sector support in the United Kingdom would be called on to help with a bailout.

In 1990, the Bank of Credit and Commerce International (BCCI) was the largest privately owned bank in the world, with 417 offices in 73 countries.[151] Two of its main holding companies were incorporated in Luxembourg and the Cayman Islands, and its principal shareholders were wealthy families from South Asia and the Middle East. However, its operational headquarters were in London. BCCI was closed by bank regulators operating in tandem in July 1991 because it was clear that it was fraud-ridden.[152] No bailout was forthcoming from the United Kindgom for three reasons: (1) BCCI had only 6,500 depositors in the United Kingdom; (2) it was a global (rather than British) bank that was not even incorporated in the United Kingdom; and (3) although its failure may have raised questions about the Bank of England's regulatory regime, it did not raise any about the security of British banking.

However, after the failure of BCCI, several small banks experienced difficulties (the most notable being the National Mortgage Bank) and required support from the Bank of England.[153] The provisions made by the Bank in respect to these loans reached a maximum of £115 million in 1993 (equivalent to 0.4 per cent of the Bank of England's total assets in 1993). The Bank acquired the National Mortgage Bank – the institution that required most of the Bank's support – for the nominal sum of £1 in 1994 to facilitate its control over realising the National Mortgage Bank's assets. The Bank intervened on the grounds that the risk of contagion to larger banks was high enough to justify it.[154]

Barings Brothers and Co. collapsed (again) in February 1995 after Nick Leeson, a derivatives trader in the bank's Singapore office, amassed losses of approximately £827 million in futures contracts on Japan's Nikkei-225 Index; the losses exceeded Barings' capital.[155] On the week-end before its collapse, the leaders of the foremost clearing and invest-ment banks were summoned to a meeting at the Bank of England to

---

[151] *The Economist*, 27 January 1990, p. 96.
[152] See House of Commons, *Inquiry into the Supervision of the Bank of Credit and Commerce International*.
[153] See Logan, 'The early 1990s small banks crisis'. According to Ackrill and Hannah, *Barclays*, p. 211, Barclays lent money, with a Bank of England indemnity, to several of these stricken banks.
[154] Hoggarth and Soussa, 'Crisis management', p. 183.
[155] For the details, see Bank of England, *Report of the Board of Banking Supervision into the Circumstances of the Collapse of Barings*.

determine whether a rescue package could be put together.[156] The banks were willing to put in only £600 million, but such was the extent of Barings' potential losses that an additional £450 million may have been required. The Bank of England stated that it was unwilling to cover these losses and risk taxpayers' money.

Why did the Bank of England and the British government break with their long tradition of rescuing failed banks? First, on the grand scale, Barings was a small institution and was not a deposit-taking bank.[157] Second, because Barings was not closely interconnected with the rest of the British banking system via bilateral exposures, its failure posed no systemic threat to the wider financial system.[158] Third, its collapse occurred in a benign macroeconomic environment and it was an idiosyncratic failure (i.e., it was due to fraud). Fourth, the Bank of England may have wanted to 'puncture the notion that any famous bank can rely on public money to protect it from its own mistakes'.[159]

Dealing with banking Armageddon

As a result of the difficulty in raising funds in the money markets in August 2007, British banks requested special liquidity assistance from the Bank of England. In the case of Northern Rock, there was daily contact with the Bank and the FSA from early August onwards.[160] When news of the Bank of England's liquidity support to Northern Rock was released on 14 September, there was a run on the bank by retail depositors, which was stopped only when the Chancellor of the Exchequer announced a government guarantee for Northern Rock's deposits and certain wholesale liabilities.[161]

The perilous state of Northern Rock at the beginning of 2008 was such that in February, it was taken into temporary public ownership under the Banking (Special Provisions) Act of 2008. This Act gave the Treasury the ability to nationalise deposit-taking institutions or transfer their business to a private-sector institution. As part of this nationalisation, the Treasury repaid the Bank of England's emergency support funds and injected new funds into Northern Rock so that at the time of its nationalisation, it had received more than £25 billion of emergency support loans from the government (i.e., 1.7 per cent of 2008 GDP).[162] An additional injection

---

[156] *The Economist*, 4 March 1995, pp. 19–21.   [157] *The Economist*, 22 July 1995, pp. 14.
[158] Hoggarth and Soussa, 'Crisis management', p. 184.
[159] *The Economist*, 4 March 1995, p. 12.
[160] House of Commons Treasury Committee, *The Run on the Rock*, pp. 35–9.
[161] House of Commons Treasury Committee, *Banking Crisis*, p. 45.
[162] National Audit Office, *The Creation and Sale of the Northern Rock plc*, p. 6.

of funds was required in January 2010 when the Treasury decided to split the bank into Northern Rock plc and Northern Rock (Asset Management) plc. The latter was a bad-asset vehicle into which the bank's £54 billion portfolio of lower-quality mortgages was placed, as well as £23 billion of the outstanding taxpayer loan.

The Treasury also used its powers under the Banking (Special Provisions) Act of 2008 to deal with the failure of the Bradford and Bingley on 27 September 2008. The bank's branches and retail-deposit business were transferred to Abbey, whilst the remainder of the bank's assets and liabilities were taken into public ownership to wind up its operations. The Financial Services Compensation Scheme (FSCS) paid Abbey £14 billion to cover the deposits of Bradford and Bingley, and the Treasury paid an additional £4 billion for deposits not covered by the FSCS – a total package equivalent to 1.2 per cent of 2008 GDP. The £14 billion from the FSCS was financed via a short-term Bank of England loan, which was subsequently replaced by a loan from the Treasury.[163] The Treasury also established temporary guarantee arrangements to safeguard Bradford and Bingley's wholesale borrowings and deposits.[164]

On 8 October 2008, with the financial system deteriorating at a rapid pace, the government announced a package of measures to deal with the financial crisis. First, it extended the Special Liquidity Scheme (SLS) by £200 billion. The SLS, which had initially been set up in April 2008, was how the Bank of England, indemnified by the Treasury, swapped Treasury bills for a bank's illiquid assets (mainly securities) for up to three years.[165] Second, it established the Bank Recapitalisation Fund, which enabled banks to strengthen their capital positions through the government rather than the private sector. Third, the Credit Guarantee Scheme, which was open to those banks that increased their capital levels, was a government guarantee of interbank lending that was established to enable banks to refinance maturing debt.

After the public release of this package, Lloyds Banking Group (i.e., the product of the Lloyds-TSB and HBOS merger) announced a £17 billion capital-raising scheme; however, because the shares were not taken up, the government acquired a 43 per cent stake in the bank. Similarly, only 0.24 per cent of the shares in the Royal Bank of Scotland were taken up by the public, with the result that the government acquired a 57.9 per cent stake in the bank.

---

[163] House of Commons Treasury Committee, *Banking Crisis*, p. 50.
[164] House of Commons Treasury Committee, *Banking Crisis*, p. 50.
[165] Bank of England Statement on Special Liquidity Scheme, 21 April 2008.

Table 6.3 *Support provided in cash to UK banks from the Treasury, 2007–2011*

	Gross capital injections and loans advanced 2007–2011 (£ billion)
Royal Bank of Scotland shares	45.80
Lloyds Banking Group shares	20.54
Northern Rock plc shares	1.40
Northern Rock (Asset Management) loan	27.44
Bradford and Bingley working-capital facility	8.55
Other loans to support deposits	29.12
Total cash outlay	132.85

Source: HM Treasury Annual Report and Accounts, 2010–11, p. 93.

The Asset Protection Scheme (APS), announced in January 2009, was designed to afford participating banks insurance (for a fee) against future credit losses on distinct, large portfolios of assets. Both Lloyds Banking Group and the Royal Bank of Scotland initially agreed to participate; however, Lloyds exited the scheme towards the end of 2009 as a result of improved market conditions and the confidence given by the implicit subsidy under the APS.

Tables 6.3 and 6.4 show the level of support provided by the Treasury to the UK banking system as a result of the crisis. Table 6.3 shows that £132.85 billion of cash was injected directly into the UK banking system between 2007 and 2011. In terms of contingencies arising from the various schemes launched to save the banking system, Table 6.4 shows that at its peak, the Treasury's contingent liabilities totalled slightly more than £1 trillion. At its peak, the total Treasury support to the banking system was 82.4 per cent of GDP.

Table 6.5 shows the effect of these financial interventions on net public-sector debt. If we exclude the financial interventions, net public-sector debt as a proportion of GDP increased from 35.8 per cent in 2006–7 to 66.2 per cent in 2011–12. However, when we include the financial interventions (i.e., the nationalisation of banks and other measures), net public-sector debt as a proportion of GDP increased from 35.8 per cent in 2006–7 to 139.9 per cent in 2011–12.

The Bank of England's response to the rescue of the banking system also has been unprecedented. The bank rate was reduced to 0.5 per cent, its lowest-ever level, at the beginning of March 2009. Simultaneously, the Bank commenced its programme of asset purchases financed by the

Table 6.4 *Contingent liabilities of the Treasury arising out of financial crisis, 2007–2011*

	Peak support (£ billion)	Outstanding guarantee commitments as of 31 March 2011 (£ billion)
Sector-wide schemes		
Credit Guarantee Scheme	250.00	115.00
Special Liquidity Scheme	200.00	71.00
Asset-Backed Securities Scheme	50.00	–
Recapitalisation fund	13.00	–
Facilities for loans to support deposits	0.31	0.56
Royal Bank of Scotland and Lloyds Banking Group		
Asset Protection Scheme	456.57	110.00
Contingent capital in Royal Bank of Scotland	8.00	8.00
Northern Rock		
Guaranteed liabilities	24.00	15.40
Contingent capital	3.40	1.60
Unused working-capital facility	3.80	2.50
Bradford and Bingley		
Guaranteed liabilities	17.00	5.39
Unused working-capital facility	2.95	2.95
Total guarantees	1,029.03	332.40

Source: HM Treasury Annual Report and Accounts, 2010–11, p. 91.

issuance of central-bank reserves. The programme was to include private- and public-sector assets, but the majority of asset purchases were UK government bonds. Between March and November 2009, the Bank's Monetary Policy Committee (MPC) authorised the purchase of £200 billion worth of assets. The MPC subsequently authorised additional purchases: £75 billion in October 2011, £50 billion in February 2012, and another £50 billion in July 2012.

As shown in Figure 6.3, the expansion of the Bank of England's balance sheet in response to the crisis, when viewed during a 222-year period, has been phenomenal. At the end of 2011, the Bank's balance sheet relative to nominal GDP was larger than it had ever been in the previous 222 years and had surpassed the high levels reached during World War II. Notably, the expansion of the Bank's balance sheet in previous financial crises was minor compared to that which occurred after 2007. The only other time when the Bank's balance sheet expanded rapidly during peacetime was

Table 6.5 *Effect of financial interventions on UK net public-sector debt*

	Net public-sector debt excluding financial interventions (£ billion)	Net public-sector debt excluding financial interventions (as a percentage of GDP)	Net public-sector debt including financial interventions (£ billion)	Net public-sector debt including financial interventions (as a percentage of GDP)
2004–5	422.1	33.9	422.1	33.9
2005–6	461.7	35.1	461.7	35.1
2006–7	497.8	35.8	497.8	35.8
2007–8	527.2	36.4	621.9	43.0
2008–9	624.0	44.5	2,108.3	150.4
2009–10	770.0	53.1	2,226.0	153.5
2010–11	909.8	60.4	2,247.8	149.1
2011–12	1,025.4	66.2	2,168.8	139.9

Source: Office for National Statistics, *Public Sector Finances*, October 2012.

during the Great Depression in the early 1930s, when its assets doubled – compared to their quadrupling in the 2007–8 crisis.

The radical policy measures adopted by the British government and the Bank of England during the 2007–8 crisis were also used to varying extents in other economies that experienced the 2007–8 crisis. Notably, radical policy measures were adopted even in Canada, a country that many observers claim escaped the 2007–8 crisis unscathed.[166] Extensive liquidity support was offered in every economy that experienced the crisis, and significant guarantees on bank liabilities were offered in almost all of them.[167] Of the thirteen economies that had the severest crisis experience in 2007–8, all had significant bank nationalisations or government injections of capital similar to the United Kingdom.[168] However, substantial asset purchases (i.e., exceeding 5 per cent of GDP) occurred only in the United States and the United Kingdom, the two major economies that suffered most during the crisis.[169]

---

[166] The total support package in Canada at its peak was estimated at 7 per cent of Canada's 2009 GDP (Macdonald, 'The big banks' big secret'). This support package included extensive liquidity support from both the US Federal Reserve and the Bank of Canada, as well as substantial purchases of mortgages by the government-owned Canada Mortgage and Housing Corporation.

[167] Claessens et al., 'Crisis management and resolution'; Laeven and Valencia, 'Resolution of banking crises'.

[168] Laeven and Valencia, 'Resolution of banking crises', p. 9.

[169] Laeven and Valencia, 'Resolution of banking crises', pp. 7–9.

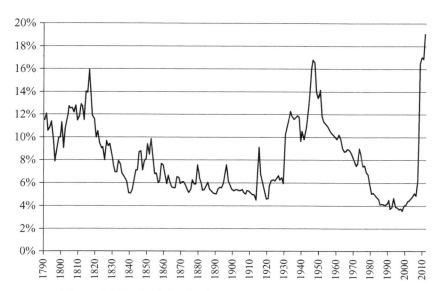

Figure 6.3 Bank of England assets as a percentage of nominal GDP, 1790–2011

Sources: Nominal GDP data are from Broadberry and van Leeuwen, 'British economic growth'; Mitchell, *British Historical Statistics*, pp. 836–7; Solomou and Weale, 'Balanced estimates'; and *Office for National Statistics*, available at http://www.ons.gov.uk/ons/datasets-and-tables/data-selector.html?cdid=YBHH&dataset=md&table-id=1.1. Bank of England assets for 1790–1980 are from Mitchell, *British Historical Statistics*, pp. 656–61. Assets from 1980 to 2011 are from the Bank of England, available at http://www.bankofengland.co.uk/boeapps/iadb/newintermed.asp.

Notes: Bank of England assets for 1790–1844 are based on the mean of the Bank's February and August balance sheets. Assets up to 1971 are based on weekly averages; thereafter, the Bank's balance sheet at the end of December is used.

Summary

Did the Bank of England act as an effective LLR in the nineteenth century? During the crisis of 1825, the Bank was hesitant to do so without suspending convertibility, but the Treasury put it under intense pressure to act as an LLR; once it started lending freely, the crisis began to subside. The Bank of England had accepted that it was an LLR. However, the Bank Charter Act did not allow the currency to expand during periods of stress in the money markets. Following the 1847 crisis, the practice of the

Treasury to issue a relaxatory letter in times of stress became accepted, enabling the Bank to respond to sudden increases in demand for cash.

Over time and starting with the bailout of Barings Brothers and Co., the Bank of England (backed and supported by the Treasury) became reluctant to allow banks to fail. By the 1920s, it was clear to both the Bank and the Treasury that they would not countenance the failure of any of the main clearing banks. This belief, although not publicly articulated by the Bank or the Treasury, was probably also held by the banks as well as their depositors. Indeed, with each successive rescue scheme, the belief that clearing banks would not be allowed to fail was reinforced.[170] The fact that banks and depositors were unconcerned about the decline in the capital-to-deposits ratio after 1914 is consistent with this belief. Notably, in its evidence to the Wilson Committee in 1978, the Bank admitted that its history of interventions during crises had the result that it and the world at large regarded 'the taking of prompt and decisive action to prevent a loss of confidence as one of the essential roles of a central bank'.[171] Before the same committee, Jack Revell, a leading academic expert on banking at the time, stated that the big clearing banks were safe because 'everybody knows that no central bank will ever let one of them fail'.[172]

The social underwriting of bank losses has two implications. First, depositors and other creditors of banks are significantly less concerned about restraints on risk shifting and about the incentives for bankers not to risk shift. Second, because the costs of risk shifting are now borne by taxpayers, they become concerned about the restraint of risk shifting. If taxpayers do not restrain risk shifting, the moral hazard is so great that banks can take huge risks that ultimately result in substantial costs for taxpayers. In effect, implicit and explicit bank guarantees subsidise the use of borrowing by banks, which, in turn, results in increased leverage and risk taking.[173] Chapter 7 examines how risk shifting was restrained when the social underwriting of bank losses became an established principle and how those restraints were systematically weakened in the decades leading up to the 2007–8 financial crisis.

[170] Alessandri and Haldane, 'Banking on the state', p. 8.
[171] *Bank of England Quarterly Bulletin*, 18 (1978), p. 231.
[172] Revell, 'Competition and regulation of banks'.
[173] Admati and Hellwig, *The Bankers' New Clothes*, pp. 129–30.

7 Banking stability and bank regulation

> Our tradition in Britain is of a less formal system of supervision than is customary in some other developed countries; and my long experience has not weakened my faith in this tradition.[1]
>
> Lord O'Brien of Lothbury

> HBOS has prudent corporate credit provisions in place. Issue closed.[2]
>
> Financial Services Authority evaluation, October 2007

Introduction

In Chapters 5 and 6, we discovered the following: (1) shareholder capital started declining during World War I and by the 1950s, it had reached exceptionally low levels; and (2) by the early twentieth century, the Bank of England and the Treasury were reluctant to see banks collapse; as a result, a policy emerged that meant that the banking system (and the major clearing banks in particular) were essentially insured by the Bank and taxpayers. As a consequence of these two developments, the potential for risk shifting was accentuated because shareholders (and depositors) stood to lose relatively little if their bank collapsed, with taxpayers ultimately bearing a substantial proportion of the downside risk. However, this chapter describes how bank regulation acted as a check on risk shifting by banks for four decades or more after 1939.

In this chapter, we perceive bank regulation as rules that constrain banks from risk shifting even if the stated or actual rationale for the rules is unrelated to constraining bank risk taking.[3] Bank regulation takes three

---

[1] *Bank of England Quarterly Bulletin* 11 (1971), p. 227.

[2] Parliamentary Commission on Banking Standards, *'An Accident Waiting to Happen': The Failure of HBOS*, p. 23.

[3] Of course, bank regulation is not always conducive to banking stability. For example, as described in Chapter 5, the regulation that restricted banks to the partnership form contributed to England's banking crisis in 1825–6. In addition, as discussed in Chapter 6, the regulations of the Bank Charter Act were unhelpful during periods of stress in the money markets.

forms in this chapter. First, there is the informal and nonstatutory regulation of banks by the Bank of England, with the Bank making its wishes known through 'nods, winks and raised eyebrows' rather than regulatory edicts.[4] Second, there is economic regulation, whereby banks are subject to nonstatutory controls as an integral part of the government's monetary, credit and fiscal policies. Third, there is statutory regulation that is prudential in nature; that is, its rationale is to prevent banks from taking excessive risks.

This chapter discusses how nonstatutory and informal regulation and economic regulation played an important role before the 1970s in keeping the banking system stable. Surprisingly, the regulation that underpinned the stability of the system did not have banking stability as its rationale. After the 1970s, statutory and formal regulation was developed that had as its rationale the stability of banks as well as of the banking system. Ironically, it is under such a regime that the British banking system had its greatest-ever crisis.

The genesis of informal control, 1914–1939

Although the Bank of England's leadership of other banks was particularly recognised after its expeditious handling of the Baring Brothers Co. crisis,[5] the amalgamation process led to the development of several large joint-stock banks that were comparable in size.[6] As a result of the growing size of joint-stock banks, several joint-stock bankers immediately before World War I began to demand a Royal Commission to examine the authority and dominance of the Bank of England. However, when the war was over, the banks seemed 'to have exhausted the assertive spirit of 1913–14, and to have settled to a passive acceptance of the Bank of England's sole authority'.[7] They did so possibly because they no longer viewed it as a competitor pursuing profit maximisation but rather as a central bank acting for the public good.[8] Goodhart suggested that the noncompetitive nature of the Bank of England from 1914 onwards was

---

[4] Jones, 'Competition and competitiveness in British banking', p. 126.

[5] Sayers, *Bank of England*, vol. I, p. 60.

[6] Sykes, *Amalgamation Movement*, p. 169, illustrates the shift in the relative size of the Bank and joint-stock banks by highlighting the fact that the Bank in 1863 had the capital strength to absorb all English joint-stock banks.

[7] Sayers, *Bank of England*, vol. II, p. 553. This leadership of the Bank was publicly acknowledged by the clearing banks and the Bank itself (Bank of England Archives, G13/1, Speech of Montagu Norman at Lord Mayor's Dinner, 1 October 1935; Bank of England Archives, G1/10, Extract from an Address by Walter Leaf, March 1927).

[8] Cairncross, 'The Bank of England', p. 45.

the key development in its effective leadership and guidance of the banking system.[9]

Several features of the banking system may have aided the Bank of England in its leadership and guidance of other banks. First, the small number of banks would have made communication, cooperation and coercion relatively easy.[10] Second – as is widely recognised – the close social relationships among many of the leading bankers may have aided the Bank in its control of other banks.[11]

Deliberately fostered by the Bank of England, a third feature of the banking system that aided it in assuming its leadership role was the oligopolistic structure of banking. Indeed, the Bank appears to have reinforced the market power of the banks by discouraging new entrants into the banking market.[12] It also supported and encouraged banks in their interest-setting cartel, which emerged during World War I. This can be viewed as a quid pro quo to the banks for allowing the Bank to act as leader. However, by limiting competition among banks, the cartel may have contributed to the stability of the banking system in the interwar period and beyond. The banking cartel also may have been encouraged by the Bank because it reduced the interest costs of financing the government's debt.[13]

The Bank of England's leadership of other banks may have been reinforced by the threat of nationalisation, which hung over the banking system from the interwar period until the 1970s. The Bank played on this fear when it made suggestions and gave directions to banks, which were all too ready to comply whenever the Bank advised that taking a contrary course would raise the spectre of nationalisation.

During the interwar years, the Bank of England began to take greater interest in the practices and behaviour of the clearing banks, becoming the central and dominant institution in an informal regulatory system.[14] Montagu Norman, the Bank's Governor from 1920 to 1944, was hostile to bank regulation imposed by the state because he believed that a system

---

[9] See Goodhart, *Evolution*, pp. 44, 55.

[10] Morgan, *The Theory and Practice of Central Banking*, p. 210; Hirsch, 'Bagehot problem', p. 248.

[11] See Cassis, *City Bankers*, for an excellent sociological study of the relationships among the individuals who controlled the country's leading financial institutions. The social relationships among actors in the financial system traditionally are seen as a source of stability (Hirsch, 'Bagehot problem', p. 244).

[12] Capie, 'Structure and performance in British banking', p. 7; Hirsch, 'Bagehot problem', p. 244.

[13] Griffiths, 'The development of restrictive practices'.

[14] Capie, 'The evolving regulatory framework', p. 131, is correct to suggest that describing this informal regulatory system as 'self-regulation' may be an exaggeration.

of informal regulation, with the Bank at the centre, was superior.[15] He also believed that freedom from regulation required that the banking system should 'act in the interests of the community and in the interests of the State'.[16]

Formal approaches to banks were usually made through the conduit of the Committee of London Clearing Bankers, which occasionally held its meetings at the Bank of England and, from 1919 onwards, lunched with the Governor.[17] However, the Bank was also 'in frequent formal intercourse with the representatives of all the important banks'.[18] For example, in 1934, at least thirty-six meetings were recorded between Montagu Norman and the chairmen, deputies, or general managers of all of the major banks.[19] During the Norman era, banks provided monthly breakdowns of their balance sheets. However, it is evident that further investigations into a bank's position occurred at the annual interviews that Norman held in his parlour with the general managers or directors of the major banks and the 'routine reports' from the chairmen of the clearing banks.[20] According to John Fforde, a Bank of England economist and the Chief Cashier from 1966 to 1970, 'the function being performed was often supervisory; but it was exercised through the Bank's evolved power as central banker de facto and not through specific powers granted it by statute'.[21]

From this evidence, it appears that the Bank of England developed an informal protosupervisory role under Norman. Nevertheless, it may be asked whether the Bank had the power to enforce its wishes on other banks because it had no formal or absolute control over them. As Fforde succinctly stated, the Bank could 'persuade or cajole, but it had to be very careful about giving orders'.[22] In some instances, Norman suggested a particular course of action and it was ignored. For example, in late 1930, Norman asked bankers to consider reducing their dividends for the

---

[15] Bank of England Archives, G13/1, Speech of Montagu Norman at the Centenary Luncheon of *The Economist*, 2 September 1943; Bank of England Archives, G13/1, Speech of Montagu Norman at Lord Mayor's Dinner, 1 October 1935.

[16] Bank of England Archives, G13/1, Speech of Montagu Norman at Lord Mayor's Dinner, 1 October 1935. Indeed, by the 1920s, banks were regarded by some as public utilities. For example, when asked in 1927 about Labour's proposal to nationalise banks, Keynes quipped in his inimitable way that they already were (Ackrill and Hannah, *Barclays*, p. 100).

[17] Sayers, *Bank of England*, p. 554.

[18] Evidence of Harvey to the Macmillan Committee, quoted in Sayers, *Bank of England*, vol. II, p. 553.

[19] Bank of England Archives, ADM34/23, Montagu Norman's Diary 1934.

[20] Clay, *Lord Norman*, pp. 276–8.   [21] Fforde, *The Bank of England*, p. 695.

[22] Fforde, *The Bank of England*, p. 696.

half-year, but only Lloyds Bank adopted the suggestion.[23] Ultimately, the Bank's role as an LLR may have given it some leverage over the banks because there was always the implicit threat of its removal.[24]

In addition to this protosupervisory function, the Bank influenced banking structure during the interwar years.[25] One fear of the Colwyn Committee on Bank Amalgamations (1918) was that large banks would make it more difficult for the Bank of England to exercise control over the banking system. As a result, the major banks – in return for having no formal or statutory barriers to mergers – agreed to the Bank's informal control of future mergers as well as the Treasury's. Norman was vehemently opposed to the Big Five banks amalgamating *inter se* or with any other bank. He even went as far as opposing the amalgamation of one of the Big Five with the Northern Bank.[26] Apparently, his main concern was that, other than leading to something uncontrollable and unwieldy, further amalgamation 'was not practical politics'[27] because it might 'stimulate the policy of a State Bank'.[28] In other words, Norman was concerned that further amalgamations would strengthen the call for the nationalisation of banks. Norman's policy was officially approved when the Chancellor of the Exchequer announced in December 1925 that no further amalgamations by the larger banks would be tolerated.

Norman was so strict in his adherence to this policy that he even opposed the National Provincial taking over the distressed Halifax Equitable Bank in 1927. In robust terms, he stated, 'I should be forced to use every means in my power to stop this or any amalgamation with one of the "Big Five" and should therefore assume a most unfriendly and hostile attitude towards the National Provincial and its Directors'.[29] In response, the National Provincial immediately terminated merger negotiations.

At the same time he prevented the five largest clearing banks from becoming any larger via acquisitions, Norman was eager to encourage amalgamations between the smaller joint-stock banks because this would enhance the stability of the banking system.[30] In particular, he wanted

---

[23] Bank of England Archives, G8/59, Committee of Treasury Minutes, 7 January 1931.
[24] Hirsch, 'Bagehot Problem', p. 243.   [25] Sayers, *Bank of England*, vol. I, p. 236.
[26] Bank of England Archives, G1/10, Bank Amalgamations – Letter from Norman to J. B. Pease, 22 November 1926.
[27] Bank of England Archives, G1/9, Bank Amalgamations – Norman memo on meeting with Sir Christopher Needham (District Bank), 3 November 1926.
[28] Bank of England Archives, G1/9, Bank Amalgamations – Norman memo, 10 August 1925.
[29] Bank of England Archives, G1/10, Bank Amalgamations – Norman memo, 13 April 1927.
[30] Bank of England Archives, G1/11, Bank Amalgamations – Notes on interview at the Bank of England on 20 June 1934.

to create a 'Big Six' by encouraging the small Lancashire banks to amalgamate and compete with the Big Five.[31] Despite his best efforts during many years, Norman was unable to achieve this end. However, there were several other cases in which Norman's direct intervention resulted in the successful merger of a distressed bank with a strong partner. For example, he was responsible for the amalgamation of the Equitable Bank with the Bank of Liverpool and Martin's.[32] He also was instrumental in encouraging the Royal Bank of Scotland to take over the troubled Williams Deacon's.[33]

Another way in which Norman sought to influence banking structure was in the area of overseas extensions. Like his grandfather G. W. Norman, he had an immense distrust of banks engaging in overseas business.[34] He believed that overseas extension was merely a case of greed and megalomania on the part of banks,[35] thereby imposing unnecessary risks on the banking system.[36] Notably, the Midland Bank claimed that it refrained from foreign participation for fear of the risks that it might impose on its depositors.[37] Norman's fear was that crises overseas could pose a risk to the credit of a clearing bank and that foreign extension placed risk onto the Bank of England and government in their role as an underwriter of the banking system.[38]

As a result of foreign extensions by Barclays and Lloyds, Norman's policy was that foreign banks that were owned by clearing banks should have their accounts closed with discrimination against their acceptances.[39] Indeed, it was suggested that this policy discouraged other banks from foreign extensions: during Norman's suzerainty, no other bank dared to defy the Bank of England on this matter.[40] Although Norman did

---

[31] Bank of England Archives, ADM20/15, Montagu Norman's Diary, 3 November 1926.

[32] Bank of England Archives, G1/10, Bank Amalgamations – Norman memo, 12 May 1927; and Letter from Manager of Equitable Bank, 4 May 1927.

[33] Bank of England Archives, G1/10, Letter from Norman to Duke of Buccleuch, 21 August 1930.

[34] Clay, *Lord Norman*, p. 6.

[35] Bank of England Archives, G1/9, Bank Amalgamations – Letter from Farrer (Economic Advisor) to Lord Colwyn, copied to Norman, 15 February 1923.

[36] Ackrill and Hannah, *Barclays*, p. 83; Clay, *Lord Norman*, p. 280. Norman was concerned to see how 'easily trouble can arise among these excitable Latin races' (Bank of England Archives, G1/9, Bank Amalgamations – Letter from Farrer [Economic Advisor] to Lord Colwyn, copied to Norman, 15 February 1923).

[37] Sykes, *Present Position*, p. 28.

[38] Bank of England Archives, G1/9, Bank Amalgamations – Norman memo, 10 August 1925.

[39] Bank of England Archives, G8/56, Committee of Treasury Minutes, 19 August 1925, 30 September 1925, and 27 May 1925.

[40] Ackrill and Hannah, *Barclays*, p. 84.

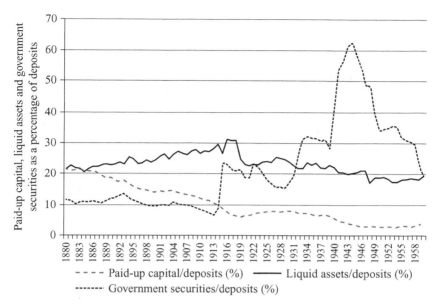

Figure 7.1 Total paid-up capital, liquid assets and government securities held by UK banks, 1880–1960
Source: Sheppard, *Growth and Role of UK Financial Institutions,* pp. 126–7.

not obtain explicit government support for his opposition to overseas extensions,[41] the Committee of Treasury approved of his discriminating policies against these banks.[42]

From the available archival evidence, it appears that Norman's interest in banking structure was motivated by a concern for banking safety and stability. The Big Five were large, stable institutions and he did not want them to participate in overseas banking in case it undermined their stability. Furthermore, his arranging of amalgamations among domestic banks arose from a concern for the stability of the banking system.

Before 1939, neither the Bank of England nor the Treasury made any formal attempt to regulate the cash and liquidity ratios of banks. As shown in Figure 7.1, the liquidity ratio gradually increased from slightly more than 20 per cent in 1880 to slightly more than 30 per cent during

---

[41] Cottrell, 'The financial system of the United Kingdom', p. 47.
[42] Bank of England Archives, G8/56, Committee of Treasury Minutes, 3 June 1925.

World War I. Thereafter, it declined steadily, reaching 20 per cent during World War II.

The most notable feature of Figure 7.1, however, is the stepwise change in banks' holdings of long-term government securities during World War I. Although the government securities-to-deposits ratio fell in the late 1920s, there was another stepwise change during the Great Depression; by the eve of World War II, it was at 30 per cent. Given that most of the assets that comprised a bank's liquidity ratio consisted of Treasury bills, money at call (which had gone to discount houses and was typically invested in Treasury bills) and cash reserves (a proportion of which had been invested by the Bank of England in government securities),[43] almost 50 per cent of total deposits in 1939 were directly or indirectly financing the government.

There does not appear to have been explicit pressure on banks to buy government bonds. However, the Bank, using its power of moral suasion, undoubtedly convinced banks that it was in their interest and the country's to help the government finance the war effort and the economic difficulties of the interwar period. Given the important role of banks in financing the government debt, it is perhaps unsurprising from a purely pragmatic viewpoint that banks were permitted and encouraged to maintain their cartel. Indeed, the banking cartel would have resulted in lower nominal interest rates, enabling the government to finance its debt at a lower cost than otherwise would have been the case. The increased holdings of government debt implied that banks had significant liquid and safe assets on their balance sheets, which further implied that they had less room for manoeuvre concerning risk shifting. Notably, the increased holdings of government debt coincided with a decrease in the capital-to-deposits ratio of banks, which explains why banks remained stable despite increased leverage.

In terms of credit policy, before 1939, there was little in the way of explicit directives from the government or the Bank of England regarding bank lending. However, the Bank did pressure the clearing banks to reduce their interest rates on loans in the 1930s, when companies were facing difficulties during the Great Depression.[44] Reporting in 1931 and possibly anticipating future policy, the Macmillan Committee suggested that the relationship with clearing banks should be closer and more of a two-way conversation so that they would clearly know whether the Bank was trying to expand or contract credit.[45]

---

[43] See Johnson, 'Clearing bank holdings of public debt'.
[44] Ackrill and Hannah, *Barclays*, p. 106.
[45] House of Commons, *Report of Committee on Finance and Industry*, pp. 160–1.

Economic regulation: Financial repression and directives

As discussed previously, two features stand out in the development of the UK banking system in the interwar years. First, there was the Bank of England's development of an informal regulatory system. Second, banks held more UK government debt on their balance sheets than previously. Both developments were taken to an entirely new level with the advent of World War II.

As a direct result of World War II, the United Kingdom's public debt reached 237.7 per cent of GDP. To reduce this debt, the government pursued the politically palatable policy of financial repression. In other words, the government attempted to regulate the financial system to generate low nominal rates and negative real-interest rates, thereby reducing the government's debt-servicing costs and the real value of its debt. Estimates produced by Reinhart and Sbrancia suggested that the UK government was able to reduce its public-debt-to-GDP ratio from a high of 237.7 per cent in 1947 to 138.2 per cent in 1955, resulting entirely from financial repression.[46] Without financial repression, they estimated that the public-debt-to-GDP ratio in 1955 would have been a staggering 246.9 per cent. The policy of financial repression helped to reduce the debt burden to 100 per cent of GDP by 1967.

Monetary policy from World War II until the early 1970s had one key objective: maintaining the demand for long- and short-term government debt, an objective that was achieved by preventing fluctuations in interest rates.[47] The banking cartel that had developed before 1939 was conducive to the government's monetary policy; thus, government policy underpinned and sanctioned the cartel.[48] The cartel helped in two ways. First, there was a strong demand from banks for government debt and, as a consequence, the Bank of England had 'no anxiety as to how the Government's requirements for finance for the following week were going to be met'.[49] Second, the interest-rate setting by the cartel ensured that nominal interest rates were low and stable.[50]

As Figure 7.1 shows, from an historical perspective, banks held substantial amounts of government debt from 1939 through to the end of the 1950s. Given that the majority of banks' liquid assets were indirectly or directly invested in government debt (as explained previously), almost 83 per cent of bank deposits in 1944 were tied up in government

---

[46] Reinhart and Sbrancia, 'The liquidation of government debt'.
[47] Rowan, 'The monetary system'; Fletcher, 'Cash base control of bank deposits'.
[48] Pressnell, 'Cartels and competition', p. 397.
[49] Nobay, 'The Bank of England', p. 47.   [50] Fletcher, 'Cash base control', p. 9.

securities – and even by 1958, almost half of bank deposits were helping to finance the government. As Harry Johnson noted in 1951, 'it may be safely concluded that much the larger part of banking operations over the past decade has consisted in the creation of deposits against government debt'.[51] In 1939, the percentage of Treasury bills issued by the government that were held by the London clearing banks was 47.7 and, by 1956, it was 71.5; in terms of long-dated government stocks, the percentages were 15.3 and 30.4, respectively.[52]

One of the main tools of financial repression was the repeated request made by the Bank of England for banks to hold a certain proportion of their deposits as Bank reserves (i.e., the cash ratio) and a certain proportion in liquid assets (i.e., the liquidity ratio). Liquid assets consisted of cash, money at call with discount houses, bills of exchange and British government Treasury bills. In other words, most of a bank's liquid assets was either short-term government securities or ultimately would be held in this form (e.g., money at call at discount houses). The sole purpose of these ratios was not prudential or to control deposits but rather to simply ensure a guaranteed market for short-term government debt.[53] Consistent with this is that bankers generally considered the liquidity ratios required by the Bank to be much higher than those dictated by the canons of banking prudence.[54]

From 1946 until 1971, the daily cash ratio maintained by the banks at the Bank of England's request and with the explicit agreement of the Committee of the London Clearing Bankers was 8 per cent. Because the cash ratio was a daily requirement, there was no scope for window dressing – that is, artificially increasing the cash ratio on monthly makeup days.[55]

In 1951, the Bank of England indicated that a bank's liquidity ratio was expected to be between 28 and 32 per cent and that it would be totally unacceptable if the ratio dropped below 25 per cent.[56] In practice, if the liquidity ratio fell below 30 per cent, the Bank would remonstrate with the errant bank.[57] From 1955, the minimum liquidity ratio was set at 30 per cent; from 1963 to 1971, it was 28 per cent. It appears that the minimum liquidity ratio truly was viewed as a minimum by the Bank and

[51] Johnson, 'Clearing-bank holdings of public debt', p. 107.
[52] Bank of England Archives, EID1/15, Statistics prepared for Radcliffe Committee.
[53] Nobay, 'The Bank of England', pp. 48–9; Fletcher, 'Cash base control', 10.
[54] House of Commons, *First Report from the Select Committee on Nationalised Industries: Bank of England*, p. xxiii; Nevin and Davis, *The London Clearing Banks*, p. 154.
[55] Bank of England Archives, C48/350, Memo by H. Clarke (Chief Cashier), 24 July 1957.
[56] Webber, 'Reserves and reserve ratios', p. 33.
[57] House of Commons, *Report of Committee on Working of the Monetary System*, p. 119.

the Big Five: from 1950 to 1970, this ratio fluctuated at approximately the 40 per cent level for clearing banks.[58]

The Bank of England also requested 'special deposits' from banks in 1958, 1960–2 and 1965–71. Special deposits were a supplement to the cash ratio, whereby banks were requested to deposit a certain percentage of their deposits with the Bank for an indefinite time. Interest was paid on those special deposits at a rate close to the prevailing Treasury bill rate, but they did not qualify as liquid assets. The stated purpose of the special deposits was to 'restrict the liquidity of the banking system and thus the ability of the banks to extend credit'.[59]

In addition to maintaining high cash and liquidity ratios, banks faced government directives – communicated and enforced by the Bank of England – concerning their lending business.[60] In general, these directives were not supervisory in nature and were not usually concerned with the security of the banking system.[61] Rather, they concerned the government's attempts to influence the economy via credit and monetary policy. Lending directives originated in the policies implemented at the beginning of World War II. In September 1939, John Simon (Chancellor of the Exchequer) wrote to Montagu Norman requesting that banks immediately restrict their advances to other than strategic sectors, including government contractors, armament companies, the export trade and agriculture.[62] This policy lasted until after the war and its sole purpose was the conserving of the nation's savings exclusively for government purposes. This system of wartime controls was carried over into the postwar economy and applied to banks even more rigorously.[63]

Directives regarding lending were both quantitative and qualitative. Quantitative requests, which were infrequent, involved banks reducing

---

[58] Ross, 'Domestic monetary', p. 312.

[59] Bank of England Archives, C48/350, Discount Office (Banking Supervision) Files – Letter from C. F. Cobbold to Chancellor, 3 July 1958.

[60] From 1939 onwards, the Treasury attempted to control capital issues and large borrowings. These regulations were part and parcel of the government's financial-repression policies because they potentially limited the competition for savings that they hoped to monopolise. The Defence Regulations and Statutory Rules (1939) required borrowers to obtain Treasury permission for any bank loan exceeding £10,000 that was not borrowed in the ordinary course of its business. These regulations were superseded by the Borrowing (Control and Guarantees) Act (1946), in which borrowings – other than those unsecured or in the ordinary course of business – were limited to £50,000 every year. This Act was effectively nullified for most borrowers, other than foreigners and local authorities, by an order of the Treasury in 1961. See Jones, 'Business of banking', p. 11.

[61] Fforde, Bank of England, p. 21.

[62] Bank of England Archives, G14/149, Letter from John Simon to Montagu Norman, 26 September 1939.

[63] Wadsworth, 'The commercial banks', p. 17.

the volume of loans or constraining the growth of lending.[64] For example, in July 1955, banks were requested to make a substantial reduction in advances and, in May 1965, they were directed that advances to the private sector should not increase by more than 5 per cent per annum. Qualitative directives guided banks to lend to specific industries, encouraging loans to defence contractors, exporters and agriculture; lending for personal expenditure, property development, hire purchase, and speculation in shares, real estate and commodities was highly constrained – or even, in the last case, forbidden altogether.[65] Lending in regions of high unemployment and in Northern Ireland also was encouraged.[66] Qualitative directives typically went along with quantitative directives in that certain categories of borrower (e.g., exporters) were to be exempted from or treated favourably during credit contractions or freezes.[67]

As in the pre-1939 period, the Bank of England was to be consulted and its approval sought for any proposed bank mergers. For example, in 1961, the Chairman of the Westminster Bank asked about the possibility of its merging with Martin's, but the Bank opposed it.[68] However, the Bank was not opposed to the two mergers that occurred in Scotland in the 1950s or the merger of the National Provincial and District in 1962. Following the press announcement of this latter merger, the Deputy Chairman of Lloyds Bank, Sir Jeremy Raisman, came to see the Bank's Governor and asked what powers could be used to prevent Lloyds from merging with Martin's.[69] The Governor thought it unlikely that the Bank would use a direction under the 1946 Act because it had not done so hitherto, but he indicated that the Bank could close Lloyds account or that the government could introduce legislation to prevent the merger.

In this era of financial repression, banks received directives that primarily concerned the asset side of their balance sheets. However, these directives were nonstatutory and had no force in law; they simply were made informally by the Bank of England. According to the *First Report from the Select Committee on Nationalised Industries*, no bank ever refused

---

[64] Nevin and Davis, *The London Clearing Banks*, p. 274; Wadsworth, *The Banks and the Monetary System*, p. 106.

[65] Bank of England Archives, C48/350, Discount Office (Banking Supervision) Files – Letter from C. F. Cobbold to the Chairman of Committee of London Clearing Bankers, 3 July 1958; Wadsworth, *The Banks and the Monetary System*, p. 106; Grady and Weale, *British Banking*, p. 48.

[66] Bank of England Archives, C48/350, Discount Office (Banking Supervision) Files – Letter from D. Heathcoat Amory, 1 July 1958.

[67] House of Commons, *First Report from the Select Committee on Nationalised Industries: Bank of England*, p. xxv.

[68] Bank of England Archives, G1/13, Governor's note, 9 May 1961.

[69] Bank of England Archives, G1/13, Governor's memo, 15 August 1962.

a request from the Bank of England.[70] Why then did banks comply with the Bank's stringent requests and directives?

One possibility is that the Act that nationalised the Bank of England in 1946 contained the following section: 'The Bank, if they think it necessary in the public interest, may request information from and make recommendations to bankers and may, if so authorised by the Treasury, issue directions to any banker for the purpose of securing that effect to any such request or recommendation'.[71] However, the Bank never needed to resort to this Act to compel banks, and bankers attest to the Bank's power of moral suasion.[72] Nevertheless, it is perhaps a testament to the Act's efficacy that it was never invoked.[73] There was at least one occasion when a Chancellor of the Exchequer, who was trying to convince banks to curtail their advances, threatened to use the power against the advice of the Bank, but the banks were able to placate him by reducing their advances.[74]

A second possibility is that the Bank of England had sanctions to use if a request or directive was disobeyed. It is generally believed that the Bank had three sanctions available: (1) closing the discount window to an erring bank, (2) withdrawing its right to hold a balance with the Bank of England, and (3) removing its authorisation under the Exchange Control Act (1947).[75]

A third possibility is that the banks obeyed the requests of the Bank because it was profitable to do so. Notably, bank profits in the 1950s and 1960s were viewed as excessive by the National Board for Prices and Incomes.[76] The banks enjoyed monopoly profits in the era of financial repression, and they may have been willing to comply with directives as a quid pro quo for being permitted to operate their cartel unhindered.[77]

A final possibility is that banks complied with directives and requests because they realised that if they did not, there would be calls for their nationalisation. The nationalisation of the Bank of England by the Labour

[70] House of Commons, *First Report from the Select Committee on Nationalised Industries: Bank of England*, p. xxvi.

[71] Bank of England Act, 1946 (9 & 10 Geo. c.27).

[72] House of Commons, *Report of Committee on Working of the Monetary System*, p. 118.

[73] Wadsworth, *The Banks and the Monetary System*, p. 106.

[74] Bank of England Archives, G14/149, Extracts from the minutes of the Committee of Treasury, 12 September 1957.

[75] Bank of England Archives, G12/1, Committee on the Working of the Monetary System, Memoranda of Evidence, Bank of England, p. 5, June 1957; House of Commons, *First Report from the Select Committee on Nationalised Industries: Bank of England*, p. xxviii.

[76] National Board for Prices and Incomes, *Bank Charges* (London: HMSO, 1967), para. 43. See also Capie and Billings, 'Profitability in English banking'.

[77] Griffiths, 'The development of restrictive practices', p. 15.

Party took legislative precedence over all other nationalisations because control of credit was of paramount importance in economic planning.[78] The nationalisation of the clearing banks, however, was deemed unnecessary because the newly nationalised and empowered Bank, as controller of the credit system, could move banks in any direction that the government wished to take them. Nevertheless, if banks did not comply with the Bank's directives, they faced the real threat of nationalisation. In a note written in 1962, the Bank's Governor acknowledged that the threat of nationalisation was always hanging over the banks.[79]

The high liquidity ratios and large holdings of government debt in the era of financial repression resulted in a low proportion of deposits actually being lent to borrowers. Ultimately, this would severely constrain a bank's ability to risk shift. In addition, banks had large cushions of liquid assets to deal with panics or deterioration in the quality of their loan portfolios. Furthermore, because of the credit constraints discussed previously, bank lending was extremely conservative and safe (e.g., loans for property development were strictly discouraged), with the result that from 1945 until the early 1970s, there was little credit risk in banking.[80] In other words, the economic regulations imposed on banks in a nonstatutory and informal manner gave them no room to manoeuvre when it came to risk shifting. This explains why the banking system was stable despite low capital ratios and why the Bank of England was unconcerned by the low capital-to-deposits ratios at the time.

The end of financial repression and the rise of prudential regulation

Financial repression in the United Kingdom began to ease in the early 1970s and came to an end by the early 1980s. There were two reasons for its demise. First, by 1967, the ratio of public debt to GDP had been reduced to the politically palatable 100 per cent level, implying that the ongoing need for financial-repression policies was much diminished. Second, competition from foreign banks and nonregulated institutions undermined the regulatory regime underpinning financial repression.

---

[78] Cairncross, 'The Bank of England', p. 48. Keynes presciently made the metaphorical comment to the Bank's Governor, Lord Catto, that when a Labour Government came into power, 'the head of the Governor of the Bank of England would be cut off: and then firmly planted on his shoulders with a slight turn to the left' (Bank of England Archives, G13/1, Speech of Lord Catto at the Lord Mayor's Dinner, 1946).

[79] Bank of England Archives, G1/13, Governor's memo, 17 September 1962.

[80] Goodhart, 'The Bank of England', p. 342.

Table 7.1 *Distribution of deposits of UK residents with UK institutions in 1962 and 1970*

	1962		1970	
	£ million	share (%)	£ million	share (%)
London clearing banks	7,168	46.9	10,297	36.2
Other UK banks	1,317	8.6	3,688	13.0
Building societies	3,510	23.0	10,142	35.6
National savings banks	1,760	11.5	1,752	6.2
Trustee savings banks	1,529	10.0	2,542	9.0
Total	15,284	100.0	28,421	100.0

Source: House of Commons, *Committee to Review the Functioning of Financial Institutions, Evidence on the Financing of Industry and Trade*, vol. 5, pp. 111–3.

The system of financial repression had several unintended consequences, which eventually came to undermine the quid pro quo relationship between the banks and the government, whereby the former were allowed by the latter to operate a cartel in exchange for compliance with its official requests. Such a system worked well when the banking system was dominated by the Big Five clearing banks. However, from the mid 1950s onwards, there was increased competition for deposits and lending coming from (1) building societies and trustee savings banks; (2) consumer-credit institutions, such as hire-purchase companies; and (3) foreign banks. In terms of deposits, as shown in Table 7.1, in 1962, the London clearing banks had less than 50 per cent of the UK market. By 1970, they had slightly more than a third of the market, with building societies increasing their market share during the 1960s.[81] In terms of lending, foreign banks and secondary banks – borrowing on the recently expanded money markets – had captured some of the clearing banks' lending market.

The growth of banking activity outside of the clearing-bank system undermined the ability of the Bank of England and the government to control the banking system via directives.[82] First, newcomers in the deposit-taking market were not amenable to Bank directives, which 'exposed the inability of customary authority to cope with important changes at the periphery of the banking community'.[83] Although the

---

[81] Wadsworth, 'Big and little banks', pp. 5, 13; Jones, 'Competition and competiveness', p. 124.
[82] House of Commons, *Report of the Committee to Review the Functioning of Financial Institutions*, pp. 69–70.
[83] Fforde, *The Bank of England*, p. 699.

Bank extended its system of requests to consumer-finance houses through the auspices of the Finance Houses Association, it was less able to do so with the many foreign banks that came into London in the 1960s and the secondary banks that emerged in the same decade. Indeed, the Bank's claim before the Select Committee on Nationalised Industries that non-bank financial institutions were 'now fully susceptible' to the requests of the Bank appears to have been unjustified.[84]

Second, the clearing banks increasingly were at a competitive disadvantage and losing business because of the cartel and the costs of complying with the Bank of England's requests. In particular, branches of US and other foreign banks operating in London faced no regulations whatsoever, giving them a huge competitive advantage over the repressed clearing banks.[85] As a result, the clearing banks sought to have greater freedom to compete with the parvenus.[86] Even as early as 1958, it was realised by the Bank of England that quantitative restrictions on bank advances placed the clearing banks at a competitive disadvantage vis-à-vis other financial institutions.[87] In an internal Bank memo in 1962, the Governor (i.e., the Earl of Cromer) stated that the size and eminence of the Big Five made them the continuous target of official requests, which simply resulted in promoting the growth of other institutions.[88]

The rise of new deposit-taking institutions and their position outside the Bank of England's circle of influence meant that there were few constraints of any kind on the ability of some of the institutions to risk shift. In addition, the Bank's power of moral suasion had little influence on the new institutions. According to Fforde, the rise of institutions just outside the boundaries of banking meant that the Bank lobbied for a Banking Act in 1957, but the Treasury was too 'keen on closing gaps in the credit squeeze and too little concerned with the protection of depositors'.[89] Fforde maintained that had a Banking Act been passed in 1957, the secondary-banking crisis fifteen years later might have been avoided.[90]

Given the pressure from the clearing banks to be free of controls that were causing them to lose market share and the growing political hostility to the bank cartel (e.g., the National Board for Prices and Incomes

---

[84] House of Commons, *First Report from the Select Committee on Nationalised Industries: Bank of England*, p. xxii.

[85] Goldberg and Saunders, 'The causes of U.S. bank expansion overseas', p. 639.

[86] Ross, 'Domestic monetary policy', p. 320.

[87] Bank of England Archives, C48/350, Discount Office (Banking Supervision) Files – Aide Memoire, June 1958.

[88] Bank of England Archives, G1/13, Governor's memo, 17 September 1962.

[89] Fforde, *The Bank of England*, p. 777.   [90] Fforde, *The Bank of England*, p. 777.

in 1967 had advocated its abolition), it is not surprising that a new approach was taken in an attempt to control the banking system and at the same time make it more competitive. The new approach, introduced in September 1971, was Competition and Credit Control (CCC). The objective of this new policy was twofold. First, the authorities treated equally all institutions recognised as banks (including foreign banks) concerning credit control and reserve requirements.[91] Second, the clearing banks abandoned their interest-rate cartel to coincide with the introduction of CCC.[92] In keeping with the informal and nonstatutory approach of the Bank of England and the Treasury towards banks, CCC was a gentleman's agreement without any legislative basis.

As part of CCC, quantitative lending restrictions were abolished, as were the clearing banks' 8 per cent cash and 28 per cent liquidity ratios. In their place, a 12.5 per cent minimum reserve-asset ratio against total eligible liabilities was imposed on all recognised banks. Reserve assets consisted of balances at the Bank of England, Treasury bills, gilts with a maturity of less than one year, and high-quality local authority and commercial bills. In the case of the clearing banks, 1.5 per cent of total eligible liabilities had to be in the form of balances at the Bank of England. All banks were also subject to calls to place special deposits with the Bank. As with the liquidity ratio before it, the reserve-asset ratio was imposed as a means of subsidising government-debt sales rather than being imposed for monetary policy or prudential reasons.[93] In other words, financial repression – although much reduced – still existed even after the introduction of CCC.

CCC freed bank lending for the first time since the war and did so at a time of increased demand. Consequently, some banks found it profitable to finance their reserve assets by borrowing on the sterling money markets. What resulted was a lending boom, and the Bank of England was frustrated in its attempts to exert control over the M3 monetary aggregate.[94] In December 1973, seeking to exercise more control over bank lending, the Bank introduced the Supplementary Special Deposit Scheme. This scheme was nicknamed the 'corset' because attempts to control one part of the monetary aggregate had previously resulted in the unexpected 'popping out' of another part elsewhere in the system. Under the scheme, if banks exceeded a fixed rate of growth of interest-bearing

---

[91] House of Commons, *Report of the Committee to Review the Functioning of Financial Institutions*, p. 70.
[92] 'Competition and credit control', *Bank of England Quarterly Bulletin* 11 (1971), p. 189.
[93] Batini and Nelson, 'The U.K.'s rocky road to stability', p. 63.
[94] Capie, *The Bank of England*, p. 521.

eligible liabilities, they had to deposit a proportion of their interest-bearing deposits with the Bank at a zero rate of interest. This system of monetary control lasted until 1980, when special deposits, supplementary special deposits and the reserve-asset ratio were abolished. Instead, banks were required to have not more than 0.5 per cent of eligible liabilities held as a non-interest-bearing cash balance with the Bank.[95] This ratio was later reduced to 0.45 and then 0.35 and, by the 2000s, it was zero.

The Bank of England believed (or hoped) that CCC would once again give the clearing banks the dominant position in British banking and eventually eliminate the growing secondary-banking sector that was not under its control or influence.[96] However, in the short run, CCC had the actual effect of contributing to the expansion of this sector due to the rapid expansion of wholesale money markets that resulted from the new monetary regime.

According to the Bank of England, the secondary-banking crisis demonstrated the need for it to intensify and extend its regulatory oversight of the banking system.[97] Pressure for change also was building from the United Kingdom's membership of the European Union (EU) and the EU's directive on banking, which aimed to harmonise banking regulation across member states.[98] The Bank and the banking system reacted almost immediately to the need for greater oversight by inaugurating a new regulatory system in the summer of 1974. However, this rapid response may have been an attempt (ultimately unsuccessful) by the Bank to ward off legislation that would undermine its informal, nonbureaucratic and nonstatutory approach to banking supervision.

The banking-supervision problem facing the Bank of England in 1974 was one of scale and scope. The growth in the number of banks (i.e., 323 full banks in 1973) meant that with a staff of only twelve in 1973, the Discount Office – the traditional means through which the Bank monitored the banking system – could not cope with the scale of the task.[99] In addition, there were 133 'section 123' banking companies; these companies, which experienced the most trouble during the secondary-banking crisis, were unsupervised and made no statistical returns to the Bank or

---

[95] 'Monetary control: Next steps', *Bank of England Quarterly Bulletin* 21 (1971), p. 38.

[96] Grady and Weale, *British Banking*, p. 147.

[97] House of Commons, *Committee to Review the Functioning of Financial Institutions, Second Stage Evidence*, vol. 4, p. 97; Gardner, 'Supervision in the United Kingdom', p. 74; Goodhart, 'The Bank of England', p. 345.

[98] 'The supervision of the UK banking system', *Bank of England Quarterly Bulletin* 15 (1975), p. 190; Capie, *The Bank of England*, p. 604.

[99] Reid, 'Lessons for bank supervision', p. 102.

any other agency.[100] The scale problem was overcome in 1974 by abolishing the Discount Office and creating a new division, Banking and Money Market Supervision, staffed by thirty-seven people, which increased to seventy-seven by 1979.[101] The scope problem was overcome by identifying companies in the United Kingdom that held substantial deposits and inviting them to voluntarily submit to Bank supervision, which, by 1975, most had agreed to do.[102]

An integral part of the new supervisory regime was the quarterly submission of statistical returns by all nonclearing banks to the Bank of England. In the case of troubled banks, the Bank required monthly or six-weekly returns.[103] The statistical returns were followed by an interview between the senior management of each bank and the Bank's supervisors. In 1977, after ten sets of prudential returns, the Bank began to categorise banks by their riskiness and to reduce the frequency of interviews for those that were perceived to be safe.[104] The clearing banks did not submit quarterly prudential returns to the Bank but instead were subject to annual prudential reviews and interviews. This exemption arose because the Bank had a long-standing and close relationship with them and, as a result, had more information.[105]

The Bank of England's supervisory philosophy, as articulated by George Blunden, the first head of the Bank's new supervisory division, had four essential characteristics: it was flexible, personal, progressive and participative.[106] Supervision, as practised by the Bank, was flexible in that the Bank did not like the rigid standards and ratios with which banks had to comply. Although the Bank looked at capital adequacy, liquidity ratios, foreign exposures, and so on, it perceived these 'only as yardsticks, not as categorical imperatives'.[107] The Bank's approach was personal in that it developed personal relationships with bank staff, thereby forming a judgement of the quality of a bank's management. The Bank's supervision had progression built into it in that the greater the formal recognition of a bank, the greater was the degree of supervisory oversight to which it was subject. The supervisory approach was also participative

[100] Grady and Weale, *British Banking*, pp. 38–9.
[101] Capie, *The Bank of England*, p. 611.   [102] Robb, 'The genesis of regulation', p. 30.
[103] 'The supervision of the UK banking system', *Bank of England Quarterly Bulletin* 15 (1975), p. 190.
[104] Capie, *The Bank of England*, pp. 613–4.
[105] 'The supervision of the UK banking system', *Bank of England Quarterly Bulletin* 15 (1975), p. 192.
[106] The supervision of the UK banking system', *Bank of England Quarterly Bulletin* 15 (1975), pp. 188–94.
[107] The supervision of the UK banking system', *Bank of England Quarterly Bulletin* 15 (1975), p. 189.

because supervision was voluntarily accepted by banks and the views of the banking community were considered. As a result, the Bank did not approve of inquisitorial inspections or examinations as practised in other jurisdictions.[108]

Although banks voluntarily allowed the Bank of England to examine their business, the question arises about what power of direction the Bank had when asking banks to become more prudent: on the face of it, none.[109] However, there was always the implicit threat that the Bank would remove an institution's formal recognition as a bank, and this may have made the banks amenable to Bank 'requests'.[110]

Statutory prudential regulation

Despite the bolstering of the supervisory system after the secondary-banking crisis, Treasury officials were concerned that the Bank of England's control of the fringe-banking institutions would weaken once the crisis was a distant memory.[111] Because they were also concerned about the call for European Economic Community (EEC) harmonisation of banking regulation, the Treasury decided to place banking supervision on a statutory basis. The Bank, for its part, was opposed to any attempts to codify regulation and supervision, believing that its light touch and informal approach was superior.[112] The Bank was fully aware of the need to deal with secondary-banking institutions, but it simply proposed a strengthening of the 1963 Protection of Depositors Act to limit deposit taking to institutions that were banks.

The 1979 Banking Act had three main planks.[113] First, there was a two-tier authorisation process for all deposit takers. If an institution wanted to operate as a deposit taker in the United Kingdom, it had to gain prior authorisation from the Bank before it could do so. Under the authorisation procedures, the Bank had the ability to confer two levels of status – recognised banks and licensed deposit takers – and it also had the power to revoke authorisation. Recognised banks were institutions that had earned a good reputation for a period of time and that offered the full complement of banking services, whereas licensed deposit takers did not have either. As a result, the latter were not permitted to use the banking label. This two-tier authorisation process allowed the

---

[108] The supervision of the UK banking system', *Bank of England Quarterly Bulletin* 15 (1975), p. 191.

[109] Moran, *The Politics of Banking*, p. 117.

[110] Revell, 'Solvency and regulation of banks', p. 46.

[111] Capie, *The Bank of England*, p. 617.   [112] Capie, *The Bank of England*, p. 588.

[113] Banking Act 1979, c. 37.

Bank to discriminate against the types of institutions that had precipitated the secondary-banking crisis; this no longer put 'banks proper' at a competitive disadvantage to their less-regulated and aggressive rivals.[114]

The second plank of the 1979 Act was the Deposit Protection Scheme (DPS) that from February 1982 guaranteed 75 per cent of the first £10,000 of sterling deposits made by nonbank customers in any institution authorised under the Banking Act. To make this guarantee effective, all authorised institutions paid a premium that was tied to the size of their deposit base. The DPS undermined the aims of the authorisation process and tipped the competitive balance in favour of small deposit takers. Consequently, the big banks lobbied intensely but – in the end – unsuccessfully against the DPS.[115] The opposition of the big banks was based on the fact that they, who contributed most to the Deposit Protection Fund and were unlikely to call on it, were subsidising smaller competitors to take imprudent risks, which ultimately would take business from them.

The third plank of the Banking Act was that once an institution was authorised, it was subject to the Bank of England's supervisory oversight. However, the Act did not undermine the approach that the Bank had developed in the aftermath of the secondary-banking crisis; if anything, it enhanced the Bank's approach by compelling all authorised deposit takers to be subject to its supervision.[116] The Bank succeeded in ensuring that the Act was in accordance with its supervisory philosophy by convincing the Treasury that it did not need powers of entry and search, which were common in other jurisdictions.[117]

The main emphasis of the Bank of England's supervision after the Banking Act remained the statistical analysis of prudential returns and the subsequent management interviews. The interviews were held every six to nine months for all clearing banks and UK branches of overseas banks, whereas other institutions authorised under the Act met with the Bank every quarter.[118] In addition, after the Act and consistent with the Bank's approach before its passage, the lower tier of authorised banks – that is, the licensed deposit takers – was subject to greater supervisory scrutiny than recognised banks.

The Bank of England continued to eschew the use of categorical balance-sheet ratios as part of its supervisory approach. For example, following the abolition of the 12.5 per cent reserve-asset ratio in 1980,

---

[114] Moran, *The Politics of Banking*, p. 123.   [115] Moran, *The Politics of Banking*, p. 127.
[116] Gardner, 'Supervision in the United Kingdom', p. 77; Cooke, 'Self-regulation and statute', p. 74; Goodhart, 'The Bank of England', p. 345.
[117] Capie, *The Bank of England*, p. 630.
[118] Hall, *Handbook of Banking Regulation and Supervision*, p. 15.

the Bank, with no ratio in mind, stated that its supervisory objective was to ensure that banks had prudent liquidity policies as well as adequate management-control systems to ensure that such policies were implemented.[119]

Capital adequacy was one of several important issues addressed by the Bank of England in its supervisory interviews with banks. The Bank employed a risk-asset ratio, which weighted assets in a bank's balance sheet by its perceived riskiness.[120] The weights used were as follows: commercial loans = 1, connected lending = 1.5, property lending = 2, and UK government bonds = 0.5. No minimum risk-asset ratio was stipulated by the Bank, but the ratio was used with individual banks on a case-by-case basis as part of the overall supervisory process.

Following the deficiencies highlighted by the failure in 1984 of JMB (see Chapter 6), a recognised bank under the 1979 Act authorisation scheme, the Bank of England immediately intensified its supervisory visits along several dimensions.[121] First, the lighter supervisory touch that applied to large and complex banks was abandoned and they became subject to more frequent visits. Second, the regular prudential reviews were augmented by informal visits. Third, the range of topics covered in supervisory visits was extended beyond prudential statistical returns to include a bank's plans, forecasts and strategies. As a result of this intensification of supervisory visits, the number of staff in the Bank of England's supervisory department grew from seventy-seven in 1979 to two hundred in 1989.[122]

The collapse of JMB also led to the 1987 Banking Act, which introduced several changes to the regulatory system.[123] First, two-tier authorisation was abandoned for a single process with a higher minimum threshold for becoming an authorised bank. Second, all institutions authorised under the Act had to appoint an independent auditor who was to furnish the Bank of England with an annual report on the bank's internal management and accounting control systems and, when requested by the Bank, to report on the prudential returns made by a bank. Third, all exposures greater than 10 per cent of a bank's capital base had to be reported to the Bank, and prior notification had to be given for all exposures greater than 25 per cent. Fourth, the provision of false or misleading supervisory information was made a criminal offence. Fifth, the Bank was given new powers to gain information on any aspect of a

---

[119] 'Monetary control: Next steps', *Bank of England Quarterly Bulletin* 21 (1981), p. 38; 'The liquidity of banks', *Bank of England Quarterly Bulletin* 21 (1981), p. 40.

[120] Blackhurst, 'What lurks behind UK bank supervision?', p. 8.

[121] See Hall, *Handbook of Banking Regulation*, pp. 18–19.

[122] Capie, *The Bank of England*, p. 611.   [123] Banking Act 1987, c. 22.

bank's business. Sixth, the Bank was given power over banks' corporate governance in that it decided the number of nonexecutive directors and whether a bank had an audit committee. Seventh, the coverage of deposit insurance was doubled to £20,000.

The termination of stringent regulations related to monetary control in 1980 had been preceded by the codification of prudential supervision. Because the disappearance of monetary controls meant that banks now had greater latitude to engage in risk shifting, it may be asked what constrained them. Because shareholder capital was still relatively small relative to assets or deposits, the burden of preventing risk shifting fell to the Bank of England as supervisor. Under the Banking Acts, the Bank was given access to banks' private information, and it was also given power to enforce its views on banks insofar as it could revoke or threaten to revoke a bank's authorisation. However, we must question whether the threat of revocation for large banks was credible and whether supervisors could detect risk shifting in large and complex banks by simply using prudential statistical returns and management interviews.

Capital adequacy and the global harmonisation of prudential regulation

After the economic instability of 1973–4, the politicians of the G-10 economies encouraged their central-bank governors to establish a standing committee, which became known as the Basel Committee on Banking Supervision (BCBS).[124] During the 1980s, there was broad agreement in the BCBS that the decline in capital ratios needed to be reversed harmoniously so as to ensure a level competitive playing field for global banks.[125] In particular, some members of the BCBS were worried about the rapid growth of undercapitalised and state-underwritten Japanese banks, which gave them a distinct competitive advantage over their Western counterparts.[126] The growth of Japanese banks in the 1980s was phenomenal: in 1981, only one of the largest ten banks in the world (in terms of total assets) was Japanese; by 1988, nine of the top ten were Japanese.[127]

---

[124] The original members of the G-10 were Belgium, Canada, France, Germany, Italy, Japan, the Netherlands, Sweden, the United Kingdom and the United States. Switzerland joined in 1964, but the name of the group remained the G-10. See Goodhart, *The Basel Committee on Banking Supervision*, for an excellent history of the BCBS.

[125] Goodhart, *The Basel Committee*, p. 195.

[126] Dewatripont, Rochet and Tirole, *Balancing the Banks*, p. 78.

[127] Tarullo, *Banking on Basel*, p. 47.

The two economies most concerned and threatened by competition from Japanese banks and most frustrated by attempts of the BCBS to harmonise capital-adequacy standards were the United States and the United Kingdom. Consequently, in 1987, the US federal supervisory authorities and the Bank of England published a proposal on standardising capital-adequacy rules.[128] This proposal outlined the risk-weighting methodology but suggested that it be used only to inform supervisory decision making and that the actual capital-adequacy ratio should be set much higher than the minimum ratio. This bilateral accord was made redundant when the other G-10 governors agreed to a harmonisation of capital-adequacy requirements in the 1988 Basel Accord.[129]

The Basel Accord, which was fully operational by the end of 1992, required banks to have a minimum of total capital equal to 8 per cent of risk-weighted assets. The risk weights (i.e., 0, 20, 50 and 100 per cent) were meant to reflect the credit risk of a bank's assets, including those held off the balance sheet. For example, cash, central-bank reserves and government debt all carried a zero weight, whereas claims on other banks carried a 20 per cent weighting. Loans fully secured by mortgage on residential property carried a 50 per cent weighting, whereas commercial lending carried a 100 per cent weighting. As a result, banks held no capital against zero-weighted assets; £1.60 of capital for each £100 of assets weighted at 20 per cent; £4 of capital for each £100 assets weighted at 50 per cent; and £8 of capital for each £100 of assets weighted at 100 per cent.

Capital was subdivided into high-quality (Tier 1) and second-rate (Tier 2), and at least 50 per cent of the capital base had to consist of Tier 1 capital. The former included paid-up ordinary capital, preferred shares and disclosed reserves, whereas the latter included undisclosed reserves, revaluation reserves, hybrid instruments and subordinated debt.

It is widely believed that the 1988 Basel Accord largely achieved its stated aims.[130] First, following the Accord, most G-10 countries increased their capital-adequacy ratios: in the United Kingdom, for example, most of the increase in the ratio resulted from increased capital rather than a reduction in risk-weighted assets.[131] Second, the Accord is believed to have increased the equality of cross-border

---

[128] Bank of England, *Agreed Proposal of the United States Federal Banking Supervisory Authorities and the Bank of England on Primary Capital and Capital Adequacy Assessment*, 1987.
[129] Goodhart, *The Basel Committee*, p. 195.
[130] Secretariat of Basel Committee on Banking Supervision, *The New Basel Capital Accord: An Explanatory Note*.
[131] Jackson, 'Capital requirements'.

competition,[132] but the empirical evidence on this is not conclusive and the pre-Accord pricing advantage of Japanese banks did not disappear.[133]

The risk-weighting methodology of Basel I was ad hoc, crude and based on political judgements.[134] More serious, however, is that it created all types of opportunities for regulatory capital arbitrage. For example, to increase their return on equity, banks engaged in 'cherry-picking' by shifting the composition of their loan portfolios towards riskier credits. Even though banks were taking more risk, their regulatory capital ratios were unchanged. Securitisation was another and more sophisticated way by which banks engaged in regulatory capital arbitrage. In effect, securitisation is another form of cherry-picking because banks typically securitise high-quality loans when the required economic capital is much less than the Basel requirement.[135]

Another weakness with Basel I, which was recognised by the BCBS, was that its sole focus was on credit risk and it ignored market- and interest-rate risk. In 1996, to address this weakness, the BCBS issued its market-risk amendment to the 1988 Basel Accord. Banks were permitted to use their own internal-risk models to assess their market risk and interest-rate exposure. The models used were value-at-risk (VaR) models – a VaR measure is an attempt to provide a single figure that encapsulates the total risk of a portfolio of financial assets. The VaR of a portfolio of financial assets is the maximum loss that will not be exceeded during the next N days with an X per cent certainty.[136] The market-risk amendment to the 1988 Basel Accord operated as follows. First, the VaR was calculated for a bank's portfolio when N equals 10 and X equals 99. Second, the capital that banks were required to hold against their market risk was a multiple of this figure greater than 3 and was determined on a case-by-case basis by individual regulators.

The Bank of England and, subsequently, the FSA made the Basel Accord capital-adequacy approach the cornerstone of their supervisory regime.[137] Banks were required to have a risk-asset ratio greater than the individual trigger ratio determined for them by the Bank and the FSA, with the trigger ratio being set above the 8 per cent minimum recommended under the Basel Accord. Banks had to meet their trigger

---

[132] Goodhart, *The Basel Committee*, p. 195; Dewatripont, Rochet and Tirole, *Balancing the Banks*, p. 79.

[133] Jackson, 'Capital requirements', pp. 41–2; Wagster, 'Impact of the 1988 Basel Accord'.

[134] Goodhart, *The Basel Committee*, p. 196.   [135] Jackson, 'Capital requirements', p. 24.

[136] Hull, *Risk Management and Financial Institutions*, p. 196.

[137] See Richardson and Stephenson, 'Some aspects of regulatory capital'; and Singh, *Banking Regulation of UK and US Financial Markets*, chaps. 1–2. On why responsibility for bank supervision switched from the Bank to the FSA in June 1998, see Briault, 'The rationale for a single national financial services regulator'.

ratio at all times, but the supervisory authorities put a buffer between this ratio and the actual target ratio set for banks. The target ratio was typically set at 0.5 to 1.0 per cent above the trigger ratio, depending on the volatility of a bank's business. Banks were also required to demonstrate that they had adequate systems in place to monitor their capital adequacy, and they had to inform the supervisory authorities of any breach of either their trigger or target ratio.

During the late 1990s, the international-banking industry became extremely vocal in its criticism of the Basel Accord and the BCBS. As a result, the BCBS commenced a consultative process in June 1999 in its first move towards a new Accord. The new Accord, which was finally published in 2004, was implemented in Europe via the Capital Requirements Directive, which came into force at the beginning of 2007. The core idea of Basel II was that banks could use their own proprietary VaR models for credit as well as market risk to determine how much capital they needed to hold. The role of the supervisors was simply to assess the adequacy of these models and ensure that they were properly implemented. As an incentive to encourage the use of these internal ratings-based (IRB) approaches, Basel II permitted banks that had adopted them to hold less regulatory capital.

Because the Great Crash occurred several months after the introduction of Basel II, it is unlikely that much direct blame can be attributed to the change in regulatory regime because substantial degrees of risk shifting had occurred before its introduction. However, the introduction of Basel II may have exacerbated the already dire situation. The case of Northern Rock is instructive. In June 2007, the FSA approved Northern Rock's IRB model. As a result of this approval, Northern Rock's risk-weighted assets fell from £34 billion under Basel I to £19 billion under Basel II, with the result that the bank's minimum required capital fell from £2.72 billion to £1.52 billion.[138] There also is an argument that the attempts to implement Basel II from 2004 onwards imposed a huge opportunity cost on the FSA, in that regulatory effort was put into implementing Basel II rather than looking out for prudential risks.[139]

If the rationale of bank regulation is to prevent banks from risk shifting and the banking system from collapsing, then the Basel approach to capital regulation failed dramatically. One reason for this failure was the regulatory arbitrage described previously, whereby capital regulation

---

[138] Dewatripont, Rochet and Tirole, *Balancing the Banks*, p. 88.
[139] Parliamentary Commission on Banking Standards, '*An Accident Waiting to Happen*': *The Failure of HBOS*, p. 23; *The Failure of the Royal Bank of Scotland*, p. 269.

perversely incentivised banks to become riskier. Indeed, much bank lending to the residential-property market could have been partially due to regulatory arbitrage because such lending had a 50 per cent weighting in a Basel risk-weighted asset calculation, compared to 100 per cent for a commercial loan.

A second reason that Basel capital regulation failed was the seriously flawed belief that risk can be captured and measured by risk-management techniques such as VaR. There are three major problems with the VaR-type approach. (1) It makes the heroic assumption that the present and future volatility of an asset can be predicted from historic volatilities.[140] The 2007–8 crisis exposed this weakness, for risk weights at the time were decreasing as actual risk was increasing.[141] (2) The co-variances and correlations that determine a bank's portfolio risk are not stable over time; during crises, asset correlations change dramatically. (3) It assumes that financial risks (i.e., the statistical distribution of asset returns) are exogenous and do not arise from the behaviour of those participating in financial intermediation.[142] In other words, the risk-measurement approach assumes away risk shifting. It simply turns banking and capital regulation into an engineering problem and ignores human behaviour.

This misplaced confidence resulted in the supervisory authorities relying on risk metrics and not using their judgement about the riskiness of a bank's overall position. The flexible and judgement-based supervisory system operated by the Bank of England until the early 1990s, which used risk-asset ratios as a heuristic, was replaced by a rules-based system that was over-reliant on banks' self-assessments of their own risk.

The myopic focus on risk management and control systems is illustrated by the case of HBOS – the most risk-loving of all of the UK banks – which failed in 2008. In late 2002, an FSA review of HBOS identified weaknesses in its control systems and risk-management procedures. At the end of 2003, as a direct result of HBOS not adequately addressing the FSA's concerns, the FSA increased its capital requirement by 0.5 per cent to 9.5 per cent, believing that HBOS was an 'accident waiting to happen'.[143] However, following reports by two leading accounting firms, KPMG and PwC, which indicated that HBOS's risk-management and control processes were working well, the FSA reversed its capital-raising decision in December 2004. By October 2007, the FSA concluded that

---

[140] Bhide, *A Call for Judgment*, pp. 122–4.
[141] Independent Commission on Banking, *Final Report*, p. 8.
[142] Dewatripont, Rochet and Tirole, *Balancing the Banks*, pp. 82–4.
[143] Parliamentary Commission on Banking Standards, '*An Accident Waiting to Happen*': *The Failure of HBOS*, p. 23.

Table 7.2 *Regulatory capital of UK banks in 2001 and 2006*

	Regulatory capital/total assets (%)		Risk-weighted assets/total assets (%)		Tier 1 capital ratio (%)		Total capital ratio (%)	
	2001	2006	2001	2006	2001	2006	2001	2006
Abbey National	4.6	4.1	39.4	32.8	8.4	8.0	11.6	12.6
Alliance and Leicester	5.8	4.8	49.1	46.9	8.8	7.9	11.9	10.2
Barclays	5.6	3.2	44.6	29.9	7.8	7.7	12.5	11.7
Bradford and Bingley	6.8	6.0	49.2	45.0	9.7	7.6	13.9	13.2
HBOS	5.4	5.6	50.5	46.7	7.9	8.1	10.6	12.0
HSBC	6.0	4.8	56.2	43.3	6.8	7.5	10.7	11.2
Lloyds-TSB	4.0	4.8	45.8	45.4	7.7	8.2	8.8	10.7
Northern Rock	7.4	3.6	56.3	30.5	8.4	8.5	13.2	11.6
Royal Bank of Scotland	6.6	5.4	57.1	45.9	7.1	7.5	11.5	11.7
Mean	5.8	4.7	49.8	40.7	8.1	7.9	11.6	11.7

Source: Annual Abstract of Banking Statistics 2007.
Notes: Regulatory capital includes Tier 1 capital (i.e., paid-up ordinary capital, preferred shares and disclosed reserves) and Tier 2 capital (i.e., undisclosed reserves, revaluation reserves, hybrid instruments and subordinated debt).

HBOS had addressed all of its concerns regarding its risk management and control processes and that the issue was closed.[144]

Another reason that Basel Accord capital regulation may have failed is that it required too little of shareholders and did not give them adequate incentives to not risk shift. Table 7.2 shows that the average ratio of regulatory capital (which, as discussed previously, is broadly defined) to total assets was low in 2001 and had declined even further by 2006. However, the regulatory capital of banks, both in terms of Tier 1 and total-capital ratio (i.e., Tier 1 plus Tier 2) was well above the Basel minimum regulatory levels of 4 and 8 per cent. Furthermore, these ratios did not change significantly between 2001 and 2006. Part of the reason is that banks were able to reduce the proportion of risk-weighted assets in their balance sheets during this period (see Table 7.2). Thus, on the eve of the Great Crash, British banks were highly leveraged but had equity capital well above the regulatory minimum.

[144] Parliamentary Commission on Banking Standards, '*An Accident Waiting to Happen*': *The Failure of HBOS*, pp. 24–5, 27.

Another problem with the Basel Accord approach to capital regulation was that large banks and those with a high degree of interconnectedness typically faced lower capital requirements because they adopted their own IRB models.[145] However, these are the same institutions that have the greatest incentive to risk shift and whose failure results in large negative externalities.

Yet another weakness of the Basel approach is that subordinated debt is viewed as capital. However, because subordinated debt-holders are not residual claimants, they have less incentive and ability than shareholders to ensure that bank management does not engage in risk shifting. Although subordinate debt-holders are less risk averse than depositors, they nevertheless face the same moral-hazard problems. This suggests that there is a conceptual problem with the Basel approach to capital regulation in that capital is viewed as a buffer in the event of shocks to asset portfolios rather than as something that incentivises managers and shareholders to act prudently.

From its inception, the Basel Accord approach to capital regulation was flawed and, as argued herein, further defects were introduced into the system over time. A possible explanation for these flaws is that the BCBS and national regulators were captured by the banking industry so that capital regulation was not an onerous burden on banks. Goodhart suggested that regulatory capture became an issue only towards the end of the 1990s, when regulators began to adopt the internal-risk-measurement models of the regulated.[146] With the distribution of the second consultative document on the new Basel Accord in January 2001, 'the scales tipped decisively in favour of regulatory capture'.[147]

A global perspective on bank regulation and stability

Before 1913, bank regulation in the United Kingdom was minimal. Except for restrictions on note issue, which were imposed to strengthen the Bank of England's monopoly note-issuing position, the authorities made few attempts to control banks until World War II. Nevertheless, the UK banking system was stable during the Great Depression, unlike those in many other nations.[148] Why was the UK banking system stable? As described in Chapter 5, the extended liability of British banks combined with the larger size of UK banks made them more robust than those in

---

[145] Dewatripont, Rochet and Tirole, *Balancing the Banks*, p. 86.
[146] Goodhart, *The Basel Committee*, pp. 416, 564.
[147] Dewatripont, Rochet and Tirole, *Balancing the Banks*, p. 81.
[148] Grossman, 'The shoe that didn't drop'.

other economies, especially in the United States. Notably, Canada had a similar banking structure and its banking system also weathered the Great Depression.[149]

The protosupervisory regime established by the Bank of England also may have contributed in a small way to interwar banking stability. This regime was nonstatutory, which was in stark contrast to other leading economies at the time, which imposed statutory regulation on banks and subjected them to periodical examinations. Another factor that contributed to the stability of the British banking system during the Great Depression was the substantial amount of government debt held by banks. However, the question remains of whether banks voluntarily invested in government bonds or moral suasion was brought to bear.

From 1939 through the early 1970s, UK banks were subject to financial repression to help finance the large debts that had accumulated to defend the nation in World War II. Britain's experience with financial repression was by no means unique because most other developed as well as several emerging nations experienced a similar set of circumstances at the time.[150] Although financial-repression policies around the globe differed, they had the same aim: to keep nominal interest rates at low levels and real-interest rates negative to help governments restructure and finance their debts.[151] Most economies induced demand for government debt via reserve requirements; many placed interest-rate controls on deposits (e.g., Regulation Q in the United States) and lending; and some directed credit to certain sectors. Similar to the United Kingdom's experience, financial-repression policies played a major role in reducing government-debt levels in the advanced and emerging economies that adopted them.[152]

Financial repression meant that banks across the globe had little scope for risk shifting, with the result that banking systems were stable. Remarkably, according to Reinhart and Rogoff's data, the quarter-century after 1945 was the most stable period during the past two centuries in terms of banking crises around the world – they were extremely rare.[153] Financial repression, however – with the inefficiencies that it induces in the financial system – may be too high a cost to pay for banking stability.[154]

Financial-repression policies across the developed world came under pressure as the repressed banks faced stiff competition from foreign banks

---

[149] Bordo, Redish and Rockoff, 'Why didn't Canada have a banking crisis'.
[150] Reinhart and Sbrancia, 'The liquidation of government debt'.
[151] Reinhart and Sbrancia, 'The liquidation of government debt'.
[152] Reinhart and Sbrancia, 'The liquidation of government debt'.
[153] Reinhart and Rogoff, *This Time Is Different*, p. 156.
[154] McKinnon, *Money and Capital*; Shaw, *Financial Deepening*.

and domestic depository institutions, neither of which were subject to regulation. This competition, as well as the fact that government-debt levels had fallen, resulted in the gradual removal of financial repression. The demise of financial-repression policies in the United Kingdom was followed by the secondary-banking crisis in 1974. The United Kingdom's experience in this regard did not differ much from that of other countries, for many economies in the post-1970 era experienced banking instability after liberalising their financial systems.[155] The UK banking system faced two problems after liberalisation, the first of which was unique and the second of which was common to many other developed economies. First, it lacked a rigorous regulatory and bank supervisory system. Second, banks had extremely low levels of capital relative to deposits and assets. This low level gave banks the incentive to engage in risk shifting, and the absence of a rigorous regulatory and supervisory system gave them the latitude to take greater risks. Consequently, banking regulation and supervision in the United Kindgom was placed on a statutory footing, for the first time, in 1979.

The rise of global banks from the 1970s onwards and the political desire to create a level playing field for such banks resulted in the Basel Accord, which was an attempt to harmonise capital-adequacy regulation across the G-10 nations. This Accord required supervisors to impose on banks a minimum 8 per cent risk-weighted capital ratio. As argued in the previous section, the Basel approach to regulation was deeply flawed, for a multitude of reasons. Ultimately, the Basel approach was a dismal failure, as witnessed by the banking crises experienced in many economies in 2007–8. Indeed, the adoption of the Basel approach explains why the 2007–8 crisis was global, affecting simultaneously most developed economies: every major developed nation had adopted the Basel regulatory system, whereas most emerging nations had adopted only elements of it but had kept more onerous economic regulations and constraints in place (e.g., Brazil, China and India).

---

[155] See Kaminsky and Reinhart, 'The twin crises'; Diaz-Alejandro, 'Good-bye financial repression'; and Demirgüç-Kunt and Detragiache, 'The determinants of banking crises'.

8 Restoring banking stability: Policy and political economy

Banks and governments have always had a symbiotic relationship.[1]
Anat Admati and Martin Hellwig

Humpty Dumpty sat on a wall.
Humpty Dumpty had a great fall.
All the king's horses and all the king's men
Couldn't put Humpty together again.

History and the Great Crash

From the long-run perspective developed in this book, it is relatively easy to understand why the 2007–8 crisis happened. Although popular opinion places the blame at the feet of reckless bankers and their huge bonuses, these are only symptoms of a much deeper problem. This book argues that bankers simply respond to the prevailing incentive structures – the culture of greed and excessive compensation were simply endogenous to the institutional setting.

The concept of risk shifting is endemic to banking and has had to be addressed by bankers, depositors and governments from earliest times. Until the interwar period, risk shifting in the United Kingdom was curtailed by the fact that bank shareholders had not only invested substantial amounts of capital in banks, they also were liable beyond what they had paid in through unlimited liability, reserve liability or uncalled capital. There was a substantial decline in this contingent capital, as well as paid-up capital relative to deposits or bank assets, during the interwar era and the 1940s. However, the low levels of capital and contingent capital that were reached in the 1950s did not concern the Bank of England, the Treasury or depositors. Why not? Quite simply, from 1939 onwards, the banking system was in lockdown due to financial-repression policies put in place to reduce the huge debt incurred fighting World War II. This meant that banks were induced to hold large amounts of safe government

[1] Admati and Hellwig, *The Bankers' New Clothes*, p. 201.

debt on their balance sheets and restricted from lending to riskier sectors, such as property development. Consequently, banks could not risk shift. However, once financial repression was brought to an end in 1980, what restrained poorly capitalised banks from risk shifting?

Depositors and other debt-holders of banks may have potentially provided much-needed discipline, but their incentives to do so were greatly diminished by the belief that had existed and been consistently confirmed during a century or more: that is, the Treasury and the Bank of England would bail out troubled banks. As demonstrated in the 2007–8 crisis, this belief by depositors and bank debtors was correct because both the Bank and the Treasury were willing to adopt extreme measures to prevent banks from failing.

The other potential constraint on banks was prudential regulation. However, as argued in Chapter 7, this proved ineffectual at restraining risk shifting and preventing a banking crisis. Consequently, the institutional environment that bankers inhabited in the years leading up to the Great Crash of 2007–8 was one in which they were not constrained by either shareholder capital or government regulations. Compounding this problem was the belief that large banks were too big to fail – this simply resulted in bankers taking even greater risks.

History provides a perspective on why the Great Crash occurred. However, does history also provide answers or even suggestions as to how to restore banking stability? The following section of this concluding chapter explores possible ways to restore banking stability. Ultimately, there are two alternatives that are suggested by history. We either impose stringent controls on banking systems – as was the case during the era of financial repression – or we require shareholders to have more 'skin in the game' by requiring banks to have more capital and shareholders to have some form of extended liability. These lessons are not only from the United Kingdom's history of banking stability but also from a global perspective. As emphasised throughout this book, the United Kingdom's experience with extended liability and post–World War II constraints on banking were not unique. The history of UK banking stability, however, provides a clear example of how these two alternatives have underpinned banking stability.

Policy lessons from history: Extended-liability redux

Prudential regulation with risk-capital ratios as the centrepiece clearly has not prevented systemic banking crises across the globe. Thus, in the aftermath of the Great Crash, policy makers around the world had an opportunity to be radical in the restructuring of banking systems.

However, regulatory changes in the aftermath of the crisis have not been radical and tend to preserve the status quo.[2] Reform has focused instead on macroprudential regulation and ring fencing.[3]

The BCBS introduced reforms, known as Basel III, that are broadly macroprudential in nature. A primary aim of macroprudential regulation is to counteract the tendencies of banks to hold too thin a capital buffer before a crisis occurs and to substantially shrink assets once a crisis is underway.[4] There are five main components of this macroprudential approach. First, there will be a greater focus on banks with larger amounts of common-equity capital (i.e., a minimum of 7.0 per cent of risk-weighted assets under Basel III and possibly higher for systemically important banks from a global perspective). Second, a countercyclical capital buffer, with a range of 0–2.5 per cent under Basel III reforms, will be imposed when authorities believe that credit growth is at an unacceptable level. Third, recapitalisation will be prewired by allowing authorities to convert capital instruments into common shares when a bank becomes nonviable or its capital ratio falls below a certain level. Fourth, a non-risk-based limit on leverage will be imposed. Fifth, liquidity ratios will be imposed on banks to ensure that they have sufficient liquidity.

Although these reforms are certainly a substantial tightening of pre-crisis regulation, they fail to address most of the inherent problems with capital regulation identified in Chapter 7, and it is doubtful whether they will curb risk-shifting behaviour by banks. Indeed, Table 7.2 in Chapter 7 shows that British banks had high Tier 1 ratios in 2006, with an average of 7.9, which is above what is proposed in Basel III. Furthermore, the stronger rules do not address the core problems of regulatory arbitrage and the ability of banks and regulators to calculate risk weights. Compared to previous versions, Basel III places even more stress on capital as a buffer rather than as something that incentivises managers and shareholders to act prudently.

In the United Kingdom, the *Independent Commission on Banking* recommended that the UK retail activities of banks be conducted in separate subsidiaries, which would be 'legally, economically and operationally separate from the rest of the banking groups to which they belonged'.[5] The

---

[2] Admati and Hellwig, *The Bankers' New Clothes*, chap. 13.

[3] *The Turner Review*, for example, recommended the adoption of a macroprudential approach. There also have been recommendations made by the Parliamentary Commission of Banking Standards regarding bankers' remuneration and punishments for reckless behaviour, which at the time of this writing have not been implemented (Parliamentary Commission on Banking Standards, *Changing Banking for Good*).

[4] Hanson, Kashyap and Stein, 'A macroprudential approach to regulation', p. 7.

[5] Independent Commission on Banking, *Final Report*, p. 9.

idea behind the 'ring fence' is to make it easier and less costly to rescue banks that experience trouble and to insulate retail banking from external financial shocks.[6] However, this proposal misdiagnoses the causes of the Great Crash because the lending on the part of retail banks (e.g., Northern Rock and HBOS) to retail and commercial-property sectors was a major contributor to the crisis. This ring-fencing proposal may make resolution easier in a future crisis, but it is doubtful whether its purpose will be met because banks will innovate around the ring fence. More important, ring fencing does not address the propensity of banks to risk shift. For example, almost all of the risky activities of HBOS before the Great Crash would have fallen within the proposed ring fence because HBOS did not have an investment-banking wing and was largely uncontaminated by an investment-banking culture.[7]

The policy choice that emerges from our study of British banking stability in the long term is that stable banking is possible under two different scenarios. First, banks are stringently regulated, as they were during the era of financial repression, and are induced to hold large amounts of government debt. Alternatively, bank shareholders face some form of extended liability and governments credibly commit to not bailing out errant banks.

The stringent regulations associated with financial repression may have delivered stability but at what cost? Financial-repression regulations were highly inefficient in that capital was misallocated. They also were open to abuse, with governments potentially using policies to favour their constituencies or political allies. Financial-repression policies are appropriate only when a country has come through a war and has accumulated substantial debt in the process. There is also a question of whether stringent regulations can be imposed on banks operating in a global environment; there may be regulatory competition among countries to attract banking business.

Consequently, the history of British banking, as well as the history of other economies' banking systems, teaches that stability can be attained only if bankers are given adequate incentives to not engage in risk shifting. British banking was relatively stable when shareholders and managers faced some form of extended liability, which meant that there was a substantial downside to their risk taking. The experience of the United States appears to provide additional support for this view. For example, Macey and Miller argued that double liability in the US national

---

[6] Independent Commission on Banking, *Final Report*, pp. 9–10.
[7] Parliamentary Commission on Banking Standards, '*An Accident Waiting to Happen*': *The Failure of HBOS*, p. 44.

banking system fostered prudent banking and was effective in protecting depositors.[8]

Before the Great Crash, some scholars suggested that extended liability should be reintroduced into banking systems.[9] In the aftermath of the 2008 crisis, Conti-Brown suggested that systematically important financial institutions should have *pro rata* unlimited liability.[10] Although these policy proposals may be viewed as interesting curiosities of financial history and somewhat anachronistic, this may be the only route back to a stable banking system.

Extended shareholder liability would achieve some of the outcomes of those who advocate narrow banking (i.e., restricting banks to operating the payments system whilst lending is carried on by other institutions) without the cost of implementing such strict regulations. In particular, given the risks associated with real estate lending, banks with extended liability would be likely to substantially reduce their exposure to this volatile sector, with the result that other institutions would arise to fill the void.[11] This was the case historically; when shareholders had extended liability, British banks rarely advanced credit to the property sector.

The economic arguments against extended liability largely revolve around the issue of the cost of bank capital. Because extended liability would reduce the marketability of bank shares – due to the need to have an administrative structure large enough to ensure that bank shares are not sold to impecunious individuals – bank capital might become overly costly. These costs, however, may not be so very great. For example, in the nineteenth century, bank shares traded relatively freely on the London and regional stock exchanges even when most banks had unlimited liability, and the dilution of liability regimes after 1878 had little effect on the liquidity of shares.[12] However, the fact that, in the modern context, banks have shareholders numbering in the hundreds of thousands may make the administrative costs prohibitively high.[13] Nevertheless, the advent of information technology and personal-credit-scoring systems means that it has never been easier to assess whether an individual has adequate wealth to cover a call on shares. That said, shareholder numbers may have to contract if extended liability were reintroduced. This could have implications for the size of banks.

---

[8] Macey and Miller, 'Double liability'.

[9] Macey and Miller, 'Double liability'; Grossman, 'Double liability'.

[10] Conti-Brown, 'Unlimited shareholder liability'.

[11] See Offer, 'Narrow banking', who stressed the need for banks to return to their historical policy in which they largely avoid lending to the property sector.

[12] Acheson and Turner, 'The secondary market'; Acheson, Hickson and Turner, 'Does limited liability matter?', pp. 263–4.

[13] Acheson, Hickson and Turner, 'Does limited liability matter?', p. 270.

The reintroduction of extended liability also might affect the composition of investors. Pension funds, mutual funds and other institutional investors hold the stock of modern banks. If unlimited liability were reintroduced, such companies might be reluctant to own bank shares because the entire fund would potentially be in jeopardy. However, if the liability were defined (e.g., double or triple liability), there is no reason to believe that institutional investors would retreat from owning bank shares.

Another potential difficulty with reintroducing extended liability is that calling capital in the middle of a crisis may exacerbate it because shareholders must sell assets to meet calls, which could result in a downwards spiral of asset prices. However, the entire purpose of extended liability is to prevent a crisis occurring in the first instance. Because extended liability incentivises banks to not risk shift, there will be no bank-credit-fuelled asset-price booms followed by crashes. One way to think of extended liability is as an ex-ante commitment that in most cases will not be called on ex-post. However, even in the middle of the minor crises in the nineteenth century, substantial calls were made on shareholders of the few banks that had failed. There is no evidence that these calls exacerbated the situation; in fact, the evidence points to the opposite: depositors' confidence in banks was strengthened when they saw the ability of wealthy shareholders to meet calls.

A major difficulty with introducing anything less than unlimited shareholder liability is that inflation can dilute the incentives associated with extended liability because it erodes the real value of contingent (and paid-up) capital. Indeed, Chapter 5 describes how inflation weakened extended-liability regimes in the United Kingdom as well as in Canada and the United States. One solution to this problem would be to index-link extended liability so that although paid-up capital might not expand following a bout of inflation, the amount of callable capital would. An alternative way to achieve this is to make the amount callable in the event of bankruptcy a fixed proportion of deposits rather than paid-up capital. Another solution is for the government to make a credible commitment to keep inflation near zero in the long run by adopting a commodity standard or fixed-exchange-rate regime. This possibility is discussed in greater detail in the following section.

Another potential problem with reintroducing extended liability is that banks could become more conservative in their lending. This fear was expressed by Andrew Haldane of the Bank of England in evidence before the House of Commons Treasury Committee in 2010.[14] However, there

---

[14] House of Commons Treasury Committee, *Too Important to Fail – Too Important to Ignore*, p. 57.

is a balance to strike between banking stability on the one hand and the availability of bank credit on the other. As the aftermath of the Great Crash highlights, credit availability is highly dependent on a stable banking system.

It is interesting that there is a body of literature suggesting that banks failed British industry by being overly conservative in the Victorian and Edwardian eras, the heyday of extended liability.[15] However, there is substantial evidence that suggests that British banks were not conservative towards British industry.[16] The lack of involvement of banks in the long-run financing of industry appears to have been caused more by a lack of demand for bank lending and the availability of an active debenture and equity market rather than any supply problems.[17] In any case, extended-liability regimes have not been directly blamed for this conservatism because the allegation is that banks became particularly conservative after the demise of unlimited liability.

Another objection to the reintroduction of extended liability is that modern banking is far too complicated. In other words, the objection is that extended liability worked well when banking was simple but would not work today. However, much of the complexity of modern banking has arisen because of the Basel regulatory system and the attempts to avoid regulation. If anything, the complexity of modern banking may facilitate the reintroduction of extended liability. In the past, bank directors needed to gather information on a candidate shareholder. However, with the advent of information processing, data analysis and credit scoring, prospective shareholders' wealth could be easily checked before they were admitted to the constituency. In addition, a subsequent deterioration in their wealth or credit standing could be uncovered easily. Conceivably, credit-rating agencies could even rate banks on the basis of the wealth or creditworthiness of their individual shareholders.

The call for a return to extended liability is not a call for the implementation of free-banking proposals, wherein all government interference in money and banking is removed.[18] Neither is it a call for the elimination of the LLR role played by central banks. A classical LLR simply prevents substantial increases in demand for high-powered money from turning

---

[15] Kennedy, 'Institutional response' and *Industrial Structure*; Best and Humphries, 'The City and industrial decline'.

[16] Capie and Collins, 'Industrial lending'; Collins, 'English bank development'; Collins and Baker, *Commercial Banks and Industrial Finance*; Fohlin, 'The balancing act'.

[17] Michie, *The London and New York Stock Exchange*; Coyle and Turner, 'Law, politics and finance'.

[18] The main advocates of free banking are Dowd, *The State and the Monetary System*; Selgin and White, 'How would the invisible hand handle money?'; and White, *Free Banking in Britain*.

into a full-blown liquidity crisis.[19] This is an important role. However, towards the end of the nineteenth century, the Bank of England and the Treasury began to bail out or to coordinate the bailout of insolvent banks. This created a major moral hazard and ultimately undermined the stability of the banking system because large banks knew that tax-payers would come to their rescue if they became insolvent. Because this social underwriting of the banking system contributed to its instability and blunts the incentives of shareholders and bankers, taxpayer-funded underwriting and government-mandated deposit insurance also needs to cease. Because implicit and explicit deposit insurance can be viewed as substitutes for extended liability or contingent capital, they would no longer be required if extended liability were reintroduced.

Political economy of banking

The proposal to reintroduce extended liability to banking as well as removing deposit insurance and implementing a credible commitment to not bailing out banks, however, is unrealistic because it does not consider the political economy of banking. Therefore, this section briefly explores the politics of banking stability and concludes that politics is the ultimate determinant of banking stability.

To suggest that there is a connection between banking and politics is not necessarily novel; there is a growing literature that emphasises how political economy has shaped banking and bank regulation in the United States.[20] For example, Johnson and Kwak argued that politics has shaped the US banking system throughout history for good and for ill,[21] and Haber showed how political institutions shaped the early development of banking systems in the United States and Mexico.[22]

---

[19] Capie, 'The evolving regulatory framework'; Schwartz, 'Real and pseudo-financial crises'.

[20] See, for example, Rajan and Zingales, 'The great reversals'; Claessens and Perotti, 'Finance and inequality'; Mian, Sufi and Trebbi, 'The political economy'; and Perotti, 'The political economy of finance'.

[21] Johnson and Kwak, 13 Bankers. Benmelech and Moskowitz, in 'The political economy of financial regulation', found that usury laws across the United States in the nineteenth century favoured wealthy political incumbents and that usury laws weakened with the broadening of suffrage within states. Rajan and Ramcharan's 'Land and credit' found that the existence of large agricultural and landed elites as an interest group adversely affected the development of banking across early twentieth-century states in the United States. Kroszner and Strahan, in 'What drives deregulation?', found that the timing of branch deregulation across US states in the 1970s and 1980s was driven by a private-interest theory whereby states dominated by large banks and small firms (i.e., winners from deregulation) deregulated branching earlier than in states dominated by small banks and insurance firms (i.e., losers from deregulation).

[22] Haber, 'Political institutions and financial development'.

Political economy also may be a determinant of the stability of banking systems. For example, Rajan argued that the deregulation and rapid expansion of banking in the United States in the early twentieth century was a response to the Populist movement, which resulted in the excessive extension of rural credit and ultimately was a contributory factor to the Great Depression.[23]

Chapter 7 discusses how government policy towards banking control and regulation may be either mediate – in that government policy towards banks is a response to their pursuit of a monetary or fiscal or overtly political objective – or immediate, in that the policy is directly targeted to the banking system. Regardless of its overtness (or otherwise), the basic argument advanced in this chapter is that government policy towards banking reflects the interests of the political and economic elite. These elite are not stationary but rather can change over time due to technological or institutional changes, such as the extension of the electoral franchise.[24] At times, government policy towards banks may even reflect the power of the banking lobby if bankers are part of the economic and political elite. It also could reflect the political power of other industries and firms. Furthermore, banking policy may reflect the demands of the nation's citizenry (or a subset thereof) voiced through its elected representatives. In addition, government policy towards banks at times may reflect national defence needs.

This view of regulation differs from the economic theory of regulation, which argues that well-organised interest groups (mainly industries and professions) influence the nature of regulation through political influence on the government and politicians.[25] According to the economic theory, regulation exists primarily because it protects industry incumbents from competition, allowing them to earn rents. However, it is difficult to explain financial deregulation and the time-series variation in bank regulation from this perspective.

In the case of the 1825–6 crisis, Chapter 5 explains that one of the proximate causes of the crisis was the existence of small, poorly capitalised banks. The reason for the existence of these banks was the chartering privileges of the Bank of England, which restricted the organisation of all other banks to partnerships and note-issuing banks to a maximum of six partners. The Bank was given this monopoly of joint-stock banking in England as a quid pro quo for providing finance to the government.

---

[23] Rajan, *Fault Lines*, p. 9.

[24] Allen, 'A theory of pre-modern British aristocracy'; Acemoglu and Robinson, 'Why did the West extend the franchise?'

[25] Stigler, 'The theory of economic regulation'; Peltzman, 'Toward a more general theory'; Becker, 'A theory of competition'.

According to Thompson and Hickson, William III and the promoters of the Bank of England – informed by the failure of the Bank of Amsterdam in 1672 to expand its currency to provide emergency war finance at the beginning of the Franco–Dutch War – were completely aware of the historical reluctance of independent parliaments to supply emergency war finance.[26] Hence, they created a national paper currency – monopolised by a state bank – that could expand flexibly during military emergencies. They could do so without creating proportionate increases in the price level because the independent common-law judges would force the state bank to resume gold payments at the pre-war rate once the military emergency had passed.[27] In other words, the Bank of England and its near-monopoly of note issuance was a vital institution that contributed to the survival of the country and its fledgling democracy.

The political elite of the United Kingdom – which before the Great Reform Act of 1832 had been dominated by the aristocracy and landed gentry – may have had an incentive to support the Bank's monopoly because this kept banks small and restricted credit to small farmers. In this way, large landowners were perhaps helped to maintain power and control over small farmers and their tenants. For example, large landowners may have perceived banks as competitors in terms of granting credit to small farmers and tenants.[28] They also may have been less able to take advantage of small farmers and tenants during periods of agricultural adversity as long as farmers could be assisted through their difficulties by banks. In addition, large landowners needed a large pool of unskilled workers, and bank credit may have made it easier for small farmers and tenants and their offspring to become educated.[29]

After the 1825–6 crisis, banks were permitted to incorporate as joint-stock companies, but they were not permitted to have limited liability or to establish within a 65-mile radius of London. However, when the Bank of England's charter was renewed in 1833, its monopoly of London banking was substantially weakened because nonissuing banks were now permitted to establish there.[30] Notably, the reforms made in the aftermath of the 1825–6 crisis are consistent with the political-economy explanation. The post-1825 reforms weakened the Bank's monopoly on banking; however, the government was able to institute them for several reasons. First, by the early 1800s, Parliamentary support for the issuance of long-term national debt during military emergencies was widespread,

---

[26] Thompson and Hickson, *Ideology and the Evolution of Vital Economic Institutions*, p. 190.
[27] Thompson and Hickson, *Ideology and the Evolution of Vital Economic Institutions*, p. 191.
[28] Rajan and Ramcharan, 'Land and credit', 1896.
[29] See Galor, Moav and Vollrath, 'Inequality in land ownership'.
[30] Bank of England Privileges Act (1833) – 3 & 4 Will. 4, c.98.

which meant that the government was less dependent on the Bank of England for emergency war finance.[31] Second, the development of bond and annuity markets meant that the government had alternative sources of finance and was less reliant on the Bank for loans during normal times.[32] Third, the power of the aristocracy and landed interests in Parliament had waned; the Parliamentary session of 1826 was a watershed in the demise of the power and influence of the landed class.[33] As a result, there was little Parliamentary opposition to post-1825 banking reforms.

In 1826, the Bank of England effectively blocked any move to allow joint-stock banks to have limited liability, and it persisted in its opposition to limited liability in banking for another four decades.[34] According to William Clay, a contemporary Parliamentarian, the Bank was simply seeking to preserve its monopoly status.[35] However, although its opposition may have been based on its own narrow self-interest, the presence of unlimited liability underpinned the stability of the UK banking system in the decades after 1825. It is interesting that in 1858, when banks were eventually permitted to have limited liability, the Bank of England's suggestion – that it should be only on condition that banks had a large extended liability – was ignored.[36] Nevertheless, in practice, this is what banks adopted after unlimited liability was abandoned.

If unlimited liability had such an important stability-enhancing role in British banking, why did it disappear after the collapse of the CGB in 1878? The commonly accepted view that there were deficiencies with the system of unlimited liability has been debunked.[37] However, there may be a political-economy dimension to its demise. First, middle-class investors in Victorian Britain did not like unlimited liability, especially after the crisis of 1866 and the CGB collapse.[38] Given their increased political influence, it is likely that they pressured politicians to pass the 1879 Companies Act, which facilitated the conversion of banks to limited liability. Second, the political elite, in desiring big banks to compete with their empire-building rivals, may have been satisfied to eliminate the main obstacle to the growth of bank concentration.[39]

---

[31] Thompson and Hickson, *Ideology and the Evolution of Vital Economic Institutions*, p. 191.

[32] Broz and Grossman, 'Paying for privilege', p. 69.

[33] Gash, *Aristocracy and People*, pp. 121–3.

[34] Headlam, *A Speech on Limited Liability*, p. 13. See Hunt, *Development of the Business Corporation*, p. 50.

[35] Clay, *Speech of William Clay*, pp. 14, 43.   [36] Turner, 'Last acre and sixpence', p. 122.

[37] Acheson and Turner, 'The death blow to unlimited liability'.

[38] Jefferys, *Business Organisation*, pp. 121, 178.

[39] See Alhadeff, *Competition and Controls in Banking*, pp. 237–8; and House of Commons Treasury Committee, *Too Important to Fail – Too Important to Ignore*, p. 56.

War and postwar economic policy had a major, if indirect, effect on the stability of the UK banking system in the twentieth century. First, the financial-repression policies, which were adopted during World War II and maintained for nearly three decades, restrained banks from risk shifting. Second, the decline in the capital-to-deposits ratio after 1913 was principally due to high wartime inflation. The decline in this ratio left banks with few incentives to curb risk shifting when government controls were removed in the 1970s.

Both Rajan and Galbraith argued that there is a political-economy explanation for the Great Crash.[40] Galbraith opined that 'inequality was the heart of the financial crisis'.[41] He argued that the rise in inequality since the 1970s was mainly due to the enrichment through the capital markets of a small number of people, including financiers and company executives.[42] This new capital-market elite preyed on those with little wealth by lending them money that they could never hope to repay. For Galbraith, this extension of credit was akin to a Ponzi scheme that only results in a bubble economy and instability.

Rajan's basic argument was that easy credit is used as a palliative by governments unable to address directly the deeper concerns of the middle classes.[43] In particular, in the years before the Great Crash, government policies made credit more easily available to alleviate the rise in inequality for the middle classes and for those left behind by economic growth and technological progress. In other words, 'an important political response to inequality was populist credit expansion, which allowed people the consumption possibilities that their stagnant incomes otherwise could not support'.[44] This credit expansion created a housing bubble that eventually collapsed with catastrophic consequences for those who had been extending the credit. However, the available empirical evidence does not support Rajan's inequality-credit-crisis nexus, and financial crises typically are followed rather than preceded by rising inequality.[45] Rajan's explanation may fit the United States, with its government-sponsored enterprises (e.g., Freddie Mac and Fannie Mae), mortgages insured by the Federal Housing Administration Community Reinvestment Act, and high-level affordable-housing mandates. However, it does not neatly fit

---

[40] Rajan, *Fault Lines*; Rajan, 'The true lessons of the recession'; Galbraith, *Inequality and Instability*.

[41] Galbraith, *Inequality and Instability*, p. 4.

[42] Galbraith, *Inequality and Instability*, p. 149. For evidence on this, see Bivens and Mishel, 'The pay of corporate executives'.

[43] Rajan, *Fault Lines*, p. 9.   [44] Rajan, *Fault Lines*, p. 42.

[45] Bordo and Meissner, 'Does inequality lead to a financial crisis?'; Atkinson and Morelli, 'Economic crises and inequality'; Claessens and Perotti, 'Finance and inequality', p. 749.

the United Kingdom, where the government has no such initiatives or agencies to promote homeownership among those in the lower deciles of income distribution.

It is possible to reconcile Galbraith's and Rajan's views in that government policy towards the banking sector in democracies is vulnerable to being captured by private interests, mostly when governments are under pressure from rising inequality to facilitate broader credit access for marginal borrowers.[46] This deadly combination of regulatory capture and populist policies can result in lax standards and regulation, which then results in excessive credit creation followed by a crisis. Notably, there is evidence that suggests that the same deadly combination was at work in the United States. Mian, Sufi and Trebbi found that beginning in 2001–2, there was a sharp increase in mortgage-industry electoral campaign contributions to politicians from districts with large shares of subprime borrowers.[47] However, their explanation is too nuanced to claim that politicians were being bought: they found that the fraction of subprime borrowers in a district is an important determinant of politicians voting in favour of subprime-related legislation. In other words, US politicians responded to private (or special) and constituent interests in the run-up to the Great Crash.

In the UK case, income inequality has increased during the past three decades. For example, in 1987, the income share of the top 1 per cent in the United Kingdom was 7.78; by 2007, it was 15.44.[48] However, there may be no causal connection between rising inequality and the dangerous expansion of credit that culminated in the Great Crash. They simply may be manifestations of a diminished concern for the middle classes from the political establishment, which has continued since the end of the Cold War and possibly earlier.[49] This diminished concern chiefly manifests in less-egalitarian tax policies that penalise the middle classes.[50] However, it also manifests in deregulation, favouring financial and other elites, which makes asset-price bubbles more likely. Asset-price bubbles have distributive consequences; for example, the housing bubble resulted in many middle-class households (particularly younger

---

[46] Perotti, 'The political economy of finance', p. 32.

[47] Mian, Sufi and Trebbio, 'The political economy'.

[48] *The World Top Incomes Database*, available at http://topincomes.g-mond. parisschoolofeconomics.eu/.

[49] See Thompson and Hickson, *Ideology and the Evolution of Vital Economic Institutions*, pp. 86–7, for possible reasons for this diminished concern and the way in which imperial centralisations throughout history eventually impoverished the vibrant middle classes in their midst.

[50] See Piketty and Saez, 'How progressive is the U.S. federal tax system?', p. 21, on the reduced egalitarianism of the UK tax system since 1970.

households) being made less wealthy as they lost capital. Ultimately, the cost of bailing out the banking system is borne by the middle classes in terms of conventional taxes, inflation and artificially suppressed interest rates.

Inequality may have made regulatory capture much easier.[51] For example, a disproportionate number of top income earners from the financial sector may have used their influence to lobby for deregulation, which ultimately led to the crisis.[52] According to the Parliamentary Commission on Banking Standards, politicians in the United Kingdom succumbed to the lobbying efforts of banks.[53] However, this raises the question of how this could happen in a constitutional democracy with strong political and legal institutions. A major explanation is that the huge earnings of the City of London and its banks in the decade or more before the Great Crash gave the financial system undue power and influence with politicians.[54] First, the City and its banks generated huge invisible earnings for the UK economy. Second, the financial sector grew relative to the rest of the economy in the decade before the crisis: from 1997 to 2007, the average annual growth of output in the UK financial sector was 6 per cent, compared with the average GDP growth of 3 per cent. The share of nominal GDP accounted for by financial services was slightly less than 6 per cent in 1997; by 2007, it was contributing almost 9 per cent.[55] As a result of this growth, banking-sector assets grew from almost 300 per cent of GDP in 1997 to approximately 500 per cent in 2007.[56] The Parliamentary Commission on Banking Standards suggested that successive governments were simply 'dazzled by the economic growth and tax revenues promised from the banking sector'.[57] Third, the banking sector in the United Kingdom was extremely profitable in the decade before the crisis: in 2007, banks contributed more than 15 per cent of the economy's profits as a whole, up from about 6 per cent in 1997.[58]

The success of the City was vital to the Labour Government's economic policy and facilitated the growth of government spending on

---

[51] Claessens and Perotti, 'Finance and inequality', p. 749.

[52] On the rise of income in the UK financial sector, see The High Pay Commission, *Cheques With Balances*, p. 34. See Igan, Mishra and Tressel, 'A fistful of dollars', for the lobbying efforts by lenders in the United States in the run-up to the 2008 crisis. They argue that these lobbying efforts contributed to the financial crisis.

[53] Parliamentary Commission on Banking Standards, *Changing Banking for Good*, p. 62.

[54] Dow and Dow, in 'Economic history', made a similar point.

[55] Burgess, 'Measuring financial-sector output', p. 234.

[56] 'Evolution of the UK banking system', *Bank of England Quarterly Bulletin* (2010), pp. 325, 329.

[57] Parliamentary Commission on Banking Standards, *Changing Banking for Good*, p. 12.

[58] Haldane, 'The contribution of the financial sector', 4.

health, education and social welfare, which enabled it to strengthen its power base among public-sector workers and welfare recipients. Thus, to gain power and influence, the financial sector did not need to 'bribe' UK politicians by bankrolling election campaigns or post-politics careers as advisers or nonexecutive directors – although, of course, this does not mean that this did not happen.

The symbiotic relationship between the banks and the government meant that the FSA was under pressure to be nonintrusive and light touch in its regulation.[59] The oft-stated policy of Gordon Brown as Chancellor and of his government was to foster the international competitiveness of the UK financial sector by limiting restrictive and intrusive regulation.[60] In Brown's words, 'not just a light touch but a limited touch'.[61] As a result, Lord Turner had argued that if the FSA had acted decisively to reign in bank-credit expansion in 2004, politicians would have told them that they 'should not be holding back the extension of mortgage credit to ordinary people', thereby 'preventing the democratisation of homeownership'.[62] Similarly, the FSA Board has argued that if the FSA had proposed to tighten regulation just before the first signs of the crisis, 'their proposals would have been met by extensive complaints that the FSA was pursuing a heavy-handed, gold-plating approach which would harm London's competitiveness'.[63]

Not only were the banks able to capture the government's regulatory policy towards them, they also might have been able to capture the Bank of England's monetary-policy decisions. For most of the two centuries covered in this study, the value of the United Kingdom's currency was tied directly or indirectly to gold via the Gold Standard, the gold-exchange standard and the Bretton Woods regime. This essentially meant that the Bank of England was free from pressure from governments and banks to lower interest rates. However, after the collapse of the Bretton Woods arrangement, the Bank was susceptible to capture by the political elite and/or banks. The greater operational independence granted to the Bank in 1997 may have left it less susceptible to political exploitation but more open to being captured by the banking system.[64] One possibility is that

---

[59] *The Failure of the Royal Bank of Scotland*, p. 261; House of Commons Treasury Committee, *Banking Crisis: Regulation and Supervision*, p. 11; Parliamentary Commission on Banking Standards, *Changing Banking for Good*, p. 62.

[60] *The Failure of the Royal Bank of Scotland*, pp. 261–2.

[61] *The Failure of the Royal Bank of Scotland*, p. 262.

[62] House of Commons Treasury Committee, *Banking Crisis: Regulation and Supervision*, p. 11.

[63] *The Failure of the Royal Bank of Scotland*, p. 262.

[64] Dow and Dow, 'Economic history', p. 11.

bankers pushed for low interest rates to assist their expansion of credit. The ability to push for low interest rates combined with lax regulation ultimately resulted in the housing bubble. This implies that banking reform also requires monetary reform, whereby credible commitments – such as having the currency tied to a commodity or commodity bundle – prevents central banks from setting interest rates too low. Another possibility is to adopt the free-banking policy of removing the central bank altogether and allowing banks to issue their own currency redeemable for a commodity or commodity bundle.[65] The desirability of such a policy ultimately revolves around the issue of whether the Bank of England continues to be a source of emergency government finance.

The political-economy explanation for the Great Crash in Britain is common across other economies caught up in the global banking crisis of 2007–8. The economies affected by the crisis were all Western, liberal democracies with large public sectors. Politicians of all political persuasions were dazzled by the financial alchemy of the banking sector and were happy to apply 'light-touch' regulation to their banking systems. Rising inequality was also an issue in these democracies, which left them vulnerable to regulatory capture by banks.[66] Notably, of all of the economies that experienced crises, the most unequal were the two at the epicentre of the crisis and consequently suffered the most: the United Kingdom and the United States.

Restoring and preserving banking stability is a political rather than an economic problem. Admati and Hellwig suggested that adequate reform of the banking system has not occurred because politicians somehow lack the political will.[67] Sadly, however, the corruption of popular democracy in the United Kingdom and elsewhere is not conducive to banking reform or banking stability.[68] The political elite, under the sway of the still-influential financial lobby, is reluctant to remove the safety nets that protect the banking system or to impose the necessary constraints on risk shifting by banks in the future, in case they undermine the competitiveness of their banks. The voting majority in Western democracies can live with this state of affairs, solaced by welfare payments and stable and well-paying public-sector jobs. However, it is in the interests of the

---

[65] See White, *Free Banking*; White, *The Theory of Monetary Institutions*; and Selgin and White, 'How would the invisible hand handle money?'

[66] See Bonica, McCarty, Poole and Rosenthal, 'Why hasn't democracy', for why democracy has not slowed rising inequality.

[67] Admati and Hellwig, *The Bankers' New Clothes*, p. 228.

[68] For more on the corruption of popular democracy and the rise of a political and business oligarchy in Britain, see Mount, *The New Few*.

middle classes – which have borne significant capital losses associated with the bank-induced housing boom and are ultimately paying the cost of bailing out the banks – that banking should be radically reformed and bank shareholders held to account. Only a major shift in the political calculus will bring about such a change. Failing such a change, we can expect banking instability and crises to become the new normal.

Bibliography

PARLIAMENTARY PAPERS/OFFICIAL REPORTS

Committee of Secrecy on the Bank of England Charter (P.P. 1831–32, VI)

Select Committee on Joint Stock Banks (P.P. 1836, IX)

Select Committee on Joint Stock Banks (P.P. 1837, XIV)

Select Committee on Joint Stock Banks (P.P. 1838, VII)

Select Committee on Banks of Issue (P.P. 1840, IV)

Secret Committee of the House of Lords on Causes of Commercial Distress (P.P. 1847–8, I)

Select Committee on the Bank Acts (P.P. 1858, LXXVIII)

Report of the Treasury Committee on Bank Amalgamations, London: HMSO, 1918.

Hansard House of Commons Debates (vol. XIV).

Hansard House of Lords Debates (vol. 465).

House of Commons, *Report of Committee on Finance and Industry*, London: HMSO, 1931.

House of Commons, *Report of Committee on Working of the Monetary System*, London: HMSO, 1959.

National Board for Prices and Incomes, *Bank Charges*, London: HMSO, 1967.

House of Commons, *First Report from the Select Committee on Nationalised Industries: Bank of England*, London: HMSO, 1970.

House of Commons, *Committee to Review the Functioning of Financial Institutions, Evidence on the Financing of Industry and Trade*, vol. 5, London: HMSO, 1978.

House of Commons, *Committee to Review the Functioning of Financial Institutions, Second-Stage Evidence*, vol. 4, London: HMSO, 1979.

House of Commons, *Report of the Committee to Review the Functioning of Financial Institutions*, London: HMSO, 1980.

House of Commons, *Inquiry into the Supervision of the Bank of Credit and Commerce International*, London: HMSO, 1992.

Bank of England, *Report of the Board of Banking Supervision into the Circumstances of the Collapse of Barings*, London: HMSO, 1995.

House of Commons Treasury Committee, *The Run on the Rock*, London: Stationery Office, 2008.

The Turner Review: A Regulatory Response to the Global Banking Crisis. London: Financial Services Authority, 2009.

House of Commons Treasury Committee, *Banking Crisis: Dealing with the Failure of the UK Banks*, London: Stationery Office, 2009.

House of Commons Treasury Committee, *Banking Crisis: Regulation and Supervision*, London: Stationery Office, 2009.

House of Commons Treasury Committee, *Too Important to Fail – Too Important to Ignore*, London: Stationery Office, 2010.

The Failure of the Royal Bank of Scotland, London: Financial Services Authority, 2011.

HM Treasury Annual Report and Accounts, 2010–11.

Independent Commission on Banking, *Final Report*, 2011.

National Audit Office, *The Creation and Sale of the Northern Rock plc*, London: HMSO, 2012.

Office for National Statistics, Public Sector Finances, October 2012, London: ONS.

Parliamentary Commission on Banking Standards, '*An Accident Waiting to Happen*': *The Failure of HBOS*, London: HMSO, 2013.

Parliamentary Commission on Banking Standards, *Changing Banking for Good*, London: HMSO, 2013.

NEWSPAPERS AND PERIODICALS

Annual Abstract of Banking Statistics (British Bankers' Association)
Bank of England Quarterly Bulletin
Belfast Newsletter
Course of the Exchange
Investor's Monthly Manual
Northern Whig
The Banker
The Bankers' Almanac and Year Book
The Banking Almanac and Yearbook
The Banker's Magazine
The Daily Telegraph
The Economist
The Guardian
The Manchester Guardian
The Observer
The Scotsman
The Times
Stock Exchange Official Yearbook

ARCHIVES

BANK OF ENGLAND

Extract from an address delivered by F. C. Goodenough in Sweden (9 May 1927), G1/10.

Draft of an article in *Bankers' Magazine*, May 1924, 'Bank Amalgamations – the Last Phase', G1/9.

Confidential internal memo on bank capital (30 September 1958), C40/102.

Memo on capital increases by clearing banks (5 November 1959), C40/102.

Confidential internal memo (3 November 1937), G14/75.

Memo by H. Clarke (24 July 1957), C48/350.

Confidential internal memo (10 April 1958), C40/102.

Confidential internal memo (30 April 1958), C40/102.

Confidential internal memo (8 October 1958), C40/102.

Confidential internal memo (6 February 1959), C40/102.

Capital of the Bank of Scotland secret memo (27 October 1937), C48/61.

Secretary's Index Book, G16/1.

Minutes of Court of Directors, G4/89, G4/113, G4/134.

Committee on the Working of the Monetary System, memoranda of evidence, G12/1.

Baring Brothers and Co. crisis papers, C5/183.

Yorkshire Penny Bank papers, C5/111.

Governor's file on bank amalgamations, G1/10.

Cox and Co. papers, C46/129.

Anglo-South American Bank papers, C48/68.

Committee of Treasury Minutes, G8/56, G8/57, G8/58, G8/59.

British Overseas Bank papers, C48/129.

Speech of Montagu Norman at Lord Mayor's Dinner (1 October 1935), G13/1.

Speech of Montagu Norman at the Centenary Luncheon of *The Economist* (2 September, 1943), G13/1.

Speech of Lord Catto at the Lord Mayor's Dinner (1946), G13/1.

Extract from an Address by Walter Leaf (March 1927), G1/10.

Montagu Norman's Diary 1926, ADM20/15.

Montagu Norman's Diary 1934, ADM34/23.

Committee on the Working of the Monetary System, Memoranda of Evidence, Bank of England (June 1957), G12/1.

Bank Amalgamations – Letter from Norman to J. B. Pease (22 November 1926), G1/10.

Bank Amalgamations – Norman memo on meeting with Sir Christopher Needham (3 November 1926), G1/9.

Bank Amalgamations – Norman memo (10 August 1925), G1/9.

Bank Amalgamations – Norman memo (13 April 1927), G1/10.

Bank Amalgamations – Notes on interview at the Bank of England on 20 June 1934, G1/11.

Bank Amalgamations – Norman memo (12 May 1927), G1/10.

Bank Amalgamations – Letter from Manager of Equitable Bank (4 May 1927), G1/10.

Bank Amalgamations – Letter from Norman to Duke of Buccleuch (21 August 1930), G1/10.

Bank Amalgamations – Letter from Farrer to Lord Colwyn and copied to Norman (15 February 1923), G1/9.

Bank Amalgamations – Governor's Note (9 May 1961), G1/13.

Bank Amalgamations – Governor's Memo (15 August 1962), G1/13.

Bank Amalgamations – Governor's Memo (17 September 1962), G1/13.

Discount Office (Banking Supervision) Files – Letter from D. Heathcoat Amory (1 July 1958), C48/350.

Discount Office (Banking Supervision) Files – Letter from C. F. Cobbold to Chancellor (3 July 1958), C48/350.

Discount Office (Banking Supervision) Files – Letter from C. F. Cobbold to Chairman of Committee of London Clearing Bankers (3 July 1958), C48/350.

Discount Office (Banking Supervision) Files – Aide Memoire (June 1958), C48/350.

Discount Office (Banking Supervision) Files, Memo (7 December 1960), C44/304.

Statistics prepared for Radcliffe Committee, EID1/15.

Governor's memo (15 August 1962), G1/13.

Extracts from the minutes of Committee of Treasury (12 September 1957), G14/149.

Letter from John Simon to Montagu Norman (26 September 1939), G14/149.

BANK OF IRELAND

Court of Directors Transactions, 1836.

BARCLAYS BANK ARCHIVES

Contracts of copartnership for the following: Bank of Liverpool; Birmingham Town and District; Carlisle and Cumberland; Stamford and Spalding Banking Company.

BRITISH LIBRARY

Contracts of copartnership for the following: Birmingham and Midland; City of Glasgow Bank; Lancaster Banking Company; County of Gloucester Bank; Herefordshire Banking Company; Huddersfield Banking Company; Hull Banking Company; Leeds and West Riding; Royal Bank of Liverpool; Wilts and Dorset; York Union Banking Company.

HBOS/BANK OF SCOTLAND ARCHIVES

Contracts of copartnership for Central Bank of Scotland.

HSBC ARCHIVES

Bradford Banking Company Registry of Wills, 236/4.

Contracts of copartnership for the following: Bradford Banking Company; Carlisle City and District; City Bank; Leicestershire Banking Company; London Joint Stock Bank; North and South Wales Bank; Stourbridge and Kidderminster; Yorkshire Banking Company; Yorkshire District Bank.

Press Cuttings Relating to Birmingham Banking Company, 16.F.02.

Sheffield and Hallamshire Share Registers, 598/1–2.

LLOYDS-TSB ARCHIVES

Contracts of copartnership for the following: Burton, Uttoxeter and Stafford-shire; Hampshire Banking Company.
Hampshire Banking Company Shareholders' Register, 1085.

PUBLIC RECORD OFFICE OF NORTHERN IRELAND (PRONI)

Contracts of copartnership for the following: Belfast Banking Company; North-ern Banking Company; National Bank of Ireland; Ulster Banking Company.
Ulster Banking Company's Share Transfer Journals, D/3499/CC/2–3.
Will Calendar Books, various annual issues.

ROYAL BANK OF SCOTLAND ARCHIVES

Contracts of copartnership for the following: Ashton, Stalybridge, Hyde and Glossop; Bank of Whitehaven; Bilston District Banking Company; Commercial Banking Company; London and Westminster Bank; London and County Bank; Manchester and Liverpool District Bank; National Bank of Scotland; National Provincial Bank; Sheffield Banking Company; Union Bank of London.
Sheffield and Rotherham Directors' Minute Book, SR/1/2.

BOOKS, ARTICLES AND PAMPHLETS

Acemoglu, D. and Robinson, J. A. 'Why did the West extend the franchise? Democracy, inequality, and growth in historical perspective', *Quarterly Jour-nal of Economics*, 115, 1167–99, 2000.
Acheson, G. G. and Turner, J. D. 'The impact of limited liability on ownership and control: Irish banking, 1877–1914', *Economic History Review*, 59, 320–46, 2006.
Acheson G. G. and Turner, J. D. 'The death blow to unlimited liability in Victo-rian Britain: The City of Glasgow failure', *Explorations in Economic History*, 45, 235–53, 2008.
Acheson, G. G. and Turner, J. D. 'The secondary market for bank shares in nineteenth-century Britain', *Financial History Review*, 15, 123–52, 2008.
Acheson, G. G. and Turner, J. D. 'Investor behavior in a nascent capital mar-ket: Scottish bank shareholders in the nineteenth century', *Economic History Review*, 64, 188–213, 2011.
Acheson, G. G. and Turner J. D. 'Shareholder liability, risk aversion, and invest-ment returns in nineteenth-century British banking', in D. R. Green, A. Owens, J. Maltby and J. Rutterford (eds.), *Men, Women, and Money: Perspec-tives on Gender, Wealth, and Investment 1850–1930*, Oxford: Oxford University Press, 2011.
Acheson, G. G., Hickson, C. R. and Turner, J. D. 'Organizational flexibility and governance in a civil-law regime: Scottish partnership banks during the Industrial Revolution', *Business History*, 53, 505–29, 2011.
Acheson, G. G., Hickson, C. R. and Turner, J. D. 'Does limited liability mat-ter? Evidence from nineteenth-century British banking', *Review of Law and Economics*, 6, 247–73, 2011.

Acheson, G. G., Hickson, C. R., Turner, J. D. and Ye, Q. 'Rule Britannia!: British stock market returns, 1825–1870', *Journal of Economic History*, 69, 1107–37, 2009.

Acheson, G. G., Turner, J. D., and Ye, Q. 'The character and denomination of shares in the Victorian equity market', *Economic History Review*, 65, 862–86, 2012.

Ackrill, M. and Hannah, L. *Barclays: The Business of Banking 1690–1996*, Cambridge: Cambridge University Press, 2001.

Admati, A. and Hellwig, M. *The Bankers' New Clothes: What's Wrong with Banking and What to Do about It*, Princeton, NJ: Princeton University Press, 2013.

Adrian, T. and Shin, H. S. 'The changing nature of financial intermediation and the financial crisis of 2007–2009', *Annual Review of Economics*, 2, 603–18, 2010.

Alborn, T. L. *Conceiving Companies: Joint-Stock Politics in Victorian England*, London: Routledge, 1998.

Alessandri, P. and Haldane, A. G. 'Banking on the state', Bank of England speech, 25 September 2009.

Alhadeff, D. A. *Competition and Controls in Banking: A Study of the Regulation of Bank Competition in Italy, France and England*, Berkeley: University of California Press, 1968.

Allen, D. W. 'A theory of the pre-modern British aristocracy', *Explorations in Economic History*, 46, 299–313, 2009.

Allen, W. R. 'Irving Fisher and the 100 percent reserve proposal', *Journal of Law and Economics*, 36, 703–17, 1993.

Amsler, C. E., Bartlett, R. L. and Bolton, C. J. 'Thoughts of some British economists on early limited liability and corporate legislation', *History of Political Economy*, 13, 774–93, 1981.

Anderson, B. L. and Cottrell, P. L. *Money and Banking in England: The Development of the Banking System, 1694–1914*, London: David & Charles, 1974.

Anderson, B. L. and Cottrell, P. L. 'Another Victorian capital market: A study of banking and bank investors on Merseyside', *Economic History Review*, 28, 600–15, 1975.

Anon. *The Western Bank Failure and the Scottish Banking System*, Glasgow: John Bain, 1858.

Anon. *How to Mismanage a Bank: A Review of the Western Bank of Scotland*, Edinburgh: Adam and Charles Black and John Maclaren, 1859.

Anon. *Williams Deacon's 1771–1970*, Manchester: Williams Deacon's Bank, 1971.

Arcand, J.-L., Berkes, E. and Panizza, U. 'Too much finance?', *IMF Working Paper WP/12/161*, 2012.

Atkinson, A. B. and Morelli, S. 'Economic crises and inequality', *United Nations Human Development Research Paper 2011/06*, 2011.

Bagehot, W. *Lombard Street: A Description of the Money Market*, New York: John Wiley & Sons, 1999 [1873].

Baker, M. and Collins, M. 'Financial crises and structural change in English commercial bank assets, 1860–1913', *Explorations in Economic History*, 36, 428–44, 1999.

Balogh, T. *Studies in Financial Organisation*, Cambridge: Cambridge University Press, 1950.

Bank of England, *Agreed Proposal of the United States Federal Banking Supervisory Authorities and the Bank of England on Primary Capital and Capital Adequacy Assessment*, 1987.

Baring, F. *Observations on the Establishment of the Bank of England and the Paper Circulation of the Country*, New York: Augustus Kelley, 1967 [1797].

Barrow, G. L. *The Emergence of the Irish Banking System, 1820–1845*, Dublin: Gill and Macmillan Ltd., 1975.

Batchelor, R. A. 'The avoidance of catastrophe: Two nineteenth-century banking crises', in F. Capie and G. Wood (eds.), *Financial Crises and the World Banking System*, London: Macmillan, 1986.

Batini, N. and Nelson, E. 'The U.K.'s rocky road to stability', *Federal Reserve Bank of St. Louis Working Paper 2005–020A*, 2005.

Beck, T. and Levine, R. 'Stock markets, banks, and growth: Panel evidence', *Journal of Banking and Finance*, 28, 423–42, 2004.

Becker, G. S. 'A theory of competition among pressure groups for political influence', *Quarterly Journal of Economics*, 98, 371–400, 1983.

Bell, G. J. *Commentaries on the Laws of Scotland*, Edinburgh: T. & T. Clark, 6th edn., 1858.

Benmelech, E. and Moskowitz, T. J. 'The political economy of financial regulation: Evidence from U.S. state usury laws in the 19th century', *Journal of Finance*, 65, 1029–73, 2010.

Benston, G. J. and Kaufman, G. G. 'The appropriate role of bank regulation', *Economic Journal*, 106, 688–97, 1996.

Berger, A. N., Herring, R. J. and Szegö, G. P. 'The role of capital in financial institutions', *Journal of Banking and Finance*, 19, 393–430, 1995.

Berger, A. N., Klapper, L. F. and Turk-Ariss, R. 'Bank competition and financial stability', *Journal of Financial Services Research*, 35, 99–118, 2009.

Bernanke, B. S. 'Nonmonetary effects of the financial crisis in the propagation of the Great Depression', *American Economic Review*, 73, 257–76, 1983.

Bernanke, B. S. and Gertler, M. 'Agency costs, net worth, and business fluctuations', *American Economic Review*, 79, 14–31, 1989.

Bernanke, B. S., Gertler, M. and Gilchrist, S. 'The financial accelerator and the flight to quality', *Review of Economic Statistics*, 78, 1–15, 1996.

Best, M. H. and Humphries, J. 'The City and industrial decline', in B. Elbaum and W. Lazonick (eds.), *The Decline of the British Economy*, Oxford: Clarendon Press, 1986.

Bhattacharya, S., Boot, A. W. A. and Thakor, A. V. 'The economics of bank regulation', *Journal of Money, Credit and Banking*, 30, 745–70, 1998.

Bhidé, A. *A Call for Judgment: Sensible Finance for a Dynamic Economy*, Oxford: Oxford University Press, 2010.

Bignon, V., Flandreau, M. and Ugolini, S. 'Bagehot for beginners: The making of lender-of-last-resort operations in the mid-nineteenth century', *Economic History Review*, 65, 580–608, 2012.

Billings, M. and Capie, F. 'Capital in British banks, 1920–1970', *Business History*, 49, 139–62, 2007.

Billings, M. and Capie, F. 'Financial crisis, contagion, and the British banking system between the world wars', *Business History*, 53, 193–215, 2011.

Bivens, J. and Mishel, L. 'The pay of corporate executives and financial professionals as evidence of rents in top 1 percent incomes', *Journal of Economic Perspectives*, 27, 57–78.

Blackhurst, C. 'What lurks behind UK bank supervision?', *International Financial Law Review*, February, 4–10, 1985.

Bodernhorn, H. *A History of Banking in Antebellum America: Financial Markets and Economic Development in an Era of Nation-Building*, Cambridge: Cambridge University Press, 2000.

Bonica, A., McCarty, N., Poole, K. T. and Rosenthal, H. 'Why hasn't democracy slowed rising inequality?', *Journal of Economic Perspectives*, 27, 103–24.

Booth, P. (ed.). *Verdict on the Crash: Causes and Policy Implications*, London: Institute of Economic Affairs, 2009.

Bordo, M. D. 'The lender of last resort: Alternative views and historical experience', *Federal Reserve Bank of Richmond Economic Review*, January/February, 18–29, 1990.

Bordo, M. D. and Meissner, C. M. 'Does inequality lead to a financial crisis?', *NBER Working Paper 17896*, 2012.

Bordo, M. D., Redish, A. and Rockoff, H. 'Why didn't Canada have a banking crisis in 2008 (or in 1930, or 1907, or . . .)?', *NBER Working Paper 17312*, 2011.

Boyd, J. H. and De Nicoló, G. 'The theory of bank risk taking and competition revisited', *Journal of Finance*, 60, 1329–43, 2005.

Briault, C. 'The rationale for a single national financial services regulator', *FSA Occasional Paper Series* 2, 1999.

Broadberry, S. N. and van Leeuwen, B. 'British economic growth and the business cycle, 1700–1850', University of Warwick: Department of Economics, 2009.

Bromhead, A. de, Eichengreen, B. and O'Rourke, K. H. 'Right-wing political extremism in the Great Depression', *NBER Working Paper 17871*, 2012.

Brown, R. *Early Scottish Joint-Stock Companies*, Glasgow: Carter and Pratt, 1903.

Broz, J. L. and Grossman, R. S. 'Paying for privilege: The political economy of Bank of England charters, 1694–1844', *Explorations in Economic History*, 41, 48–72, 2004.

Brunnermeier, M. K. 'Deciphering the liquidity and credit crunch 2007–2008', *Journal of Economic Perspectives*, 23, 77–100, 2009.

Bryer, R. A. 'The Mercantile Laws Commission of 1854 and the political economy of limited liability', *Economic History Review*, 50, 37–56, 1997.

Buckley, A. *Financial Crisis: Causes, Context and Consequences*, Harlow: FT Prentice Hall, 2011.

Buiter, W. *The Unfortunate Uselessness of Most State-of-the-Art Academic Monetary Theories*, available at http://blogs.ft.com/maverecon, accessed March 3, 2009.

Burgess, S. 'Measuring financial-sector output and its contribution to UK GDP', *Bank of England Quarterly Bulletin*, 234–46, 2011.

Cairncross, A. 'The Bank of England: Relationships with the government, the civil service and parliament', in G. Toniolo (ed.), *Central Banks' Independence in Historical Perspective*, Berlin: Walter de Gruyter, 1988.

Callender, W. R. *The Commercial Crisis of 1857: Its Causes and Results*, London: Longman, 1858.

Calomiris, C. W. and Kahn, C. M. 'The role of demandable debt in structuring optimal banking arrangements', *American Economic Review*, 81, 497–513, 1991.

Calomiris, C. W. and Mason, J. R. 'Consequences of bank distress during the Great Depression', *American Economic Review*, 93, 937–47, 2003.

Calomiris, C. W. and Schweikart, L. 'The panic of 1857: Origins, transmission, and containment', *Journal of Economic History*, 51, 807–34, 1991.

Cameron, R. *Banking in the Early Stages of Industrialization: A Study in Comparative Economic History*, New York: Oxford University Press, 1967.

Campbell, G. 'Myopic rationality in a mania', *Explorations in Economic History*, 49, 75–91, 2012.

Campbell, G. and Turner, J. D. 'Dispelling the myth of the naive investor during the British Railway Mania, 1845–46', *Business History Review*, 86, 3–41, 2012.

Campbell, R. H. 'Edinburgh bankers and the Western Bank of Scotland', *Scottish Journal of Political Economy*, 2, 134–148, 1955.

Campbell, R. H. 'The law and the joint-stock company in Scotland', in P. L. Payne (ed.), *Studies in Scottish Business History*, London: Frank Cass and Co., 1967.

Capie, F. 'Banking in Europe in the nineteenth century: The role of the central bank', in R. Sylla, R. Tilly and G. Tortella (eds.), *The State, the Financial System and Economic Modernization*, Cambridge: Cambridge University Press, 1999.

Capie, F. 'Structure and performance in British banking, 1870–1939', *Centre for the Study of Monetary History, City University Discussion Paper* 27, 1987.

Capie, F. *The Bank of England, 1950s to 1979*, Cambridge: Cambridge University Press, 2010.

Capie, F. 'The evolving regulatory framework in British banking', in Martin Chick (ed.), *Governments, Industries and Markets: Aspects of Government-Industry Relations in the UK, Japan, West Germany and the USA since 1945*, Aldershot: Elgar, 1990.

Capie, F. and Billings, M. 'Profitability in English banking in the twentieth century', *European Review of Economic History*, 5, 367–402, 2001.

Capie, F. and Collins, M. 'Industrial lending by English commercial banks, 1860s–1914: Why did banks refuse loans?', *Business History*, 38, 26–44, 1996.

Capie, F. and Rodrik-Bali, G. 'Concentration in British banking 1870–1920', *Business History*, 24, 280–92, 1982.

Capie, F. and Wood, G. *Money over Two Centuries: Selected Topics in British Monetary History*, Oxford: Oxford University Press, 2012.

Carr, J. L., Glied, S. and Mathewson, G. F. 'Unlimited liability and free banking in Scotland: A note', *Journal of Economic History*, 49, 974–8, 1989.

Carr, J. L. and Mathewson, G. F. 'Unlimited liability as a barrier to entry', *Journal of Political Economy*, 96, 766–84, 1988.

Cassis, Y. *City Bankers, 1890–1914*, Cambridge: Cambridge University Press, 1994.

Checkland, S. G. *Scottish Banking: A History, 1695–1973*, Glasgow: Collins, 1975.

Christie, J. R. 'Joint-stock enterprise in Scotland before the companies acts', *Juridical Review*, 21, 128–47, 1909.

Chubb, H. 'The Bank Act and the crisis of 1866', *Journal of the Statistical Society of London*, 35, 171–95, 1872.

Claessens, S., Dell'Ariccia, G., Igan, D. and Laeven, L. 'Lessons and policy implications from the global financial crisis', *IMF Working Paper WP/10/44*, 2010.

Claessens, S., Pazarbasioglu, C., Laeven, L., Dobler, M., Valencia, F., Nedelescu, O. and Seal, K. 'Crisis management and resolution: Early lessons from the financial crisis', *IMF Staff Discussion Note*, 2011.

Claessens, S. and Perotti, E. 'Finance and inequality: Channels and evidence', *Journal of Comparative Economics*, 35, 748–73, 2007.

Clapham, J. H. *An Economic History of Modern Britain: Free Trade and Steel*, Cambridge: Cambridge University Press, 1932.

Clapham, J. H. *An Economic History of Modern Britain: The Early Railway Age 1820–1850*, Cambridge: Cambridge University Press, 1930.

Clapham, J. H. *The Bank of England: A History*, 2 volumes, Cambridge: Cambridge University Press, 1944.

Clark, F. W. *A Treatise on the Law of Partnership and Joint-Stock Companies According to the Law of Scotland*, Edinburgh: T. & T. Clark, 1864.

Clay, H. *Lord Norman*, London: Macmillan, 1957.

Clay, W. *Speech of William Clay, Esq., M.P. on Moving for the Appointment of a Committee to Inquire into the Operation of the Act Permitting the Establishment of Joint-stock Banks. To Which are Added, Reflections on Limited Liability, Paid-up Capital, and Publicity of Accounts, as Applied to Such Institutions; With Some Remarks on an Article on Joint-stock Companies in the Last Number of the Edinburgh Review*, London: James Ridgway and Sons, 1837.

Cleary, E. J. *The Building Society Movement*, London: Elek Books, 1965.

Collins, M. 'English bank development within a European context, 1870–1939', *Economic History Review*, 51, 1–24, 1998.

Collins, M. *Money and Banking in the UK: A History*, London: Routledge, 1990.

Collins, M. 'The Bank of England as lender of last resort', *Economic History Review*, 45, 145–53, 1992.

Collins, M. 'The banking crisis of 1878', *Economic History Review*, 42, 504–27, 1989.

Collins, M. and Baker, M. *Commercial Banks and Industrial Finance in England and Wales, 1860–1913*, Oxford: Oxford University Press, 2003.

Conti-Brown, P. 'Unlimited shareholder liability for systematically important financial institutions', *Stanford University Rock Center for Corporate Governance Working Paper*, 2011.

Cooke, C. *Corporation, Trust and Company: An Essay in Legal History*, Manchester: Manchester University Press, 1950.

Cooke, P. W. 'Self-regulation and statute: The evolution of banking supervision', in E. P. M. Gardner (ed.), *UK Banking Supervision: Evolution, Practice and Issues*, London: Allen & Unwin, 1986.

Cottrell, P. L. *Industrial Finance, 1830–1914*, London: Methuen, 1980.

Cottrell, P. L. 'London's first big bang? Institutional change in the City, 1855–83', in Y. Cassis and P. L. Cottrell (eds.), *The World of Private Banking*, Farnham: Ashgate, 2009.

Cottrell, P. L. 'The financial system of the United Kingdom in the twentieth century', in L. De Rosa (ed.), *International Banking and Financial Systems: Evolution and Stability*, Aldershot: Ashgate, 2003.

Couper, C. T. *Report of the Trial before the High Court of Judiciary: Her Majesty's Advocate Against the Directors and the Manager of the City of Glasgow Bank*, Edinburgh: Edinburgh Publishing Company, 1879.

Coyle, C. and Turner, J. D. 'Law, politics and finance: The great reversal of the UK corporate debt market, *Journal of Economic History*, 73, 809–45, 2013.

Crafts, N. 'Regional GDP in Britain, 1871–1911: Some estimates', *Scottish Journal of Political Economy*, 52, 54–64, 2005.

Crick, W. F. and Wadsworth, J. E. *A Hundred Years of Joint Stock Banking*, London: Hodder and Stoughton, 1936.

Dawes, M. and Ward-Perkins, C. N. *Country Bankers of England and Wales: Private Provincial Banks and Bankers 1688–1953*, London: Chartered Institute of Bankers, 2000.

Deaton, A. 'The financial crisis and the well-being of Americans', *Oxford Economic Papers*, 64, 1–26, 2012.

Dell'Ariccia, G., Detragiache, E. and Rajan, R. 'The real effect of banking crises', *Journal of Financial Intermediation*, 17, 89–112, 2008.

Demirgüç-Kunt, A. and Detragiache, E. 'The determinants of banking crises in developing and developed countries', *IMF Staff Papers*, 45, 81–109, 1998.

Demsetz, R. S., Saidenberg, M. R. and Strahan, P. E. 'Banks with something to lose: The disciplinary role of franchise value', *Federal Reserve Bank of Minneapolis Quarterly Review*, Winter, 3–13, 1996.

Dewatripont, M., Rochet, J.-C. and Tirole, J. *Balancing the Banks: Global Lessons from the Financial Crisis*, Princeton, NJ: Princeton University Press, 2010.

Diamond, D. W. and Dybvig, P. H. 'Bank runs, deposit insurance, and liquidity', *Journal of Political Economy*, 91, 401–19, 1983.

Diamond, D. W. and Dybvig, P. H. 'Banking theory, deposit insurance, and bank regulation', *Journal of Business*, 59, 55–68, 1986.

Diamond, D. W. and Rajan, R. G. 'The credit crisis: Conjectures about causes and remedies', *American Economic Review Papers and Proceedings*, 99, 606–10, 2009.

Diaz-Alejandro, C. 'Good-bye financial repression, hello financial crash', *Journal of Development Economics*, 19, 1–24, 1985.

Dimson, E., Marsh, P. and Staunton, M. *Credit Suisse Global Investment Returns Sourcebook 2011*, London: Credit Suisse, 2011.

Dornbusch R. and Frankel, J. A. 'The Gold Standard and the Bank of England in the crisis of 1847', in M. D. Bordo and A. J. Schwartz (eds.), *A Retrospective on the Classical Gold Standard, 1821–1931*, Chicago: University of Chicago Press, 1984.

Dow, A. and Dow, S. 'Economic history and economic theory: The staples approach to economic development', *Cambridge Journal of Economics* (forthcoming).

Dowd, K. *The State and the Monetary System*, London: Phillip Allan, 1989.

Dowd, K. and Hutchinson, M. *The Alchemists of Loss: How Modern Finance and Government Intervention Crashed the Financial System*, Chichester: John Wiley and Sons, 2010.

Dun, J. 'The banking institutions, bullion reserves, and non-legal-tender note circulation of the United Kingdom statistically investigated', *Journal of the Statistical Society*, 39, 1–189, 1876.

England, C. 'Agency costs and unregulated banks: Could depositors protect themselves?', *Cato Journal*, 7, 771–97, 1988.

English, H. *A Complete View of the Joint Stock Companies Formed During the Years 1824 and 1825*, London: Boosey and Sons, 1827.

Esty, B. C. 'The impact of contingent liability on commercial bank risk taking', *Journal of Financial Economics*, 47, 189–218, 1998.

Evans, D. M. *The Commercial Crisis, 1847–1848*, Devon: David & Charles, 1849.

Evans, D. M. *The History of the Commercial Crisis, 1857–1858 and the Stock Exchange Panic of 1859*, London: Groombridge & Sons, 1859.

Evans, L.T. and Quigley, N. C. 'Shareholder liability regimes, principal-agent relationships, and banking industry performance', *Journal of Law and Economics*, 38, 497–520, 1995.

Ferguson, N. *The House of Rothschild: The World's Banker 1849–1999*, New York: Penguin, 1999.

Fetter, F. W. 'A historical confusion in Bagehot's Lombard Street', *Economica*, 34, 80–3, 1967.

Fetter, F. W. *The Irish Paper Pound 1797–1826: A Reprint of the Report of the Committee of 1804 of the British House of Commons on the Condition of the Irish Currency*, London: George Allen and Unwin, 1955.

Fforde, J. S. *The Bank of England and Public Policy, 1941–1958*, Cambridge: Cambridge University Press, 1992.

Flannery, M. J. 'Deposit insurance creates a need for bank regulation', *Federal Reserve Bank of Philadelphia Business Review*, 17–27, 1982.

Fleming, J. S. 'On the theory and practice of banking in Scotland', *Journal of the Institute of Bankers*, 4, 129–50, 1883.

Fletcher, G. A. 'Cash base control of bank deposits and the British banking system', *Société Universitaire Européenne de Recherches Financière (SUERF) Working Paper*, 1978.

Fohlin, C. 'The balancing act of German universal banks and English deposit banks, 1880–1913', *Business History*, 43, 1–24, 2001.

Freeman, M., Pearson, R. and Taylor, J. 'Different and better? Scottish joint-stock companies and the law, c.1720–1845', *English Historical Review*, 122, 61–81, 2007.

Freixas, X., Giannini, C., Hoggarth, G. and Soussa, F. 'Lender of last resort: A review of the literature', *Financial Stability Review* 7, 151–67, 1999.

French, E. A. *Unlimited Liability: The Case of the City of Glasgow Bank*, London: Certified Accountant Publications Ltd., 1985.

French, K., Baily, M., Campbell, J., Cochrane, J., Diamond, D., Duffie, D., *et al. The Squam Lake Report: Fixing the Financial System*, Princeton, NJ: Princeton University Press, 2010.

Friedman, M. *A Program for Monetary Stability*, New York: Fordham University Press, 1959.

Friedman, M. and Jacobson Schwartz, A. *The Great Contraction 1929–1933*, Princeton, NJ: Princeton University Press, 2008.

Frydman, R. and Goldberg, M. D. *Beyond Mechanical Markets: Asset Price Swings, Risk, and the Role of the State*, Princeton, NJ: Princeton University Press, 2011.

Galbraith, J. K. *Inequality and Instability: A Study of the World Economy Just Before the Great Crisis*, Oxford: Oxford University Press, 2012.

Galor, O., Moav, O. and Vollrath, D. 'Inequality in land ownership, the emergence of human capital promoting institutions, and the great divergence', *Review of Economic Studies*, 76, 143–79, 2009.

Gardner, E. P. M. 'Supervision in the United Kingdom', in E. P. M. Gardner (ed.), *UK Banking Supervision: Evolution, Practice and Issues*, London: Allen & Unwin, 1986.

Gash, N. *Aristocracy and People: Britain 1815–1865*. London: Edward Arnold, 1979.

Gayer, A. D., Rostow, W. W. and Jacobson Schwartz, A. *The Growth and Fluctuation of the British Economy 1790–1850*, 2 vols., Oxford: Clarendon Press, 1953.

Giannini, C. 'Enemy of none but a common friend of all? An international perspective on the lender-of-last-resort function', *Princeton Essays in International Finance* 214, 1–66, 1999.

Goldberg, L. G. and Saunders, A. 'The causes of U.S. bank expansion overseas: The case of Great Britain', *Journal of Money, Credit and Banking*, 12, 630–43, 1980.

Goldsmith, R. W. *Financial Structure and Development*, New Haven, CT: Yale University Press, 1969.

Goodhart, C. A. E. 'Myths about the lender of last resort', *FMG Special Paper* 120, 1999.

Goodhart, C. A. E. 'The Bank of England 1970–2000', in R. Michie and P. Williamson (eds.), *The British Government and the City of London in the Twentieth Century*, Cambridge: Cambridge University Press, 2004.

Goodhart, C. A. E. *The Basel Committee on Banking Supervision: A History of the Early Years 1974–1997*, Cambridge: Cambridge University Press, 2011.

Goodhart, C. A. E. *The Business of Banking 1891–1914*, London: Gower, 1986.

Goodhart, C. A. E. *The Evolution of Central Banks*, London: MIT Press, 1988.

Gorton, G. *Misunderstanding Financial Crises: Why We Don't See Them Coming*, Oxford: Oxford University Press, 2012.

Gorton, G. *Slapped by the Invisible Hand: The Panic of 2007*, Oxford: Oxford University Press, 2010.

Grady, J. and Weale, M. *British Banking, 1960–85*, London: Macmillan, 1986.

Green, D. R. and Owens, A. 'Gentlewomanly capitalism? Spinsters, widows and wealth holding in England Wales', *Economic History Review*, 56, 510–36, 2003.

Gregory, T. E. *The Westminster Bank Through a Century*, 2 vols., London: Westminster Bank Ltd., 1936.

Griffiths, B. 'The development of restrictive practices in the UK monetary system', *Manchester School*, 41, 3–16, 1973.

Grossman, R. S. 'Double liability and bank risk taking', *Journal of Money, Credit and Banking*, 33, 143–59, 2001.

Grossman, R. S. 'New indices of British equity prices, 1870–1913', *Journal of Economic History*, 62, 121–46, 2002.

Grossman, R. S. 'The shoe that didn't drop: Explaining banking stability during the Great Depression', *Journal of Economic History*, 53, 654–82, 1994.

Grossman, R. S. *Unsettled Account: The Evolution of Banking in the Industrialized World since 1800*, Princeton, NJ: Princeton University Press, 2010.

Grossman, R. S. and Imai, M. 'Contingent capital and bank risk-taking among British banks before the First World War', *Economic History Review*, 66, 132–55, 2013.

Haber, S. 'Political institutions and financial development: Evidence from the economy histories of Mexico and the United States', *Stanford University Working Paper*, 2005.

Haldane, A. 'The contribution of the financial sector: Miracle or mirage?', *Speech at Future of Finance Conference*, 2010.

Hall, F. G. *The Bank of Ireland 1783–1946*, Dublin: Hodges, Figgis & Co., 1949.

Hall, M. J. B. *Handbook of Banking Regulation and Supervision*. London: Woodhead-Faulkner, 1989.

Hall, R. E. 'Why does the economy fall to pieces after a financial crisis?', *Journal of Economic Perspectives*, 24, 3–20, 2010.

Hanson, S. G., Kashyap, A. K. and Stein, J. C. 'A macroprudential approach to financial regulation', *Journal of Economic Perspectives*, 25, 3–28, 2011.

Harris, R. *Industrializing English Law: Entrepreneurship and Business Organization, 1720–1844*, Cambridge: Cambridge University Press, 2000.

Hawtrey, R. G. *A Century of Bank Rate*, London: Longmans, Green and Co., 1938.

Headlam, T. E. *A Speech on Limited Liability in Joint Stock Banks in the House of Commons, May 8, 1849: Together With a Proposed Act of Parliament on the Subject*, London: Trelawney Saunders, 1849.

Hickson, C. R. and Turner, J. D. 'Free banking gone awry: The Australian banking crisis of 1893', *Financial History Review*, 9, 147–67, 2002.

Hickson, C. R. and Turner, J. D. 'Trading in the shares of unlimited-liability banks in nineteenth century Ireland: The Bagehot hypothesis', *Journal of Economic History*, 63, 931–58, 2003.

Hickson, C. R. and Turner, J. D. 'Free banking and the stability of early joint-stock banking', *Cambridge Journal of Economics*, 28, 903–19, 2004.

Hickson, C. R. and Turner, J. D. 'The genesis of corporate governance: Nineteenth-century Irish joint-stock banks', *Business History*, 47, 174–89, 2005.

High Pay Commission. *Cheques with Balances: Why Tackling High Pay Is in the National Interest*, available at www.highpaycommission.co.uk.

Hirsch, F. 'The Bagehot problem', *The Manchester School*, 45, 241–57, 1977.

Hodgson, G. M. 'The Great Crash of 2008 and the reform of economics', 33, 1205–221, 2009.

Hoggarth, G., Reis, R. and Saporta, V. 'Costs of banking system instability: Some empirical evidence', *Journal of Banking and Finance*, 26, 825–55, 2002.

Hoggarth, G. and Soussa, F. 'Crisis management, lender of last resort and the changing nature of the banking industry', in *Financial Stability and Central Banks: A Global Perspective*, London: Routledge, 2001.

Holmes, A. R. and Green, E. *Midland: 150 Years of Banking Business*, London: BT Batsford Ltd., 1986.

Horsefield, J. K. 'The Bank of England as mentor', *Economic History Review*, 2, 80–7, 1949.

Hüfner, F. 'The German banking system: Lessons from the financial crisis', *Organisation for Economic Co-operation and Development Economics Department Working Paper* 788, 2010.

Hull, J. C. *Risk Management and Financial Institutions*, Upper Saddle River, NJ: Pearson Prentice Hall, 2007.

Humphrey, T. M. and Keleher, R. E. 'The lender of last resort: A historical perspective', *Cato Journal*, 4, 275–321, 1984.

Hunt, B. *The Development of the Business Corporation in England 1800–1867*, Cambridge, MA: Harvard University Press, 1936.

Igan, D., Mishra, P. and Tressel, T. 'A fistful of dollars: Lobbying and the financial crisis', *NBER Working Paper 17076*, 2011.

Jackson, P. 'Capital requirements and bank behaviour: The impact of the Basel Accord', *Basle Committee on Banking Supervision Working Papers*, 1, 1999.

James, J. A. 'Panics, payments disruptions and the Bank of England before 1826', *Financial History Review*, 19, 289–309, 2012.

Jefferys, J. B. *Business Organisation in Great Britain 1856–1914*, New York: Arno Press, 1977.

Jensen, M. C. 'Agency costs of free cash flow, corporate finance, and takeovers', *American Economic Review Papers and Proceedings*, 76, 323–9, 1986.

Jensen, M. C. and Meckling, W. 'Theory of the firm: Managerial behaviour, agency costs and capital structure', *Journal of Financial Economics*, 3, 305–60, 1976.

Johnson, H. G. 'Clearing bank holdings of public debt, 1930–1950', *London and Cambridge Economic Service Bulletin*, 29, 102–9, 1951.

Johnson, S. and Kwak, J. *13 Bankers: The Wall Street Takeover and the Next Financial Meltdown*, New York: Pantheon Books, 2010.

Jones, G. *British Multinational Banking 1830–1990*, Oxford: Clarendon Press, 1993.

Jones, G. 'Competition and competitiveness in British banking 1918–1971', in G. Jones and M. Kirby (eds.), *Competitiveness and the State: Government and*

Business in Twentieth-Century Britain, Manchester: Manchester University Press, 1991.

Jones, R. W. 'The business of banking', *Gilbart Lectures on Banking, University of London King's College*, 1948.

Joplin, T. *An Essay on the General Principles and Present Practice of Banking in England and Scotland*, London: Baldwin, Cradock & Joy and J. Ridgway, 1827.

Kaminsky, G. L. and Reinhart, C. M. 'The twin crises: The causes of banking and balance-of-payments problems', *American Economic Review*, 89, 473–500, 1999.

Kareken, J. H. and Wallace, N. 'Deposit insurance and bank regulation: A partial equilibrium exposition', *Journal of Business*, 51, 413–38, 1978.

Kaufman, G. F. 'Lender of last resort: A contemporary perspective', *Journal of Financial Services Research*, 5, 95–110, 1991.

Kennedy, W. *Industrial Structure, Capital Markets, and the Origins of British Economic Decline*, Cambridge: Cambridge University Press, 1987.

Kennedy, W. 'Institutional response to economic growth: Capital markets in Britain to 1914', in L. Hannah (ed.), *Management Strategy and Business Development*, London: Macmillan, 1976.

Kerr, A. W. *History of Banking in Scotland*, London: A & C Black 1908.

Kindleberger, C. P. *Manias, Panics and Crashes: A History of Financial Crises*, 4th edition, New York: John Wiley and Sons, 2000.

King, R. G. and Levine, R. 'Finance and growth: Schumpeter might be right', *Quarterly Journal of Economics*, 108, 717–37, 1993.

King, W. T. C. 'The extent of the London discount market in the middle of the nineteenth century', *Economica*, 7, 321–6, 1935.

Kiyotaki, N. and Moore, J. 'Credit chains', *Journal of Political Economy*, 99, 220–64, 1997.

Klein, B. 'The competitive supply of money', *Journal of Money, Credit and Banking*, 6, 421–53, 1974.

Körnert, J. 'The Barings crises of 1890 and 1995: Causes, courses, consequences and the danger of domino effects', *Journal of International Financial Markets, Institutions and Money*, 13, 187–209, 2003.

Kroszner, R. S. and Strahan, P. E. 'What drives deregulation? Economics and politics of the relaxation of bank branching restrictions', *Quarterly Journal of Economics*, 114, 1437–67, 1999.

Laeven, L. 'Banking crises: A review', *Annual Review of Financial Economics*, 3, 17–40, 2011.

Laeven, L. and Valencia, F. 'Resolution of banking crises: The good, the bad, and the ugly', *IMF Working Paper WP/10/146*, 2010.

Laidler, D. 'Two views of the lender of last resort: Thorton and Bagehot', *University of Western Ontario Department of Economics Working Paper 20029*, 2002.

Lee, T. A. 'A helpless class of shareholder: Newspapers and the failure of the City of Glasgow Bank', *Accounting History Review*, 26, 143–59, 2012.

Levine, R. 'Financial development and economic growth: Views and agenda', *Journal of Economic Literature*, 35, 688–726, 1997.

Levine, R. and Zervos, S. 'Stock markets, banks, and economic growth', *American Economic Review*, 88, 537–58, 1998.

Lindert, P. H. 'Unequal English wealth since 1670', *Journal of Political Economy*, 94, 1127–62, 1986.

Logan, A. 'The early 1990s small banks crisis: Leading indicators', *Financial Stability Review*, 8, 130–45, 2000.

Lovell, M. C. 'The role of the Bank of England as lender of last resort in the crises of the eighteenth century', *Explorations in Entrepreneurial History*, 10, 8–21, 1957.

Macdonald, D. 'The big banks' big secret: Estimating government support for Canadian banks during the financial crisis', *Canadian Centre for Policy Alternatives Report*, 2012.

Macey, J. R. and Miller, G. P. 'Double liability of bank shareholders: History and implications', *Wake Forest Law Review*, 27, 31–62, 1992.

Martinez-Miera, D. and Repullo, R. 'Does competition reduce the risk of bank failure?', *Review of Financial Studies*, 23, 3638–64, 2010.

McKinnon, R. I. *Money and Capital in Economic Development*, Washington, DC: Brookings Institution, 1973.

Mian, A. and Sufi, A. 'House prices, home equity-based borrowing, and the US household leverage crisis', *American Economic Review*, 101, 2132–56, 2011.

Mian, A., Sufi, A. and Trebbi, F. 'The political economy of the subprime mortgage credit expansion', *NBER Working Paper 16107*, 2010.

Mian, A., Sufi, A. and Trebbi, F. 'The political economy of the US mortgage default crisis', *American Economic Review*, 100, 1967–98, 2010.

Michie, R. *The London and New York Stock Exchange, 1850–1914*, London: Allen & Unwin, 1987.

Miller, M. H. 'Do the M+M propositions apply to banks?', *Journal of Banking and Finance*, 19, 483–89, 1995.

Minsky, H. P. *Stabilizing an Unstable Economy*, 2nd edn., New York: McGraw-Hill, 2008.

Mishkin, F. S., 'Over the cliff: From the subprime to the global financial crisis', *Journal of Economic Perspectives*, 25, 49–70, 2011.

Mitchell, B. R. *British Historical Statistics*, Cambridge: Cambridge University Press, 1988.

Mitchener, K. J. and Richardson, G. 'Does skin in the game reduce risk taking? Leverage, liability and the long-run consequences of New Deal banking reforms', *Explorations in Economic History*, 50, 508–25, 2013.

Modigliani, F. and Miller, M. H. 'The cost of capital, corporate finance, and the theory of investment', *American Economic Review*, 48, 261–97, 1958.

Moore, G. 'Solutions to the moral-hazard problem arising from the lender-of-last-resort facility', *Journal of Economic Surveys*, 13, 443–76, 1999.

Moran, M. *The Politics of Banking: The Strange Case of Competition and Credit Control*, 2nd edn., London: Macmillan, 1986.

Morgan, E. V. *The Theory and Practice of Central Banking, 1797–1913*, Cambridge: Cambridge University Press, 1943.

Mount, F. *The New Few or a Very British Oligarchy*, London: Simon & Schuster, 2012.

Munn, C. W. *Clydesdale Bank: The First One Hundred and Fifty Years*, London: Collins, 1988.

Munn, C. W. 'The emergence of central banking in Ireland: Bank of Ireland 1814–50', *Irish Economic and Social History*, 10, 19–32, 1983.

Munn, C. W. *The Scottish Provincial Banking Companies 1747–1864*, Edinburgh: John Donald, 1981.

Neal, L. 'The financial crisis of 1825 and the restructuring of the British financial system', *Federal Reserve Bank of St. Louis Review*, May/June, 53–76, 1998.

Nevin, E. and Davis, E. W. *The London Clearing Banks*, London: Elek Books, 1970.

Newton, L. A. 'Assessment of information, uncertainty and risk: The strategies of English and Welsh joint-stock bank managements, 1826–1860', *University of Reading Discussion Paper* 431, 2001.

Newton, L. A. 'The birth of joint-stock banking: England and New England compared', *Business History Review*, 84, 27–52, 2010.

Newton, L. A. and Cottrell, P. L. 'Female investors in the first English and Welsh commercial joint-stock banks', *Accounting, Business and Financial History*, 16, 315–40, 2006.

Nobay, A. B. 'The Bank of England, monetary policy and monetary theory in the United Kingdom, 1951–1971', *The Manchester School*, 41, 43–57, 1973.

O'Brien, D. 'The lender-of-last-resort concept in Britain', *History of Political Economy*, 35, 1–19, 2003.

O'Donoghue, J., Goulding, L. and Allen, G. 'Composite price index, 1750–2003', *Economic Trends*, 604, 38–46, 2004.

Offer, A. 'Narrow banking, real estate, and financial stability in the UK, c.1870–2010', *University of Oxford Discussion Papers in Economic and Social History*, 116, 2013.

Ogden, T. 'An analysis of Bank of England discount and advance behaviour, 1870–1914', in J. Foreman-Peck (ed.), *New Perspectives on the Late Victorian Economy: Essays in Quantitative Economic History 1860–1914*, Cambridge: Cambridge University Press, 1991.

Ogden, T. *The Development of the Role of the Bank of England as a Lender of Last Resort*, City University, PhD dissertation, 1988.

Ó Gráda, C. *Ireland: A New Economic History*, Oxford: Clarendon Press, 1994.

Ó Gráda, C. 'Moral hazard and quasi-central banking: Should the Munster Bank have been saved?', in D. Dickson and C. Ó Gráda (eds.), *Refiguring Ireland: Essays in Honour of L. M. Cullen*, Dublin: The Lilliput Press, 2003.

Ó Gráda, C. 'The last major Irish bank failure before 2008', *Financial History Review*, 19, 199–217, 2012.

Orbell, J. and Turton, A. *British Banking: A Guide to Historical Records*, Aldershot: Ashgate, 2001.

Parnell, H. *Observations on Paper Money, Banking, and Overtrading*, London: James Ridgway, 1827.

Peltzman, S. 'Toward a more general theory of regulation', *Journal of Law and Economics*, 19, 109–48, 1976.

Perotti, E. 'The political economy of finance', *Tinbergen Institute Discussion Paper 13–034*, 2013.

Peston, R. and Knight, L. *How Do We Fix This Mess? The Economic Price of Having It All and the Route to Lasting Prosperity*, London: Hodder & Stoughton, 2012.

Philips, M. *A History of Banks, Bankers, and Banking in Northumberland, Durham, and North Yorkshire*, London: Effingham Wilson & Co., 1894.

Piketty, T. and Saez, E. 'How progressive is the U.S. federal tax system? A historical and international perspective', *Journal of Economic Perspectives*, 21, 3–24, 2007.

Plumptre, C. C. M. *Grant's Treatise on the Law Relating to Bankers and Banking Companies*, London: Butterworths, 1882.

Pressnell, L. S. 'Cartels and competition in British banking: A background study', *Banca Nazionale Del Lavoro Quarterly Review*, 95, 373–405, 1970.

Pressnell, L. S. *Country Banking in the Industrial Revolution*, Oxford: Clarendon Press, 1956.

Pressnell, L. S. 'Gold reserves, banking reserves, and the Baring crisis of 1890', in C. R. Whittlesey and J. S. G. Wilson (eds.), *Essays in Money and Banking in Honour of R. S. Sayers*, Oxford: Clarendon Press, 1968.

Rae, G. *The Country Banker: His Clients, Cares, and Work from an Experience of Forty Years*, London: John Murray, 1885.

Rait, R. S. *The History of the Union Bank of Scotland*, Glasgow: John Smith & Son, 1930.

Rajan, R. G. *Fault Lines: How Hidden Fractured Still Threaten the World Economy*, Princeton, NJ: Princeton University Press, 2010.

Rajan, R. G. and Ramcharan, R. 'Land and credit: A study of the political economy of banking in the United States in the early 20th century', *Journal of Finance*, 66, 1895–931, 2011.

Rajan, R. G. 'The true lessons of the recession: The West can't borrow and spend its way to recovery', *Foreign Affairs*, 91, 69–79, 2012.

Rajan, R. G. and Zingales, L. 'The great reversals: The politics of financial development in the twentieth century', *Journal of Financial Economics*, 69, 5–50, 2003.

Reid, M. *Abbey National Conversion to PLC*, London: Pencorp Books, 1991.

Reid, M. 'Lessons for bank supervision from the secondary-banking crises', in E. P. M. Gardner (ed.), *UK Banking Supervision: Evolution, Practice and Issues*, London: Allen & Unwin, 1986.

Reid, M. *The Secondary Banking Crisis 1973–75: Its Causes and Course*, London: Macmillan, 1982.

Reinhart, C. M. and Rogoff, K. S. *This Time Is Different: Eight Centuries of Financial Folly*, Princeton, NJ: Princeton University Press, 2009.

Reinhart, C. M. and Rogoff, K. S. 'The aftermath of financial crises', *American Economic Review Papers and Proceedings*, 99, 466–72, 2009.

Reinhart, C. M. and Rogoff, K. S. 'From financial crash to debt crisis', *American Economic Review*, 101, 1676–706, 2011.

Reinhart, C. M. and Sbrancia, M. B. 'The liquidation of government debt', *NBER Working Paper 16893*, 2011.

Revell, J. R. S. 'Competition and regulation of banks', *Institute of European Finance Working Paper*, 1978.

Revell, J. R. S. 'Solvency and regulation of banks: Theoretical and practical implications', *Bangor Occasional Papers in Economics* 5, 1975.

Richards, R. *The Early History of Banking in England*, London: P S King & Son, 1929.

Richardson, J. and Stephenson, M. 'Some aspects of regulatory capital', *FSA Occasional Paper Series* 7, 2000.

Robb, V. 'The genesis of regulation', *Financial Stability Review*, 29–41, 1997.

Rockoff, H. 'Walter Bagehot and the theory of central banking', in F. Capie and G. E. Wood (eds.), *Financial Crises and the World Banking System*, London: Macmillan, 1986.

Rogers, D. *The Big Four British Banks: Organisation, Strategy and the Future*, London: Macmillan, 1999.

Rosenblum, L. 'The failure of the City of Glasgow Bank', *The Accounting Review*, 8, 285–91, 1933.

Ross, D. M. 'Domestic monetary policy and the banking system in Britain 1945–1971', in R. Michie and P. Williamson (eds.), *The British Government and the City of London in the Twentieth Century*, Cambridge: Cambridge University Press, 2004.

Rothbard, M. *America's Great Depression*, 3rd ed., Kansas City: Sheed & Ward, 1975.

Rowan, D. C. 'The monetary system in the fifties and sixties', *The Manchester School*, 41, 19–42, 1973.

Rubenstein, W. D. 'The Victorian middle classes: Wealth, occupation, and geography', *Economic History Review*, 33, 602–23, 1977.

Saul, S. B. *The Myth of the Great Depression, 1873–1896*, London: Macmillan, 1969.

Saunders, A. and Wilson B. 'The impact of consolidation and safety-net support on Canadian, US and UK banks: 1993–1992', *Journal of Banking and Finance*, 23, 537–71, 1999.

Saville, R. *Bank of Scotland: A History, 1695–1995*, Edinburgh: Edinburgh University Press, 1996.

Sayers, R. S. *Lloyds Bank in the History of English Banking*, Oxford: Clarendon Press, 1957.

Sayers, R. S. *The Bank of England: 1891–1944*, 2 vols., Cambridge: Cambridge University Press, 1976.

Sayers, R. S. 'Twentieth-century English banking', *Transactions of the Manchester Statistical Society*, 1–16, 1954–5.

Schularick, M. and Taylor, A. M. 'Credit booms gone bust: Monetary policy, leverage cycles, and financial crises, 1870–2008', *American Economic Review*, 102, 1029–61, 2011.

Schwartz, A. J. 'Origins of the financial market crisis of 2008', *Cato Journal*, 29, 19–23, 2009.

Schwartz, A. J. 'Real and pseudo-financial crises', in F. Capie and G. E. Wood (eds.), *Financial Crises and the World Banking System*, London: Macmillan, 1986.

Seabourne, T. 'The summer of 1914', in F. Capie and G. E. Wood (eds.), *Financial Crises and the World Banking System*, London: Macmillan, 1986.

Secretariat of Basel Committee on Banking Supervision. *The New Basel Capital Accord: An Explanatory Note*, Basel: Bank for International Settlements, 2001.

Selgin, G. A. 'Legal restrictions, financial weakening, and the lender of last resort', *Cato Journal*, 9, 429–59, 1989.

Selgin, G. A. and White, L. H. 'How would the invisible hand handle money?', *Journal of Economic Literature*, 22, 1718–49, 1994.

Shaw, E. S., *Financial Deepening in Economic Development*, Oxford University Press: New York, 1973.

Sheppard, D. K. *The Growth and Role of UK Financial Institutions 1880–1962*, London: Methuen, 1971.

Shiller, R. *The Subprime Solution: How Today's Global Financial Crisis Happened and What to Do About It*, Princeton, NJ: Princeton University Press, 2008.

Shin, H. S. 'Reflections on Northern Rock: The bank run that heralded the global financial crisis', *Journal of Economic Perspectives*, 23, 101–19, 2009.

Simpson, N. *The Belfast Bank 1827–1970*, Belfast: Blackstaff Press, 1975.

Singh, D. *Banking Regulation of UK and US Financial Markets*, Brookfield, VT: Ashgate, 2007.

Smith, K. C. and Horne, G. F. *An Index Number of Securities, 1867–1914*, London: Royal Economic Society Memorandum, 1934.

Smith, V. C. *The Rationale of Central Banking and the Free Banking Alternative*, London: P S King & Son, 1936.

Solomou, S. N. and Weale, M. 'Balanced estimates of UK GDP 1870–1913', *Explorations in Economic History*, 28, 54–63, 1991.

Solow, R. M. 'Economic history and economics', *American Economic Review Papers and Proceedings*, 75, 328–31, 1985.

Sorkin, A. *Too Big to Fail: The Inside Story of How Wall Street and Washington Fought to Save the Financial System from Crisis – and Themselves*, New York: Viking, 2009.

Stigler, G. J. 'The theory of economic regulation', *Bell Journal of Economics and Management Science*, 2, 3–21, 1971.

Stiglitz, J. E. 'Credit markets and the control of capital', *Journal of Money, Credit and Banking*, 17, 133–52, 1985.

Stuckey, V. 'Thoughts on the improvement of the system of country banking', *The Edinburgh Review*, 63, 419–41, 1836.

Sykes, J. *The Amalgamation Movement in English Banking, 1825–1924*, London: P S King & Son, 1926.

Sykes, J. *The Present Position of English Joint Stock Banking*, London: Ernest Benn Ltd., 1928.

Tamaki, N. *The Life Cycle of the Union Bank of Scotland 1830–1954*, Aberdeen: Aberdeen University Press, 1983.

Tarullo, D. K. *Banking on Basel: The Future of International Financial Regulation*, Washington, DC: Peterson Institute for International Economics, 2008.

Taylor, J. *Creating Capitalism: Joint-Stock Enterprise in British Politics and Culture 1800–1870*, London: Royal Historical Society, 2006.

Thomas, S. *The Rise and Growth of Joint Stock Banking*, London: Sir Isaac Pitman & Sons, 1934.

Thompson, E. A. and Hickson, C. R. *Ideology and the Evolution of Vital Economic Institutions: Guilds, the Gold Standard, and Modern International Cooperation*, Boston: Kluwer, 2001.

Thornton, H. *An Enquiry into the Nature and Effects of the Paper Credit of Great Britain*, London: George Allen and Unwin, 1939.

Tobin, J. 'A case for preserving regulatory distinctions', *Challenge*, 30, 10–17, 1987.

Turner, J. D. 'Irish contributions to nineteenth-century monetary and banking debates', in T. Boylan, R. Prendergast, and J. D., Turner (eds.), *A History of Irish Economic Thought*, Oxford: Routledge, 2011.

Turner, J. D. '"The last acre and sixpence": Views on shareholder liability regimes in nineteenth-century Britain', *Financial History Review*, 16, 111–28, 2009.

Turner, J. D. 'Wealth concentration in the European periphery: Ireland, 1858–2001', *Oxford Economic Papers*, 62, 625–46, 2010.

Turner, J. D. 'Wider share ownership? Investors in English bank shares in the nineteenth century', *Economic History Review*, 62, 167–92, 2009.

Viner, J. *Studies in the Theory of International Trade*. London: Clifton, 1975.

Wadsworth, J. E. 'Big and little banks: Economic and historic influences on the size of English banks', *Société Universitaire Européenne de Recherches Financière (SUERF) Working Paper*, 1978.

Wadsworth, J. E. *The Banks and the Monetary System in the UK 1959–1971*, London: Methuen & Co., 1973.

Wadsworth, J. E. 'The commercial banks', in *British Banking Today*, London: Institute of Bankers, 1953.

Wagster, J. D. 'Impact of the 1988 Basel Accord on international banks', *Journal of Finance*, 51, 1321–46, 1996.

Wagster, J. D. 'Wealth and risk effects of adopting deposit insurance in Canada: Evidence of risk shifting by banks and trust companies', *Journal of Money, Credit and Banking*, 39, 1651–81, 2007.

Wallace, N. 'Narrow banking meets the Diamond-Dybvig model', *Federal Reserve Bank of Minneapolis Quarterly Review*, Winter, 3–13, 1996.

Watt, H. *The Practice of Banking in Scotland and England; With Observations and Suggestions on the Renewal of the Bank of England Charter, on the Principles and Regulation of Joint Stock Banks, and on the One Pound Note Circulation*, London: Simpkin and Marshall, 1833.

Webber, A. 'Reserves and reserve ratios in British banking, 1870–1960', *Centre for Banking and International Finance Discussion Paper* 19, 1985.

White, L. H. *Free Banking in Britain: Theory, Experience and Debate 1800–1845*, 2nd edn., London: Institute of Economic Affairs, 1995.

White, L. H. 'The evolution of Hayek's monetary economics', mimeo, Athens: University of Georgia, 1995.

White, L. H. *The Theory of Monetary Institutions*, Oxford: Blackwell, 1999.

Wilcox, M. G. 'Capital in banking: An historical survey', in E. P. M. Gardner (ed.), *UK Banking Supervision: Evolution, Practice and Issues*, London: Allen & Unwin, 1986.

Wilson, A. J. *Banking Reform: An Essay on the Prominent Dangers and the Remedies They Demand*, London: Longmans, Green & Co., 1879.

Winton, A. 'Limitation of liability and the ownership structure of the firm', *Journal of Finance*, 48, 487–512, 1993.

Winton, J. R. *Lloyds Bank 1918–1969*, Oxford: Oxford University Press, 1982.

Withers, H. and Palgrave, R. H. I. *The English Banking System*, Washington, DC: National Monetary Commission, 1910.

Wood, J. H. 'Bagehot's lender of last resort', *Independent Review*, 7, 343–51, 2003.

Woodward, S. 'Limited liability in the theory of the firm', *Journal of Institutional and Theoretical Economics*, 141, 601–11, 1985.

Xiao, Y. 'French banks amid the global financial crisis', *IMF Working Paper WP/09/201*, 2009.

Ziegler, P. *The Sixth Great Power: Barings 1762–1929*, London: Collins, 1988.

Index